Paul's Community Formation Preaching in 1 Thessalonians

Kwang-hyun Cho

Paul's Community Formation Preaching in 1 Thessalonians

An Alternative to the New Homiletic

PETER LANG

Bern · Bruxelles · Frankfurt am Main · New York · Oxford · Warszawa · Wien

Bibliographic information published by die Deutsche Nationalbibliothek
Die Deutsche Nationalbibliothek lists this publication in the Deutsche
Nationalbibliografie; detailed bibliographic data is available on the Internet
at ‹http://dnb.d-nb.de›.

British Library Cataloguing-in-Publication Data: A catalogue record for this book
is available from The British Library, Great Britain.

Library of Congress Control Number: 2017948968

Cover image: iStockphoto/sedmak

ISBN 978-3-0343-3089-3 pb.   ISBN 978-3-0343-3090-9 eBook
ISBN 978-3-0343-3092-3 EPUB   ISBN 978-3-0343-3091-6 MOBI

This publication has been peer reviewed.

© Peter Lang AG, International Academic Publishers, Bern 2017
Wabernstrasse 40, CH-3007 Bern, Switzerland
bern@peterlang.com, www.peterlang.com

All rights reserved.
All parts of this publication are protected by copyright.
Any utilisation outside the strict limits of the copyright law, without
the permission of the publisher, is forbidden and liable to prosecution.
This applies in particular to reproductions, translations, microfilming,
and storage and processing in electronic retrieval systems.

Printed in Switzerland

Acknowledgements

This book is a revised doctoral dissertation completed at the University of Pretoria. Dr. Cas Wepener and Dr. Ernest van Eck eminently worked together across the departments to provide insightful feedbacks and to sharpen the arguments for an interdisciplinary student across the ocean. Preaching faculty at Gordon-Conwell Theological Seminary: Dr. Haddon Robinson, Dr. Scott Gibson, and Dr. Jeffery Arthurs shared not only their homiletical wisdom but also their own personal lives with a visiting Ph. D. scholar. Likewise, I also owe the library staff at Gordon-Conwell for all the help.

I would like to express much gratitude for all my teachers at Korea Theological Seminary. Dr. Wonha Shin, Dr. Sunsung Kim, and Dr. Sungnam Kil especially have inspired me and have guided me in the right path. I would also like to give special thanks to Dr. Hongsuk Kim, senior pastor at Anyang Ilsim Presbyterian Church, who has been incredibly generous to me.

Johanna Lüder and Marina Essig at Peter Lang International Academic Publishers have been very helpful for publishing this book.

For all of these and many more I give thanks to God. When I walked through the valley of the shadow, He made a way for me. This book is the fruit of the way God made.

Soil Deo Gloria.

Table of Contents

Chapter One

Introduction 11
  1.1. Statement of the Problem and Research Gap 11
  1.2. Research Methodology and Structure 22
  1.3. The Continuity between Paul's Letters and His Preaching 24
      1.3.1. Communication to Communities of Faith 25
      1.3.2. Repetition of What Paul Preached Before 29
      1.3.3. The Use of Amanuenses 31
      1.3.4. Reading Aloud in the Communities of Faith 32
      1.3.5. A Means of the Apostle's Presence from a Distance 36
      1.3.6. Conclusion 37

Chapter Two

The New Homiletic: The Turn to the Individual Listener 39
  2.1. The Background of the New Homiletic 39
      2.1.1. The Cultural Context of 1960s: The Challenge to
            Traditional Authority 39
      2.1.2. The Dissatisfaction with Traditional Preaching 42
      2.1.3. The New Hermeneutic 47
  2.2. The Common Characteristics of the New Homiletic 50
      2.2.1. The Elevation of the Listener's Role:
            Partner of Preaching 50
      2.2.2. Experience as the Primary Purpose of Preaching 54
      2.2.3. Attention to Alternative Sermon Forms 57
  2.3. A Critical Reflection on the New Homiletic 61
      2.3.1. Critique against the Elevation of the Listener's Role 61
      2.3.2. Critique against the Primacy of the Experience 63
      2.3.3. Critique against the Attention to the Sermon Forms
            and Narrative Preaching 65
      2.3.4. Critique against the Turn to the Individual Listener 68
  2.4. Conclusion 72

Chapter Three

Paul's Main Intention of Preaching in 1 Thessalonians:
Community Formation 73
   3.1. The Pagan City of Thessalonica: The Cults 73
   3.2. The Thessalonian Community: A Newly Born
        Gentile Community 78
   3.3. The Suffering of the Community: Conflict with the
        Larger Pagan Society 86
   3.4. Paul's Writing of the Letter: Community Formation
        in the Face of Challenge 92
   3.5. Conclusion 100

Chapter Four

Paul's Preaching for Community Formation:
The Creation and Maintenance of Symbolic Boundaries 101
   4.1. Symbolic Boundaries and Community Formation 101
   4.2. Preaching of the Kerygmatic Narrative to
        Create Boundaries 108
       4.2.1. The Kerygmatic Narrative Incorporated 108
       4.2.2. The Kerygmatic Narrative Functioned as
            Symbolic Boundaries 114
   4.3. Preaching of Local Narratives to Create Boundaries 118
       4.3.1. Local Narratives Incorporated 118
       4.3.2. Local Narratives Functioned as
            Symbolic Boundaries 121
   4.4. Preaching of Ethical Norms to Create Boundaries 126
       4.4.1. Ethical Norms Incorporated 126
       4.4.2. Ethical Norms Functioned as
            Symbolic Boundaries 135
   4.5. Conclusion 140

Chapter Five

Homiletical Implications of Paul's Preaching for
Community Formation with Regard to the Post-Christian Context 141
   5.1. Connecting the Post-Christian Context to Paul's
        Pre-Christian Context 141

   5.2. Essential Task of Preaching in a Post-Christian Culture: Community Formation 146
   5.3. Preaching Methods for Community Formation 152
       5.3.1. To Preach Shared Narratives 152
       5.3.2. To Preach Ethical Norms 159
   5.4. Conclusion 162

Chapter Six

Conclusion 163
   6.1. Summary of the Findings 163
   6.2. Suggestions for Further Study 165

Bibliography 167

Chapter One
Introduction

1.1. Statement of the Problem and Research Gap

Though few scholars claim that the approach of the New Homiletic is already becoming old,[1] the New Homiletic has determined the ongoing consequence for the homiletical field, especially in North America.[2] O. Wesley Allen writes:

> Their core contributions continue to be influential in preaching and the study of preaching today. There are few preachers whose approach has not been shaped directly or indirectly by them. There are no homileticians teaching in North America today who would not name this group as the shoulders upon which we stand.[3]

Current dialogical preaching, seeker-sensitive preaching and even some preachers in the Emerging Church also find their roots in the New Homiletic.[4] Scott Gibson therefore states, "The influence of the New Homiletic in late twentieth century and early twenty-first century preaching is wide spread."[5]

---

1   James Thompson, *Preaching Like Paul: Homiletical Wisdom for Today* (Louisville: Westminster John Knox Press, 2001), 1.
2   See O. Wesley Allen, "Introduction: The Pillars of the New Homiletic," in *The Renewed Homiletic*, ed. O. Wesley Allen (Minneapolis: Fortress Press, 2010); Richard L. Eslinger, *The Web of Preaching: New Options in Homiletical Method* (Nashville: Abingdon Press, 2002); Scott M. Gibson, "Defining the New Homiletic," *The Journal of the Evangelical Homiletics Society* 5, no. 2 (2005).
3   Allen, 18.
4   See Kristopher Kim Barnett, "A Historical/Critical Analysis of Dialogical Preaching" (Ph.D. diss., Southwestern Baptist Theological Seminary, 2008), 162–209. For particularly the relationship between the New Homiletic and preaching in the Emerging Church, see Nicholas G. Gatzke, "Preaching in the Emerging Church and Its Relationship to the New Homiletic" (Ph.D. diss., Brunel University, 2008).
5   Gibson: 23.

No one denies that the homiletical approach has sparked the proliferation of new homiletical methods and stimulated the renewal of preaching. Proponents of the New Homiletic have contended that conventional styles of preaching are neither attractive nor effective for contemporary listeners and thus have sought an alternative to such preaching through a paradigm shift from the traditional framework of preaching. Richard Eslinger describes the new direction in preaching as "the Copernican Revolution in homiletics."[6] David Lose thusly comments about the influence of the New Homiletic:

> Next to the sixteenth century, the twentieth has probably seen a greater interest in the renewal and revival of preaching than any other. In the second half of the century, especially, preachers benefited from a creative "explosion" of available homiletical methods. Many of these have been grouped together under the banner of "the New Homiletic."[7]

Reflecting on the development of the New Homiletic, Paul Wilson also contends, "Not since the Middle Age or the Reformation have such mighty winds swept the homiletical highlands."[8]

It is, however, also true that the New Homiletic has been challenged by the fundamental question of whether the homiletical development by the New Homiletic has contributed to the development of the church.[9] For example, Charles Campbell claims, "One can hardly argue that these

---

6 Richard L. Eslinger, *A New Hearing: Living Options in Homiletic Methods* (Nashville: Abingdon Press, 1987), 65.
7 David L. Lose, "Whither Hence, New Homiletic?," in *the Academy of Homiletics* (Perkins School of Theology: Academy of Homiletics, 2000), 255.
8 Paul Scott Wilson, *The Practice of Preaching* (Nashville: Abingdon Press, 1995), 12.
9 See David L. Allen, "A Tale of Two Roads: Homiletics and Biblical Authority," *Journal of the Evangelical Theological Society* 43, no. 3 (2000); Charles L. Campbell, *Preaching Jesus: New Directions for Homiletics in Hans Frei's Postliberal Theology* (Grand Rapids: W. B. Eerdmans Pub., 1997); Mark A. Howell, "Hermeneutical Bridges and Homiletical Methods: A Comparative Analysis of the New Homiletic and Expository Preaching Theory 1970–1995" (Ph.D. diss., Sourthen Baptist Seminary, 1999); Grant Irven Lovejoy, "A Critical Evaluation of the Nature and Role of Authority in the Homiletical Thought of Fred B. Craddock, Edmund A. Steimle, and David G. Buttrick" (Ph.D. diss., Southwestern Baptist Theological Seminary, 1990); Randal Alan Williams, "The Impact of Contemporary Narrative Homiletics on Interpreting and Preaching the Bible" (Ph.D. diss., Southern Baptist Theological Seminary, 2006); John W. Wright, *Telling God's Story: Narrative Preaching for Christian Formation* (Downers Grove: IVP Academic, 2007).

developments have resulted in a more vital and faithful church."[10] He continues:

> Beneath the surface, however, signs of trouble can be discerned. The new preaching theories and resources do not appear to have brought new life to the church. Over the same period that homiletics has enjoyed a resurgence, mainline Protestant churches have been in decline. The multiplication of preaching theories and resources has taken place alongside a growing sense of concern, even despair, about the life and future of the church. Recently homiletical developments seem to have accomplished little more than to rearrange the proverbial deck chairs on the Titanic.[11]

Even one of their own gives a negative response to the question whether the New Homiletic stimulates the resurgence and development of the church: "Majority-culture churches in long-established denominations in North America have been in institutional decline since the beginning of the New Homiletic."[12] The wind of the New Homiletic may be mighty on the homiletical highlands as Paul Wilson stated, but the wind did not blow so strongly for the development of the church.

In addition to the development of the New Homiletic, a tendency of preaching, especially in the churches of the United States, is the scarcity of preaching on the Pauline letters. Paul's letters have been scholarly considered to be a hot place; the letters do not seem to be attractive to contemporary preachers of the ministerial fields. About the lack of preaching on Paul's letters, Robert Jewett states, "Paul's preaching is typically limited to three occasions in contemporary Protestant churches: 'on Reformation Sunday (Rom. 1:16–17), for weddings (1 Corinthians 13) and for funerals (Rom. 8:31–39)!'"[13] Jewett's observation is not quite different from those even in the twenty-first century. Brad Braxton diagnoses the pervading assumptions about Paul's letters among contemporary preachers:

> Many ministers assume that Paul is difficult to understand, overly opinionated, and supportive of, if not directly responsible for, various kinds of oppression in the church. Consequently, some preachers prefer not to drag the baggage surrounding Paul into their pulpits.[14]

---

10 Campbell, 121.
11 Ibid., xi.
12 Ronald J. Allen, "Celebration Renewed: Responses," in *The Renewed Homiletic*, ed. O. Wesley Allen (Minneapolis: Fortress Press, 2010), 79.
13 Robert Jewett, *Paul the Apostle to America: Cultural Trends and Pauline Scholarship* (Louisville: Westminster John Knox Press, 1994), 14.
14 Brad R. Braxton, *Preaching Paul* (Nashville: Abingdon Press, 2004), 14.

With these assumptions preachers tend to be reluctant to include Paul's letters in their preaching.

In addition to the scarcity of preaching on Paul's letters in the church, the legitimacy regarding Paul as a model for contemporary preaching has also been questioned. Paul's direct and authoritative style of preaching is considered inappropriate for contemporary listeners in a post-modern culture that dislikes authority. J. Christiaan Beker describes the animosity toward Paul's style: "Many intelligent church members cherish a dislike for Paul because of his presumable arrogance, his doctrinal stance, or his 'perversion' of the gospel of Jesus."[15] James Thompson thus claims, "To suggest that Paul's preaching in a pagan context of the first century is a model for preaching in the twenty-first century is to invite incredulity and resistance from most contemporary preachers."[16] Homiletical texts addressing Paul's preaching as a model for preaching ministry have been few and far between.

Some scholars admit that the New Homiletic is responsible for the disrespect towards Paul in preaching. As noticed in the subtitle of the work of Eugene Lowry, one of the leading scholars in the New Homiletic: "Why All Sermons Are Narrative,"[17] much literature of the New Homiletic treats narrative or story preaching as a primary style of preaching[18] that ignores other biblical genres, especially Paul's letters. Concerning the paucity of preaching from Paul's letters within the New Homiletic, Nancy Gross observes:

> The homiletical trend of the last twenty-five years, from which we are only just now emerging, has been narrative preaching. After generations of "three points and a

---

15 J. Christiaan Beker, *Heirs of Paul: Paul's Legacy in the New Testament and in the Church Today* (Minneapolis: Fortress Press, 1991), 101.
16 Thompson, 14.
17 Eugene L. Lowry, *The Homiletical Beat: Why All Sermons Are Narrative* (Nashville: Abingdon Press, 2012).
18 See Fred B. Craddock, *As One without Authority* (Saint Louis: Chalice Press, 2001); Fred B. Craddock, *Overhearing the Gospel* (St. Louis: Chalice Press, 2002); Eugene L. Lowry, *Doing Time in the Pulpit: The Relationship between Narrative and Preaching* (Nashville: Abingdon Press, 1985); Eugene L. Lowry, *How to Preach a Parable: Designs for Narrative Sermons* (Nashville: Abingdon Press, 1989); Eugene L. Lowry, *The Homiletical Plot: The Sermon as Narrative Art Form* (Louisville: Westminster John Knox Press, 2001); Henry H. Mitchell, *Celebration and Experience in Preaching* (Nashville: Abingdon Press, 1990); Charles L. Rice, *Interpretation and Imagination: The Preacher and Contemporary Literature* (Philadelphia: Fortress Press, 1970); Edmund A. Steimle, Morris J. Niedenthal, and Charles L. Rice, *Preaching the Story* (Philadelphia: Fortress Press, 1980).

poem," the pendulum swung far in the other direction and the narrative movement caught nearly every preacher's attention and imagination. According to conventional wisdom, the Pauline epistles clearly do not lend themselves to narrative preaching.[19]

David Bartlett simply evaluates the recent homiletical trend as follows: "In the legitimate enthusiasm for narrative preaching, we sometimes undervalue Paul."[20] In the text of the New Homiletic, Paul's preaching is normally not regarded as a model for contemporary preaching.

Despite this exclusion of Paul's preaching, some scholars have recently advocated that Paul's preaching has the potential to overcome the limitations of the New Homiletic. James Thompson, in *Preaching Like Paul: Homiletical Wisdom for Today*, first considered Paul's preaching model from the letters as a model for contemporary preaching, based on a balanced critique of the New Homiletic. In the section titled "Reflections a Generation Later" of the book, he gives an insightful comment about the New Homiletic:

> When I first read the new homileticians, beginning shortly after the publication of Fred Craddock's *Overhearing the Gospel* and *As One without Authority*, I greeted their proposals with enthusiasm, recognizing that narrative could give life to the sermon. However, with the passage of time, I am convinced that, to rescue preaching, something more is needed than the rediscovery of the narrative form. Although I have learned very much from the "new wineskins" of preaching, my earlier enthusiasm for the contributions of the past generation is now tempered by both unanswered questions and reservations about this approach.[21]

In contrast to the extensively popular interest in narrative preaching proposed by the New Homiletic, Thompson shows that Paul's letters offer an alternative model for contemporary preaching by demonstrating how Paul's style of preaching used in the pre-Christian culture is appropriate for the current post-Christian culture. He writes, "Paul is a forgotten mentor in our understanding of preaching. His preaching in a pre-Christian age has much to tell preachers who live in a post-Christian age."[22] His groundbreaking analysis of homiletical dialogue between Paul and contemporary

---

19 Nancy Lammers Gross, *If You Cannot Preach Like Paul* (Grand Rapids: W. B. Eerdmans Pub., 2002), xii.
20 David L. Bartlett, "Text Shaping Sermons," in *Listening to the Word: Studies in Honor of Fred B. Craddock*, eds. Gail R. O'Day and Thomas G. Long (Nashville: Abingdon Press, 1993), 160.
21 Thompson, 9.
22 Ibid., 18–19.

homiletics exposes a significant area for study, which has been missed under the massive influence of the New Homiletic.

Claiming that the narrative movement in homiletics catches many of scholars' attention and imagination, Nancy Gross, in *If You Cannot Preach Like Paul*, also joins the ranks Thompson begins by reclaiming Paul for contemporary preaching in the church. She also poses a problem in contemporary homiletical situation in which Paul's letters have been ignored and misused in the pulpit: "It is important to reclaim Paul for the preaching ministry of the church because without a vital preaching presence emerging from the Pauline epistles, we are depriving the church of the whole counsel of God."[23] However, it is not enough to pay attention to the Pauline letters in the same way as traditionally practiced. According to Gross, the traditional preaching approaches to the Pauline letters mainly understood Paul as a systematic theologian, using a Pauline text as a proof text or for preaching a linear, rational, deductive argument.[24] Preachers should make a paradigm shift from this traditional way of preaching Paul. To do this, she argues that contemporary preachers should do what Paul did, not just say what he said, because his letters are so specific in addressing pastoral situations. According to her, doing what Paul did is to properly consider the nature of Paul's preaching ministry as a practical theologian.

Moving beyond the broad approach to Paul's letters, David Eung-Yul Ryoo in "Paul's Preaching in the Epistle to the Ephesians and Its Homiletical Implications"[25] examines Ephesians in particular to offer Paul's preaching as a good model for contemporary preachers. Ryoo explores how Paul preached major theological themes such as God the Father, Jesus Christ, the Holy Spirit, and the Christian Life in the letter with special emphasis on his use of the Old Testament; Ryoo then examines homiletical implications for

---

23   Gross, xvi.
24   Ibid., 12–17.
25   David Eung-Yul Ryoo, "Paul's Preaching in the Epistle to the Ephesians and Its Homiletical Implications" (Ph.D. diss., Southern Baptist Theological Seminary, 2003). Scholarly opinions are sharply divided over whether Ephesians is a letter by Paul. A discussion of Paul's authorship of all thirteen letters attributed to him in the New Testament is beyond the scope of this study. The authorship of some letters such as Ephesians, 1 and 2 Timothy, Titus, Colossians, and 2 Thessalonians continues to be debated. Therefore, the following discussion on the continuity between Paul's letters and his preaching only focuses on "undisputed letters" – Romans, 1 and 2 Corinthians, Galatians, Philippians, 1 Thessalonians, and Philemon – which are widely accepted as authentic.

contemporary preachers by interacting with the New Homiletic. Based on exegetical and theological investigations, he suggests that Paul's preaching in Ephesians reflects both the "indicative-grounded and imperative-oriented preaching"[26] and the "redemptive-historical preaching,"[27] which is generally lacking in the approach of contemporary narrative preaching.

Corey Len Abney in "The Apostle Paul's Methodology of Preaching in Acts and 1 Corinthians and Its Implications for Expository Preaching"[28] also criticizes the current indifference to Pauline preaching caused by the excessive attention on narrative preaching:

> As narrative preaching increased in popularity and acceptance over the years, a new generation of preachers emerged without much exposure to the Pauline corpus. […] Proponents of narrative preaching scoffed contiunally at the notion of an authoritative text produced by an authoritative author. Even the narrative preachers who attemps to embrace Paul's letters in ther preaching ministry do so with belief that Paul's inscripturated words are not necessarily God words.[29]

To defend Paul's preaching method there should be an alternative to the narrative preaching of the New Homiletic, Abney concentrates on a hermeneutical analysis of Paul's sermons in Acts and the first letter to the Corinthians, considering their literary and rhetorical aspects. In this analysis, he argues that Paul's model of preaching should inform modern preachers how to develop an expository preaching model – biblical, Christological, applicational, adaptable, personal, colorful and sometimes confrontational.

Michael Knowles in *We Preach Not Ourselves: Paul on Proclamation* explores Paul's spirituality of preaching based on his own exegetical reading of 2 Corinthians 1:1–6:13. Discerning that the current homiletical

---

26 Ibid., 179. Traditionally, Paul's letters has been divided into two parts: (1) indicative mode as the theological exposition, (2) imperative mode as the practical application. However, this rigid dichotomy has been challenged by the view that there exists an inextricable connection between theological concepts and ethical practice. See Victor Paul Furnish, *Theology and Ethics in Paul* (Nashville: Abingdon Press, 1968), 110, 279. Also see David G. Horrell, *Solidarity and Difference: A Contemporary Reading of Paul's Ethics* (New York: T & T Clark International, 2005), 10–15.
27 Ryoo, 191.
28 Corey Len Abney, "The Apostle Paul's Methodology of Preaching in Acts and 1 Corinthians and Its Implications for Expository Preaching" (Ph.D. diss., Southern Baptist Theological Seminary, 2009).
29 Ibid., 12.

discussion has been engrossed more in sermonic form rather than content or spirituality,[30] Knowles does not demonstrate Paul's rhetorical aspects as a model of preaching but how the theology of the cross shape the preacher and the content of the sermon. Using Michael Gorman's *Cruciformity: Paul's Narrative Spirituality of the Cross*[31] as a foundation, Knowles asserts that "Paul [...] concentrates on the conclusion of Jesus's life, proposing crucifixion and resurrection as categories that provide a primary template or archetype for Christian spirituality, discipleship, and ministry."[32] According to Knowles, Paul's preaching ministry is no exception: The death and resurrection of Jesus drive the content of Paul's preaching and the means by which preaching is made possible. They also regulate the manner and method by which Paul preaches.

Steven Smith in *Dying to Preach: Embracing the Cross in the Pulpit* sets out that the Cross of Christ heavily shaped Paul's theology of preaching. Similar to Knowles, he also asserts that a style of preaching has become the ultimate question in the field of homiletics and the medium of preaching has even "trumped the message of Scripture" in the field of ministry.[33] Instead of expounding half of 2 Corinthians, Smith however goes through various selected texts from 1 and 2 Corinthians and then concludes that Paul suffered for the benefit of the Corinthian believers by identifying Paul's ministry to the Corinthians as "dying for others."[34] Following the example of Paul, Smith declares that preachers also must embrace the cross in the pulpit, which requires them to surrender to Christ, as Christ surrendered his rights for others. In order to "surrender[ing] to Christ in the preaching task,"[35] Smith proposes that contemporary preachers must surrender to the text they are preaching, surrender to the listeners as recognizing that their preaching must meet the need of the listeners to know the truth, and surrender to the labor of excellence in preaching.

Though Paul's preaching has been advocated recently as the alternative model to contemporary preaching, it is still necessary to introduce

---

30 Michael P. Knowles, *We Preach Not Ourselves: Paul on Proclamation* (Grand Rapids: Brazos Press, 2008), 19–20.
31 Michael J. Gorman, *Cruciformity: Paul's Narrative Spirituality of the Cross* (Grand Rapids: W. B. Eerdmans Pub., 2001).
32 Knowles, 15.
33 Steven W. Smith, *Dying to Preach: Embracing the Cross in the Pulpit* (Grand Rapids: Kregel Publications, 2009), 49–50.
34 Ibid., 23–59.
35 Ibid., 111.

updated Pauline studies into the homiletical debate. While many narrative homileticians, especially in the New Homiletic, have proposed the sharp distinction between narrative texts and Paul's letters, which finally lead to the neglect of Paul's letters in contemporary homiletical debate, a considerable amount of literature on Paul in fact has suggested that Paul's letters have a narrative dimension.[36] It is certain that one cannot separate Paul's letters from his pastoral relationship to his communities. James Dune writes, "With Paul's letters, however, it is impossible to escape their character as *letters*, communication from a *known* author to *specific* people in *particular* circumstances."[37] Thus, each Pauline letter contains specific issues and topics shared by between Paul and his congregants. This means that Paul's letters arose from some congregational narratives "in front of" the text.[38] In addition to the local narratives, Paul's letters also assume various levels of the grand narratives like the God of Israel who created the world, humanity who has been depraved by sin, and God's initiative of recovery through Abraham and his descendants, culminating in Jesus Christ. Not telling these stories exhaustively in many cases, Paul kept these controlling narratives in mind in his letters. Richard Hays even states, "The framework of Paul's thought is constituted neither by a system of doctrines

---

36 Richard Hays' works have had much influence on contemporary study of narrative ingredients in Paul. See Richard Hays, *Echoes of Scripture in the Letters of Paul* (New Haven: Yale University Press, 1989); Richard Hays, *The Faith of Jesus Christ: The Narrative Substructure of Galatians 3:1–4:11* (Grand Rapids: W. B. Eerdmans Pub., 2002). Norman Petersen introduces a sociological consideration to the narrative approach. See Norman R. Petersen, *Rediscovering Paul: Philemon and the Sociology of Paul's Narrative World* (Philadelphia: Fortress Press, 1985). For narrative features in Paul's thought, see Douglas A. Campbell, *The Quest for Paul's Gospel: A Suggested Strategy* (London: T & T Clark, 2005); Gorman, *Cruciformity: Paul's Narrative Spirituality of the Cross*; A. Katherine Grieb, *The Story of Romans: A Narrative Defense of God's Righteousness* (Louisville: Westminster John Knox Press, 2002); Ben Witherington, *Paul's Narrative Thought World: The Tapestry of Tragedy and Triumph* (Louisville: Westminster John Knox Press, 1994); N. T. Wright, *The New Testament and the People of God* (Minneapolis: Fortress Press, 1992); N. T. Wright, *Paul in Fresh Perspective* (Minneapolis: Fortress Press, 2009). For a critical assessment of the narrative study of Paul, see Bruce W. Longenecker, ed. *Narrative Dynamics in Paul* (Louisville: Westminster John Konx Press, 2002).
37 James D. G. Dunn, *The Theology of Paul the Apostle* (Grand Rapids: W. B. Eerdmans Pub., 1998), 11. Italics original.
38 For the distinction between the world in front and the world behind the text, see David L. Bartlett, *Between the Bible and the Church: New Methods for Biblical Preaching* (Nashville: Abingdon Press, 1999), 138–151.

nor his personal religious experience but by a 'scared story,' a narrative structure"; "the story provides the foundational substructure upon which Paul's argumentation is constructed."[39] N. T. Wright also claims, "The apostle's most emphatically 'theological' statements and arguments are in fact expressions of *the essentially Jewish story now redrawn around Jesus.*"[40] Though it is not necessary to believe that Paul used all levels of the grand narrative above mentioned in all of his letters, it can be said that Paul weaved elements of multiple narratives, including local and grand ones, into his letters.[41] Therefore, James Thompson writes, "Nor can one assume that narrative and letters inhabit totally different worlds, for they interact with each other at a variety of levels. Both modes of communication share a common denominator of narrative and discourse."[42] Based on this research on narrative dynamics in Paul's letters, this study aims to examine the role of narratives in Paul's preaching.

In addition, this study proposes that Paul's preaching can be considered as preaching for community formation. Preaching for community formation is critical in the contemporary homiletical field as the main emphasis of the New Homiletic is placed on *individual* listeners and appealing to them.[43] As far as preaching for community formation is concerned, this study also considers recent sociological studies that have examined how the early Christian communities, including those begun by Paul, were formed.[44] This

---

39 Hays, *The Faith of Jesus Christ: The Narrative Substructure of Galatians 3:1–4:11*, 6, 7.
40 Wright, *The New Testament and the People of God*, 79. Italics original.
41 Ben Witherington speaks of four distinct stories: (1) the story of a world gone wrong, (2) the story of Israel, (3) the story of Christ, and (4) the story of Christians, including Paul himself. Witherington, 5. James Dunn sees talks about five narrative elements: (1) the story of God and creation, (2) the story of Israel, (3) the story of Jesus, (4) Paul's own story, and (5) the stories of those who had believed before Paul and of those who came to form the churches. Dunn, 18. Michael Bird suggests that Paul's letters contains the story of Paul's life and ministry and a grand narrative composed of six main chapters: (1) God and creation, (2) Adam and Christ, (3) Abraham, (4) Israel, (5) Jesus, and (6) the church. Michael F. Bird, *Introducing Paul: The Man, His Mission, and His Message* (Downers Grove: InterVarsity Press, 2008), 38.
42 James Thompson, "Reading the Letters as Narrative," in *Narrative Reading, Narrative Preaching: Reuniting New Testament Interpretation and Proclamation*, eds. Joel B. Green and Michael Pasquarello (Grand Rapids: Baker Academic, 2003), 85.
43 This issue will be discussed in chapter 2.
44 Two important studies relating to Paul are by Margaret Y. MacDonald, *The Pauline Churches: A Socio-Historical Study of Institutionalization in the Pauline and*

study also examines some sociological approaches adopted for the study of the New Testament into the field of homiletics, especially the concept of symbolic boundaries to explore Paul's preaching for community formation.

This study concentrates on Paul's preaching in 1 Thessalonians, which has not been adequately discussed in contemporary homiletical discussions as seen above. There are three additional reasons for choosing this book for the study. First, there is almost universal consensus that Paul wrote this letter. Although some verbs used in the letter are in the plural, which could imply multiple authors,[45] Paul's primary authorship of 1 Thessalonians is not debated.[46] As Charles Wanamaker concludes, "No contemporary scholars of repute seem to doubt the authentic Pauline character of the letter."[47]

Second, little in the letter suggests that Paul dominantly addressed complicated doctrinal subjects such as justification by faith, work of the law, and so on. Rather, Paul's central concern in 1 Thessalonians is the ongoing progress of the community. This letter reflects Paul's pastoral interest in a community more obviously than in any of Paul's other letters.[48] Due to the scarcity of doctrinal issues that would cause heated debates, this letter, compared to Paul's other ones, has been relatively neglected by scholars. However, the clear pastoral attention of Paul to his fledgling

---

Deutero-Pauline Writings (Cambridge: Cambridge University Press, 1988), and Wayne A. Meeks, *The First Urban Christians: The Social World of the Apostle Paul* (New Haven: Yale University Press, 1983). For a brief description of sociological approaches regarding Paul, see David G. Horrell, *An Introduction to the Study of Paul* (New York: T & T Clark, 2006), 98–102.

45   The use of the plural verbs may refer to Silvanus and Timothy, mentioned in 1:1, but it may be also be Paul's characteristic style to use it to refer to himself. See C. E. B. Cranfield, "Change of Person and Number in Paul's Epistles," in *Paul and Paulinism: Essays in Honour of C.K. Barrett*, eds. Hooker M. D. and Wilson S. G. (London: SPCK, 1982), 280–289. It is also possible that Paul dictated his letter to Silvanus. For a brief discussion Silvanus's potential influence, see Ernest Best, *A Commentary on the First and Second Epistles to the Thessalonians* (New York: Harper & Row, 1972), 23–29.

46   A number of scholars in the nineteenth century, such as Clement Schrader and F. C. Baur, challenged its authorship. The chief ground for their objection against Pauline authorship was lack of doctrinal emphasis, See F. F. Bruce, *1 and 2 Thessalonians* (Waco: Word Books, 1982), xxxiii.

47   Charles A. Wanamaker, *The Epistles to the Thessalonians: A Commentary on the Greek Text* (Grand Rapids: W. B. Eerdmans Pub., 1990), 17.

48   Abraham J. Malherbe, *Paul and the Thessalonians: The Philosophic Tradition of Pastoral Care* (Philadelphia: Fortress Press, 1987), 2.

community as shown in 1 Thessalonians makes this letter an effective source for discovering his preaching strategy for community formation.

Lastly, when compared with the other Pauline letters, 1 Thessalonians lacks internal conflict within the believing community. The challenges are mainly related to external pressures that were due to the Thessalonians' conversion and their new life style in a pagan context of a larger society.[49] Thus, Paul's main attention in 1 Thessalonians is not to be in opposition to a heretical group in his community, as seen in his other letters, but in facing the harsh external situation that the community struggled against to form a communal identity and community solidarity. Therefore, Paul's preaching in 1 Thessalonians can be a useful model for preaching about community formation.

1.2. Research Methodology[50] and Structure

The primary purpose of the study is to explore Paul's preaching for community formation in 1 Thessalonians as an alternative to contemporary homiletics, particularly the New Homiletic.

To conduct this study, it is first necessary to investigate whether or not continuity exists between Paul's letters and his preaching. By examining Paul's preaching contained in his letters and the oral aspects of his letters within the wider context of letter writing protocol in the Greco-Roman world, the preliminary section will attempt to show that Paul normally utilized the rhetorical and homiletical devices in his letter writing and his letters show a strong echo of his preaching. By proving that Paul's letters are very much related to his preaching, this homiletical study on Paul's preaching model in 1 Thessalonians for contemporary preachers can be justified.

Chapter 2 will provide a description and critical evaluation of the New Homiletic. First, the chapter will probe some background features from

---

49   This issue will be again discussed at greater length in chapter 3.
50   The methodology of this study is quite similar to the tasks of practical theology as argued by Richard R. Osmer. These are: (1) What is going on? (descriptive-empirical task), (2) Why is this going on? (interpretive task), (3) What ought to be going on? (normative task), and (4) How might we respond? (pragmatic task). See Richard R. Osmer, *Practical Theology: An Introduction* (Grand Rapids: W. B. Eerdmans Pub., 2008), 4.

whence the New Homiletic originated. The chapter then will describe the common characteristics of the New Homiletic by analyzing the homiletical theories of main figures within the homiletical approach. The chapter then will provide a critical evaluation of the New Homiletic, particularly a critique against the individualistic approach for preaching. This criticism will show the neglected task of preaching in contemporary homiletical approaches and emphasize the need for a study on preaching for community formation.

Chapter 3 aims to show that Paul's primary task in 1 Thessalonians is to form and maintain the young Thessalonian community in a hostile environment. The chapter will introduce the pagan context of the city of Thessalonica and the profile of the community established in the pagan city. Then, it will be demonstrated that the Thessalonian community experienced suffering as a result of conflicts with pagan compatriots. Finally, the chapter will show that Paul in this crisis of the community wrote 1 Thessalonian to implement the process of community formation for the long-term well-being of the community. Paul's intention in 1 Thessalonians will legitimize the main focus of this study to explore his preaching for community formation in 1 Thessalonians.

The aim of chapter 4 is to explore Paul's preaching for community formation in 1 Thessalonians. First, contemporary sociological research on the role of symbolic boundaries in the formation of collective identity will be introduced. The concept of symbolic boundaries will provide the backdrop for the rest of this chapter for Paul's community formation preaching. After that, the chapter will examine how Paul in his preaching drew symbolic boundaries and made conceptual distinction between his community and outsiders to establish a cooperative identity through community solidarity. The chapter will confirm that Paul used the kerygmatic narrative, local narratives, and ethical norms as resources to construct symbolic boundaries. It will be shown that the shared narratives in Paul's preaching have a major role in discriminating between believers as insiders and non-believers as outsiders as well as establishing the cooperative identity of the community. It will be further demonstrated that Paul utilized the ethical norms different from Gentile morality as a component of the symbolic boundary, which served as the badges of communal identity and distinguished his community from Gentile outsiders.

Chapter 5 will examine the homiletical implications of Paul's community formation preaching in 1 Thessalonians by using the perspectives of the contemporary homiletics and post-Christian culture. The chapter will suggest that, in the contemporary culture, the two fundamental tasks of preaching is to provide shared narratives and communal ethical norms that are not in accordance with those in a non-Christian culture, and to build Christian communities.

1.3. The Continuity between Paul's Letters and His Preaching

Paul has been appreciated as one of the most dedicated preachers throughout Christian history: "Preaching was, in fact, his calling, and with a fine single-mindedness, he made it his life's work, everything else being subordinated to it."[51] However, what is actually contained in the Bible are not his sermons. Except for a few "sermons" in Acts,[52] the Bible contains his letters. Also, Paul was aware that he was writing letters. His references to letters, the Greek term ἐπιστολή, are founded in his letters,[53] which means that Paul knew that what he had done was to write a letter. The genre of the letter was very well-known in the Greco-Roman world; there was a good deal of commonality in Hellenistic letter writing customs. Most scholars agree that Paul's letters adhere to standard Hellenistic letter writing protocol. What we have are not his sermons, but his letters, which seems to be an obstacle as this study examines Paul's preaching in his letters, focusing on 1 Thessalonians as a model for contemporary preaching ministry. In

---

51 Martin Dibelius and Werner Georg Kümmel, *Paul* (Philadelphia: Westminster Press, 1966), 21.
52 According to Richard Wells, Luke in Acts records at least twenty evangelical preaching – ten by Paul, eight by Peter, and one each by Stephen and James. Luke also mentions more than twenty-five other events linked to preaching. See C. Richard Wells and A. Boyd Luter, *Inspired Preaching: A Survey of Preaching Found in the New Testament* (Nashville: Broadman & Holman, 2002), 76. It is necessary to note that these passages in Acts are also not verbatim sermons; they are summaries of what Paul originally preached. See William Barclay, "A Comparision of Paul's Missionary Preaching and Preaching to the Church," in *Apostolic History and the Gospel: Biblical and Historical Essays Presented to F. F. Bruce on His 60th Birthday*, eds. W. Ward Gasque and Ralph P. Martin (Grand Rapids: Eerdmans, 1970), 165.
53 See among his letters, 1 Thess. 5:27; Rom. 16:22; 1 Cor. 5:9, 16:3; 2 Cor. 3:1, 2, 3, 7:8, 10:9, 10, 11.

spite of the limitations in the knowledge about Paul's actual preaching, this preliminary section will present the continuity between Paul's letters and his preaching, and argue that his letters provide a strong echo of his actual preaching ministry.

1.3.1. Communication to Communities of Faith

Paul's letters functioned beyond that of personal correspondence. At the turn of the twentieth century, Adolf Deissmann made a sharp distinction between "letter" and "epistle" based on his investigation of ancient papyri. A "letter" was a private document written for "personal and intimate communication."[54] In contrast, an "epistle" was a document written for "published literature" with a wide audience.[55] Having made this distinction between letters and epistles, Deissmann concluded that Paul wrote letters, not epistles, and emphasized the similarities between Paul's letters and privately occasioned papyrus letters. Deissmann noted, "I have no hesitation in maintaining the thesis that all the letters of Paul are real, nonliterary letters. Paul was not a writer of epistles but of letters; he was not a literary man."[56] According to Deissmann, Paul's letters were intended to be about private matters and to address specific situations that could not be repeated or be accessed by the general public.

From the content and aim of Paul's letters, however, it seems obvious that they cannot be classified merely as occasional, private letters. His letters were primarily to believing communities. These letters were intended to address a group of people in a community of faith to greet, inform, teach, encourage, and persuade them. Even Paul's most private letter, his

---

54 Adolf Deissmann, *Bible Studies: Contributions, Chiefly from Papyri and Inscriptions, to the History of the Language, the Literature, and the Religion of Hellenistic Judaism and Primitive Christianity* (Edinburgh: T. & T. Clark, 1901), 3.
55 Ibid., 9.
56 Adolf Deissmann, *Light from the Ancient East: The New Testament Illustrated by Recently Discovered Texts of the Graeco-Roman World* (London: Hodder & Stoughton, 1909), 232. Recent scholars have criticized the public and private categories. Ben Witherington states that the sharp distinction between public and private realms is a modern invention. Ben Witherington, *The Acts of the Apostles: A Socio-Rhetorical Commentary* (Grand Rapids: W. B. Eerdmans Pub., 1998), 335. Also see Stanley K. Stowers, *Letter Writing in Greco-Roman Antiquity* (Philadelphia: Westminster Press, 1986), 19.

letter to Philemon, was addressed not just to one slave owner, but to the believing community that Philemon belonged to and congregated in his house, "the church that meets in your home" (2).[57] Paul also commands that his first letter to Thessalonians "[be] read to all the brothers" (5:27), which indicates that he intended for his letter to be read by a wider audience.[58] Therefore, Arthur Nock has suggested that Paul's letters were a new type of letter, an "encyclical," which became a pattern for later bishops in addressing their churches.[59] It is evident that Paul's letters were intended to be documents that were read in the communities, and not as personal or private documents.

Paul's letters were also copied soon after he wrote them and were probably distributed to other believing communities.[60] The communities were encouraged to exchange his letters among one another. Aware that his letters may be circulated, Paul obviously addresses his first letter to Corinth to both "the church of God in Corinth" and to "all those everywhere who call on the name of our Lord Jesus Christ" (1:2). Paul's letters certainly transcend the situation of the individual community. John Polhill therefore concludes, "Paul's letters always had an eye on the larger Christian community. [...] In short, Paul's letters were both occasional (written for specific congregations) and general (carrying the apostle's authority for all who might read them)."[61] The fact that Paul's letters were written to communicate with believing communities, and even the larger context of the Christ-following community, shows that Paul's letters and preaching share its primary function.

Paul modified the common Hellenistic letter form to accommodate preaching into this function sharing. The typical structure of the Greco-Roman letters in those days was composed of three parts: salutation, body, and closing. The salutation contained the name of the person who wrote the letter (addresser), the addressee, and a greeting. The greeting might be followed by a health wish, a prayer, or a thanks to various gods. After the body, the closing of the letter ended with a word of farewell, sometimes preceded by a wish of health for the addressee or a request for them to greet others.[62]

---

57 Biblical quotations are from the NIV unless otherwise indicated.
58 Charles B. Cousar, *The Letters of Paul* (Nashville: Abingdon Press, 1996), 25.
59 Arthur D. Nock, *St. Paul* (New York: Harper and Brothers, 1937), 146.
60 Cousar, 25.
61 John B. Polhill, *Paul and His Letters* (Nashville: Broadman & Holman, 1999), 121.
62 Stowers, 20.

Although all of the thirteen letters bearing Paul's name[63] are consistent with this standard three-part structure of letters in the Greco-Roman period, the letters go beyond the typical form by Paul's addition of a thanksgiving section and parenthetic section. Paul's letters usually have a five-part structure: salutation, thanksgiving, body, paranesis, and closing.[64]

With the exception of Galatians,[65] his letters contain a thanksgiving which indicates the basic intent or key topics of the letter.[66] The thanksgiving section also functions rhetorically as a kind of *captatio benevolentiae* intended to make the listeners or readers more receptive by winning their goodwill. In addition to the above reason, it has been suggested that Paul began his preaching with a thanksgiving to God, and that practice left its imprint on his use of the thanksgiving in his letters.[67] This idea is supported by the fact that Paul's thanksgiving sometimes has a liturgical flavor. 2 Corinthians 1:3 is one of the most obvious examples: "Praise be to the God and Father of our Lord Jesus Christ."[68]

The parenthetic section Paul grafted into the traditional letter form also reflects the practice of preaching to some extent. From the beginning, Christian preaching embraced commentary on biblical texts and applying their teaching to the lives of the people, which originated from Jewish synagogue preaching.[69] In the parenthetic section, Paul's ethical instructions[70] which follow the body of his letters show the most distinctive feature of preaching; that is application which follows explication.

---

63 See above, n. 24.
64 Stanley E. Porter, "A Functional Letter Perspective: Towards a Grammar of Epistolary Theory" in *Paul and the Ancient Letter Form*, eds. Stanley E. Porter and Sean A. Adams (Leiden: Brill, 2010), 19.
65 The absence of thanksgiving in Galatians could be due to the nature of the letter in which Paul was upset with the Galatian believers. See. Stowers, 22.
66 Stowers, 22. Also see William G. Doty, *Letters in Primitive Christianity* (Philadelphia: Fortress Press, 1973), 31–32.
67 Raymond E. Brown, *An Introduction to the New Testament* (New York: Doubleday, 1997), 415.
68 Calvin J. Roetzel, *The Letters of Paul: Conversations in Context* (Louisville: Westminster John Knox Press, 2015), 76.
69 O. C. Edwards, "History of Preaching," in *Concise Encyclopedia of Preaching*, eds. William H. Willimon and Richard Lischer (Louisville: Westminster John Knox Press, 1995), 186.
70 For three different types of ethical instructions in Paul's parenthetic section, see Roetzel, 77–79.

It can be said, therefore, that these distinctive parts in Paul's letters compared to the conventional letter form in those days – thanksgiving and paranesis – indicate a close link between the letters and preaching. Paul wisely modified the existing Hellenistic letter form to add to the function of preaching to believers.

In addition to this, Paul's letters possess many liturgical expressions that have no parallel in ancient letters. This feature illustrates that his letters were written to act as a sermon in worship settings. The standard greeting of the ancient letters is only the word "greetings." However, Paul begins his letters with the atypical expression "Grace to you and peace" (χάρις ὑμῖν καὶ εἰρήνη).[71] He adds a wish for peace that originated from the Semitic *shalom* greeting, while the word "grace" is related to the ordinary word "greetings (χάριειν)."[72] This new phrase "grace and peace" with addition of "from God our Father and the Lord Jesus Christ" reflects an early Christian worship context. Philip Tite asserts, "This innovation within early Christian epistolary style accommodates ancient conventions for the more specific context of the network of early Christian communities."[73] Paul christianized the typical greeting of the ancient letters for the use of worship setting, and Paul's style of greeting consequently became a distinctive characteristic of his letters.

In addition to the unique beginning of his letters, Paul inserts the holy kiss impossible for an individual to do without others into the closing part of his letters (Rom. 16:16; 1 Cor. 16:20; 2 Cor. 13:12; 1 Thess. 5:26). For the holy kiss, John Heil writes, "Its performance after the reading of the letter in the liturgical assembly would be a public demonstration of the communal unity, love, fellowship, and reconciliation Paul intends the letter to achieve."[74] The holy kiss was intended to be practiced in the worship of the believing community.

Instead of the ordinary farewell, Paul also closes his letters with a benediction. At the end of 2 Corinthians, for example, Paul gives the benediction:

---

71   Rom. 1:7; 1 Cor. 1:3; 2 Cor. 1:2; Gal. 1:3; Eph. 1:2; Phil. 1:2; Philem. 3.
72   Stowers, 21.
73   Philip L. Tite, "How to Begin, and Why? Diverse Function of the Pauline Prescript within a Greco-Roman Context," in *Paul and the Ancient Letter Form*, eds. Stanley E. Porter and Sean A. Adams (Leiden: Brill, 2010), 73–74.
74   John Paul Heil, *The Letters of Paul as Rituals of Worship*, (Eugene: Cascade Books, 2011), 60. Some scholars view the holy kiss as prelude to the celebration of the Eucharist. See Roetzel, 81.

"May the grace of the Lord Jesus Christ, and the love of God, and the fellowship of the Holy Spirit be with you all" (13:13). Paul's closing benedictions are taken from the liturgy of the church. Their presence suggests that Paul's own preaching contained the homiletical benediction. Robert Jewett has listed six such homiletical benedictions in the Thessalonian correspondence.[75] Paul's use of the expressions from the liturgy in the letters suggests that the letters reflects his own preaching style in a worship setting.

In summary, Paul added a function of preaching to his letters and modified the typical Hellenistic format of letters for the function. Therefore, it would not be an overstatement that Paul's letters reflect his style of preaching.

1.3.2. Repetition of What Paul Preached Before

Many parts of Paul's letters repeat what he already preached in the communities. In Galatians, for example, Paul states, "As we have already said, so now I say again: If anybody is preaching to you a gospel other than what you accepted, let him be eternally condemned!" (1:9). This statement evidently refers to what Paul preached before in the believing communities of Galatia. In 1 Thessalonians Paul's primary concern is to encourage the Thessalonians to remember what he had previously preached before while he worked in the believing community. The conspicuous formula "you know" or "as you know" (1:5, 2:1, 2:5, 2:11, 3:3, 3:4, 4:2) is repeatedly found in the letter. Paul's letters consistently repeat what he preached before and the instructions already known to the believing communities. Material of Paul's prior preaching was most likely used to write his letters. Richard Longenecker even suggests that the body of Romans can be viewed "as something of a précis of Paul's preaching in Jewish synagogues of the Diaspora and at Jewish-Gentile gatherings."[76] Paul's preaching material therefore is an important component of his letters.

75　Robert Jewett, "The Form and Function of the Homiletical Benediction," *Anglican Theological Review* 51, (1969): 18–34. The cases he identifies are 1 Thess. 3:11; 3:12–13; 5:23.
76　Richard N. Longenecker, "On the Form, Function, and Authority of the New Testament Letters," in *Scripture and Truth*, eds. D. A. Carson and John D. Woodbridge (Grand Rapids: Zondervan, 1983) Longenecker suggests that Ephesians also could be "a précis of Paul's teaching on redemption in Christ and the nature of the church."

One of the most significant elements of preaching repeatedly found in Paul's letters is his evangelistic preaching. For instance, Paul in 1 Corinthians discusses the resurrection with reminder of his earlier evangelistic preaching: "Now, brothers, I want to remind you of the gospel I preached to you, which you received and on which you have taken your stand" (15:1). The following statement is based on the crux of kerygma that he had previously preached in the believing community: "that Christ died for our sins according to the Scriptures, that he was buried, that he was raised on the third day according to the Scriptures" (15:3–4). Another obvious example is in 1 Thessalonians where Paul states, "For they themselves report what kind of reception you gave us. They tell how you turned to God from idols to serve the living and true God, and to wait for his Son from heaven, whom he raised from the dead – Jesus, who rescues us from the coming wrath" (1:9–10). This description is essentially a summary of Paul's gospel as it was first preached to the Thessalonians.[77] In his venerable work, *The Apostle Preaching and Its Development*, C. H. Dodd has indicated that the apostle had a basic structure of his gospel and weaved it into his letters.[78] It is evident that Paul's letters include aspects of what he as a missionary preached before.

With other pre-Pauline material composed on earlier occasions such as catechisms for new converts, well-known hymns and sayings,[79] Paul used his own preaching material in his letters. In this regard, James Thompson concludes that "Paul's oral communication to his churches includes catechetical instruction for the Christian life, repetition of his original preaching, and instruction about the implications of his previous instruction in the Christian life and faith."[80] Paul's letters are closely related with what he preached to the Pauline communities he established. Although they are not sermons in the technical sense, they undoubtedly contain much material that was a component of Paul's preaching.

---

77   R. H. Mounce, "Preaching, Kerygma," in *Dictionary of Paul and His Letters*, eds. Gerald F. Hawthorne, Ralph P. Martin, and Daniel G. Reid (Downers Grove: InterVarsity Press, 1993), 736.
78   C. H. Dodd, *The Apostolic Preaching and Its Developments* (New York: Harper, 1964), 9–17.
79   About preformed sources Paul used for his letters, see E. Randolph Richards, *Paul and First-Century Letter Writing: Secretaries, Composition, and Collection* (Downers Grove: InterVarsity Press, 2004), 95–99. Also see Roetzel, 85–93.
80   Thompson, *Preaching Like Paul: Homiletical Wisdom for Today*, 32.

1.3.3. The Use of Amanuenses

In antiquity it was a common practice to dictate letters to trained amanuenses. In the orally oriented culture of the first century, most people were unable to write. Writing was a specialized skill in antiquity.[81] A secretary therefore was essential for letter writing and all other forms of correspondence. The normal mode of composition of letters in the Greco-Roman world was to dictate it to a secretary.[82]

It seems that most of the New Testament letters, including those of Paul, were produced in this way. The extent to which Paul used amanuenses is debated; however, the fact that Paul used an amanuensis, like most other writers of the period, stands firm.[83] The use of such amanuenses by Paul is clearly indicated in Romans 16:22, where Tertius identifies himself as the one who "wrote" the letter. It was also normal, when a secretary had composed the letter, for the writer to add a final greeting in his own hand to indicate the letter's authenticity. Paul thus sometimes writes in his letters: "I, Paul, write this greeting in my own hand" (1 Cor. 16:21; see also Gal. 6:11; Col. 4:18; 2 Thess. 3:17 and Philem. 19). These postscripts of Paul's letters are likely indications that Paul added a few words in his own hand to letters he dictated to a secretary.

1 Thessalonians does not contain clear evidence such as a name of amanuenses or Paul's "signature" for his work to indicate that Paul used a secretary in his writing. Some scholars, however, opine that the shift from the first person plural to the first person singular in 5:27 indicates that at this point Paul himself took the pen from his secretary and authenticated the letter by his personal words.[84]

The fact that Paul used amanuenses indicates that his letter-writing process was essentially dependent on orality. John Harvey observes:

> The popular culture of the first century was, technically, a rhetorical culture. In a rhetorical culture, literacy is limited, and reading is vocal. Even the solitary reader

---

81 Pieter J. J. Botha, "The Verbal Art of the Pauline Letters: Rhetoric, Performance and Presence," in *Rhetoric and the New Testament*, eds. Thomas H. Olbricht and Stanley Porter (Sheffield: JSOT Press, 1993), 414.

82 Paul J. Achtemeier, "Omne Verbum Sonat: The New Testament and the Oral Environment of Late Western Antiquity," *Journal of Biblical Literature* 109, no. 1 (1990): 12.

83 For a comprehensive discussion, see Richards, 59–93.

84 Raymond F. Collins, *The Birth of the New Testament: The Origin and Development of the First Christian Generation* (New York: Crossroad, 1993), 124.

reads aloud (Acts 8:30). The normal mode of writing is by dictation, and that which is written down is intended to be read aloud to a group rather than silently by the individual. Such a culture is familiar with writhing, but is, in essence, oral.[85]

Paul Achtemeier also aptly asserts, "[…] *no* writing occurred that was not vocalized."[86] The letter writer was not just a writer, as we who live in a culture very different from that of the first century may guess; he was also a speaker. It is natural that the oral dimension of Paul's letter-writing process undoubtedly influenced his letters, embracing his oral preaching style. William Barclay therefore states:

> Paul's letters are sermons far more than they are theological treatises. It is with immediate situations that they deal. They are sermons even in the sense that they were spoken rather than written. They were not carefully written out by someone sitting at a desk; they were poured out by someone striding up and down a room as he dictated, seeing all the time in his mind's eye the people to whom they were to be sent.[87]

James Hester describes Paul's style of letters as "as much oral as it is written. It is as though Paul wrote speeches."[88] He continues, "If one accepts the notion that Paul's letters are rife with oral expression or style […] one had better begin to take seriously the possibility that Paul saw his letters as speeches."[89]

Paul's letters were thus a result of a series of oral events. Paul's oral presentations to amanuenses in dictating them were an integral part of his letters, just as in the writing process of other common ancient letters. Therefore, Paul's letters reflect a close relationship with his preaching.

1.3.4. Reading Aloud in the Communities of Faith

Like the practice of writing, the practice of reading was also dominated by the oral environment in antiquity. Since most people in the first century were

---

85 John D. Harvey, *Listening to the Text: Oral Patterning in Paul's Letters* (Grand Rapids: Baker Books, 1998), xv.
86 Achtemeier: 15. Italics original.
87 Barclay, 170.
88 James D. Hester, "The Use and Influence of Rhetoric in Galatians 2:1–14," *Theologische Zeitschrift* 42, no. 5 (1986): 387.
89 Ibid.: 389.

illiterate,[90] letter-receivers naturally needed to hear what the letter-writers addressed in the letters. Therefore, letters were not read silently by individuals but were read aloud in front of the audience.[91] Paul's letters were no exception. Paul had fully understood that his communication would be delivered to the believing community orally and intended for his letters to be read aloud in the community: "I charge you before the Lord to have this letter read to all the brothers" (1 Thess. 5:27). Though Paul's request that his letter be read in a gathering is only recorded in 1 Thessalonians, it is not unreasonable infer that Paul expected his other letters would also be read in the communities of faith, considering the low literacy rate in Paul's communities.[92] Due to a lack of existing information about the precise composition of early Christ-following communities, it is difficult to estimate the literacy rate among members of Pauline communities. However, it would be reasonable to assume that the rate would not be significantly different from that of other communities in antiquity. Pieter Botha notes, "Most of Paul's audience probably never even saw the text."[93] Paul's letters were written to be read aloud rather than in private.

Ancient letters, including Paul's, therefore were naturally designed for aural communication. Letter-writers composed their material and organized the structure of the letters in ways that could be followed easily by listeners or letter-receivers. John Harvey observes, "Clues to the organization of thought are, of necessity, based on sound rather than sight."[94] Paul's letters were also at times specifically organized by sound rather than sight. Ben Witherington observes, "Paul had written his words so that they might be *heard* as persuasive."[95] Paul thus employed the distinctive features of oral communication. His frequently uses repetition, inclusion, chiasm,

---

90   Most skills in the Greco-Roman world were acquired orally through apprenticeship. For this reason, the high level of illiteracy could be largely ignored. For a discussion of literacy rates among populations in the Greco-Roman world and the evidence on literacy, see William V. Harris, *Ancient Literacy* (Cambridge: Harvard University Press, 1989).
91   Joanna Dewey, "Textuality in an Oral Culture: A Survey of the Pauline Traditions," *Semeia* 65, (1994): 45.
92   Ibid.: 47.
93   Botha, 413.
94   John D. Harvey, *Listening to the Text: Oral Patterning in Paul's Letters* (Grand Rapids: Baker Books, 1998), xv.
95   Ben Witherington, *New Testament Rhetoric: An Introductory Guide to the Art of Persuasion in and of the New Testament* (Eugene: Cascade Books, 2009), 97. Italics original.

parallelism, antitheses, paradox, word play, hyperbole, alliteration, and refrain, which shows that his letter writing style reflects the common pattern of oral speech intended to be heard.[96]

It required a great skill to read aloud letters that were structurally organized not for private reading. And in antiquity, writing materials were expensive,[97] and so Greek texts were written in what was called *scriptio continua*, without separation of individual words, punctuation or accents, and without indications of paragraphs.[98] Under these circumstances, a letter-writer might have the letter delivered and read by someone familiar with its content and what the writer intended to address. This frequently occurred with Paul's letters. Because his letters are much longer in length compared to other letters of the time,[99] Paul preferred to have an appropriate person deliver and read his letters to the community, such as one of his workers who knew his mind, meaning, and even emotion included in his letter. Harvey confirms, "Letter writing was as close to face-to-face communication as first-century correspondents could come. Paul's use of emissaries also enhanced communication because the emissaries had personal knowledge of the content of the letters they carried."[100] Timothy in 1 Thessalonians and Titus in 2 Corinthians seem to have carried and read the letters to the communities.[101] William Doty thus notes,

---

96   Harvey, 97–118.
97   John D. Harvey, "Orality and Its Implications for Biblical Studies: Recapturing an Ancient Paradigm," *Journal of the Evangelical Theological Society* 45, no. 1 (2002): 102. For the cost of Paul's letters and other ancient letters, see Richards, 165–169.
98   See Harry Y. Gamble, *Books and Readers in the Early Church: A History of Early Christian Texts* (New Haven: Yale University Press, 1995), 48–54.
99   The average length of a letter of Cicero was 295 words, and that of Seneca 955; the average length of a Pauline letter is 2,500 words. See Martin R. P. McGuire, "Letters and Letter Carriers in Christian Antiquity," *The Classical World* 53, no. 5 (1960): 148.
100 Harvey, *Listening to the Text: Oral Patterning in Paul's Letters*, xv.
101 Margaret M. Mitchell, "New Testament Envoys in the Context of Greco-Roman Diplomatic and Epistolary Conventions: The Example of Timothy and Titus," *Journal of Biblical Literature* 111, no. 4 (1992): 641–662. Mitchell also demonstrates that it was expected that the envoys would transmit information not contained in the letter. After reading the letter, they could answer any follow up question a community might have concerning the letter they received from Paul. Also see Claude E. Cox, "The Reading of the Personal Letters as the Background for the Reading of the Scripture in the Early Church," in *The Early Church in Its Context: Essays in Honor of Everett Ferguson*, eds. Abraham Malherbe, Frederick Norris, and James Thompson (Leiden: Brill, 1998), 81–82.

Paul, who made such a point of indicating his trust in those carriers (co-workers), did not think of his written letters as exhausting what he wished to communicate. He thought of his associates, especially those commissioned to carry his letters, as able to extend his own teachings.[102]

Moreover, the great teachers of rhetoric dating to Paul's time considered voice, gestures, and even the face of the reader to be crucial parts of effective communication. In this respect, letter-reading in antiquity was a "performance."[103] Letters were intended to be read and performed. The letter-reader's task included the performance of vocal production and physical movement to reflect the emotional stance of the letter-writer.[104] Paul also seemed to share this interest in the performance of letter-reading. According to Randolph Richards, Paul's request in 1 Thessalonians 5:27 is considered to be a formal request for a performance of the letter, not just reading.[105] Botha concludes that in a letter of Paul, "there was someone involved in the creation and transportation of it, finally 'recreating' for others a presentation/performance of the 'message' intended for sharing."[106] The emissary's performance gave the letters fullness by "adding oral commentary in the spirit and attitude of Paul himself."[107] The performance of Paul's letter allowed it to become a more truly living voice of Paul.

Paul's letters were intended to be read aloud in the Christ-following communities so they not only reflected his oral communication style but also were structured for the ears of the congregation. Paul shaped his letters into an effective composition so that the informed readers would deliver or even perform his oral communication or preaching in the believing communities. His letters were prepared for a careful performance as a proper speech or preaching of Paul. Therefore, Paul's letters are close to his actual preaching.

---

102 Doty, 45–46.
103 Botha, 417–419.
104 Richard F. Ward, "Pauline Voice and Presence as Strategic Communication," *Semeia* 65 (1994): 104.
105 Richards, 202.
106 Botha, 417.
107 Ward: 105.

1.3.5. A Means of the Apostle's Presence from a Distance

Paul's letters were a form of his apostolic presence. In the ancient Mediterranean world, letters were considered as a means to continue the friendship between two parties after they had separated.[108] The concept such as παρουσία (presence) and ὁμιλία (company) are basic to the ancient letters. "Absent in body, but present through this letter" is a common formula reflecting this phenomenon.[109] Ancient letters were considered to be a substitute for personal presence. The same is true of Paul's letters. For Paul's apostolic παρουσία, Robert Funk has concluded that Paul preferred to visit personally. Yet, even in modern times, it is not always possible to be physically present in one's preferred location. Paul had to use alternative means to reiterate his presence. Sending an emissary to read a letter aloud was one of most effective substitutes for Paul's apostolic presence in the early churches.[110] His use of the idiomatic "to see you" in 1 Thessalonians (2:17, 3:10) clearly indicates his desire to be personally present with the Thessalonians and that the predominant function of the letter was to maintain his personal contact with the congregation. Paul's statement in 1 Corinthians 5:3, that although he is "not physically present" but "in spirit," also shows that the letter was a medium of his apostolic authority as well as a means of his presence.[111] In 2 Corinthians, Paul also notes, "Such people should realize that what we are in our letters when we are absent, we will be in our actions when we are present" (10:11). Paul's letters were an ideal surrogate for his presence and voice from a distance to satisfy the need for pastoring the congregations. Boyd Luter aptly summarizes thusly:

> If Paul could go to visit a particular church at a specific crucial time and preach related to their needs, he did. But often, he could not go [...] Thus, a letter laying out his theological and behavioral response to the church's situation was the best facsimile spiritual "presence" he could offer in lieu of his actual physical presence.

---

108 Malherbe, 69.
109 Stowers, 59.
110 Robert Funk, "The Apostolic Parousia: Form and Significance," in *Christian History and Interpretation: Studies Presented to John Knox*, eds. William R. Farmer, Charles Francis D. Moule, and Richard R. Niebuhr (Cambridge: University Press, 1967), 249–269. Funk argues that Paul had three different means in which he could make his presense felt: his physical presence, his presence via an emissary, and his presence via a letter.
111 Ibid., 264.

> And because the apostle was almost surely verbalizing his letters through dictation to an amanuensis, in a very real sense, they should be considered what could be called *written preaching*.[112]

Paul's letters thus served as his presence and voice for pastoral action to his communities when he was physically unable to visit them. Therefore, it can be assumed that Paul's letters have a strong relationship with his preaching.

1.3.6. Conclusion

The enterprise of writing and reading letters in the first century was normally shaped by the orally oriented culture. A letter-writer in antiquity dictated a letter to a secretary, who would in turn produce it into one reflecting his or her own oral communication style. An ancient letter was also expected to be read aloud; therefore, the letter had to be structured for hearing rather than private or individual reading. Moreover, the letter was read by an informed emissary who could perform the content of the letter in the letter-writers' oral communication style, physical gestures, and emotional state. Considering such a practice in letter writing and reading, it is no exaggeration to say that Paul's letters should be regarded as compositions that are close to his oral communication and preaching style.

It must be also taken into account that Paul not only utilized the existing customs of ancient letter writing but also adapted the genre for his own purpose. His letters were not written as private and personal letters; they were written for the believing communities and sent to the communities. Paul's letters functioned as a substitute for his voice and presence to the believing communities in pastoral need when he was physically unable to be with them. The function of his letters was almost the same as that of his preaching to the Christ-following communities themselves. Paul therefore weaved what he had previously preached to the communities, including his evangelistic preaching, into his letters. It can be suggested that his letters reflect his actual preaching because his letters functioned as a form of preaching in the communities made of Paul's actual preaching material.

Sidney Greidanus states, "Listening to the letter, then, was like listening to Paul. Hence one can characterize the New Testament Epistles

---

112 Wells and Luter, 122. Italics original.

as long-distance sermons."[113] Although this statement may be a slight exaggeration, it can be nonetheless concluded that Paul's letters acted as a surrogate for his voice and presence in the communities, and provided continuity for his preaching. Thus, Paul's letters provide information and insight into his preaching ministry for contemporary preachers.

---

113 Sidney Greidanus, *The Modern Preacher and the Ancient Text: Interpreting and Preaching Biblical Literature* (Grand Rapids: W. B. Eerdmans Pub., 1988), 314.

Chapter Two
The New Homiletic: The Turn to the Individual Listener

This aim of chapter is to describe and evaluate contemporary homiletics, particularly the New Homiletic.[1] To accomplish this aim, this chapter first will probe some important background features from whence the New Homiletic was birthed. Second, this chapter will describe the common characteristics of the New Homiletic by analyzing the homiletical theories of main figurers within the homiletical approach. Finally, the chapter will present a critical reflection on the New Homiletic. While considering various critiques against the New Homiletic, this chapter will highlight an individualistic orientation within the approaches to preaching of the New Homiletic. In the context of the contemporary homiletics, this criticism will show the necessity for a study on preaching for community formation, which this study undertakes.

2.1. The Background of the New Homiletic

2.1.1. The Cultural Context of 1960s: The Challenge to Traditional Authority

John Stott illustrates preaching as a widely known image: a "bridge-building."[2] This metaphor properly shows that the task of preachers is

---

[1] It cannot be said that the New Homiletic is the only one approach in the contemporary homiletics. For example, Lucy Rose suggests four major contemporary approaches for preaching: (1) traditional homiletical theory, (2) kerygmatic homiletical theory, (3) transformational homiletical theory, and (4) conversational theory of preaching. See Lucy Atkinson Rose, *Sharing the Word: Preaching in the Roundtable Church* (Louisville: Westminster John Knox Press, 1997). Others have called the trasformatonal theory the New Homiletic. See Eugene L. Lowry, *The Sermon: Dancing the Edge of Mystery* (Nashville: Abingdon Press, 1997), 31.

[2] John R. W. Stott, *Between Two Worlds* (Grand Rapids: W. B. Eerdmans Pub., 1994), 137.

not just to expose the message of a biblical text but also to communicate the message to people shaped by a specific cultural context. Given that preaching is always determined by the text and the context of the listeners, it is natural that the emerging cultural environment played a significant role in the stimulation for the new approach to preaching.

The decade of the 1960s, the period in which the New Homiletic germinated in the United States, can be described a period of change. Americans experienced tremendous social and cultural upheaval. No other decade of the twentieth century has obtained the legendary status of the 1960s. With emphasizing the cultural revolution of 1960s, scholars often name both the decade and the mood of cultural change the "Sixties."[3]

After World War II for the next decade and a half America continued to grow and develop. By this confidence in the progress, Americans consequently believed that its society could be consolidated and social conflict could be minimized. In the early 1960s, however, this consensus of Americans was undermined. A massive movement opposing the Vietnam War brought deep segmentation within the country. Minority groups such as African Americans, Hispanics, and Native Americans challenged the assumption that the nation provided equal rights for all. Women also began to protest against traditional male-dominated system of the society.[4] The hippie movement arose in the west coast and spread across the whole of the United States as a subculture rejecting the mainstream culture of the country. The notable social and cultural changes in the Sixties questioned the raveling old authority and shelved traditional assumptions. Sydney Ahlstrom has summarized this indelible shift of the period:

> The decade of the Sixties was a time, in short, when the old foundations of national confidence, patriotic idealism, moral traditionalism, and even of historic Judaeo-Christian theism, were awash. Presuppositions that had held firm for centuries – even millennia – were being widely questioned. Some sensational manifestations came and went (as fads and fashions will), but the existence of a basic shift of mood rooted in deep social and institutional dislocations was anything but ephemeral.[5]

---

[3] Peter B. Levy, ed. *America in the Sixties – Right, Left, and Center: A Documentary History* (Westport: Greenwood Press, 1998), 1.

[4] Allan M. Winkler, "Modern America: The 1960s, 1970s, and 1980s," in *Encyclopedia of American Social History Vol. 1*, eds. Mary Kupiec Cayton, Elliott J. Gorn, and Peter W. Williams (New York: Charles Scribner's Sons, 1993), 219.

[5] Sydney E. Ahlstrom, *A Religious History of the American People* (New Heaven: Yale University Press, 1972), 1080.

At the heart of the social and cultural revolution was the challenge to traditional authority.[6]

The strong challenge to authority in 1960s did not leave the church unaffected. According to historian Stephen Whitefield, churches were traditionally regarded as the most trusted institutions in America, more than the government, schools, or the media.[7] By the beginning of the 1960's, however; many Americans were skeptical about the purpose and function of religion in the transformed cultural environment,[8] and also called the settled religious authority into question with unprecedented vigor.

It was time at this period that namely the "Death of God" movement erupted. This movement was radical in a way that traditional authority of the religion was rejected. Books with daring titles such as Gabriel Vahanian's *The Death of God*,[9] Paul Buren's *Secular Meaning of the Gospel*,[10] and Thomas Altizer's *Gospel of Christian Atheism*[11] suggested that the traditional ways of thinking and speaking about God were no longer relevant, gaining media attention.[12]

The authority of preachers that was presumed in the past was also no longer the case. As Haddon Robinson aptly ponders in the 1960s, "authority – all authority – became suspect. [...] Pastors were no longer trusted as

---

6 Many scholars view the 1960's as the turning point from modernity to postmodernity. Postmodernism, while it is hard to define or delineate, is characterized by the essential belief that all truth is relative and all authority is questioned.

7 Stephen J. Whitfield, *The Culture of the Cold War* (Baltimore: Johns Hopkins University Press, 1991), 153.

8 During the 1960 the church in the United States for the first time experienced a decline in membership. See Dean M. Kelley, *Why Conservative Churches Are Growing: A Study in Sociology of Religion* (New York: Harper & Row, 1972), 1. For more detailed information on the shift of the religious landscape in 1960s, see Robert D. Putnam and David E. Campbell, *American Grace: How Relogion Divides and Unites Us* (New York: Simon & Schuster, 2012) 91–100.

9 Gabriel Vahanian, *The Death of God: The Culture of Our Post-Christian Era* (New York: G. Braziller, 1961).

10 Paul van Buren, *The Secular Meaning of the Gospel: Based on an Analysis of Its Language* (New York: Macmillan, 1963).

11 Thomas J. J. Altizer, *The Gospel of Christian Atheism* (Philadelphia: Westminster Press, 1966).

12 The cover of the April 8, 1966 edition of *Time* magazine handled with the question "Is God Dead?" and the accompanying article addressed the "Death of God" movement in America. See John T. Elson, "Theology: Toward a Hidden God," *Time*, April 8, 1966.

the authorities they had been. This anti-authority mood created suspicion of churches and their values including the authority of Scripture."[13] The cultural upheaval of 1960s undercut the authority of the church and preachers.

This challenge to the traditionally recognized authority of the church and preachers, which was influenced by the cultural revelation in 1960s, stimulated the emergence of the New Homiletic. Fred Craddock, whose work most contemporary homileticians trace the birth of the New Homiletic to,[14] in his recent article looks back the turbulent cultural situation in the Sixties which directly made an influence on his new approach to preaching as follows:

> I was aware in 1965 of the revolution of the '60s – a social revolution, a sexual revolution, a drug revolution – and the establishment of Berkeley, California, as the new capital of the New America. [I should have been aware of it earlier,] What I was not aware of was how deeply the revolution had made an attack on tradition and authority, which included the pulpit.[15]

However, as soon as he recognized that the revolution of 1960s had influenced the authority of preachers; Craddock began to move preachers into a different kind of approach to preaching. It is not surprising that Craddock entitled his book *As One without Authority*.[16] The sixties and the challenge to authority of preachers in the cultural situation caused the New Homiletic to emerge.

2.1.2. The Dissatisfaction with Traditional Preaching

Clyde Fant writes in his *Preaching for Today* that a definite cycle of preaching can be perceived over the 2,000 year history of Christian preaching.

---

13 Haddon W. Robinson, "Preaching Trends: A Riview," *Journal of the Evangelical Theological Society* 6, no. 2 (2006): 25.
14 David Reid, Stephen Bullock, and Jeffrey Fleer, "Preaching as the Creation of an Experience: The Not-So-Rational Revolution of the New Homileitc," *the Journal of Communication and Religion* 18, no. 1 (1995): 2.
15 Fred B. Craddock, "Inductive Preaching Renewed," in *The Renewed Homiletic*, ed. O. Wesley Allen (Minneapolis: Fortress Press, 2010), 41.
16 Fred B. Craddock, *As One without Authority: Essays on Inductive Preaching* (Enid: Phillips University Press, 1971). *As One without Authority* was reprinted in 1975, 1979, and 2001. Most citations of *As One without Authority* will be from the latest edition, unless the other editions are specified.

He notes that the cycle of preaching the following stages: search, discovery, excitement, routinization, boredom, and disillusionment.[17] The birth of the New Homiletic is no exception in which routinization and boredom with the methods of prior traditional preaching guided many homileticians to explore new approaches for preaching.

People in the Sixties not only expressed a doubt on the authority of preachers but also on the validation of preaching. It was discovered that both preachers and hearers were very frustrated with conventional preaching.[18] Some such as Clyde Reid in his book *The Empty Pulpit*, whose title shows the crisis of preaching in the moment, declared preaching passé.[19] Fred Craddock also complained of traditional preaching: "It is the sober opinion of many concerned Christians, some who give the sermon and some who hear it, that preaching is an anachronism."[20] This far-reaching dissatisfaction with preaching even caused that many theological schools and seminaries in the United States reduced their teaching in homiletics and instead trained pastors for counseling and psychotherapy.[21]

Except irrelevant content of sermons, the criticism of conventional preaching can be broadly summed up in two categories. First would be the critiques that traditional preaching is too preacher-centered, which assumes an authoritarian foundation for preaching. Therefore, many homileticians tagged on traditional preaching as "performance of preacher,"[22] "rhetoric of authority,"[23] and "sovereign preaching."[24] Purpose of the preacher-centered preaching is understood as "conviction and persuasion" and "teaching and exhorting."[25] As a result, the preacher is considered as a

---

17 Clyde E. Fant, *Preaching for Today* (New York: Harper & Row, 1975), 10.
18 Reuel L. Howe, *Partners in Preaching: Clergy and Laity in Dialogue* (New York: Seabury Press, 1967), 11–25.
19 Clyde H. Reid, *The Empty Pulpit: A Study in Preaching as Communication* (New York: Harper & Row, 1967), 116.
20 Fred B. Craddock, *As One without Authority* (Saint Louis: Chalice Press, 2001), 4.
21 Edwin Charles Dargan and Ralph G. Turnbull, *A History of Preaching 3* (Grand Rapids: Baker, 1974), 318.
22 Howe, 23.
23 Craig A. Loscalzo, *Preaching Sermons That Connect: Effective Communication through Identification* (Downers Grove: InterVarsity Press, 1992), 17.
24 John S. McClure, *The Roundtable Pulpit: Where Leadership and Preaching Meet* (Nashville: Abingdon Press, 1995), 30.
25 John Albert Broadus and Jesse Burton Weatherspoon, *On the Preparation and Delivery of Sermons* (New York: Harper & brothers, 1944), 270, 24. Although the first edition of this book titled by *A Treatise on the Preparation and Delivery of Sermons*

figure of authority whose "main duty is to tell people what to believe and why they should believe it."[26] The traditional preaching system well works on the presupposition in which the preacher is in an authoritative position over the listeners placed in an obedient stance. Consequently, sermons are too often perceived as the "exclusive responsibility of the ordained minister."[27] Listeners in the preaching event are assigned to only passive roles. Reuel Howe writes metaphorically about the assumed roles of preachers and listeners in traditional preaching: "The preacher looks down; the people look up. Often, as the lights in the church are turned down and a spotlight turned on the preacher, the congregation disappears into an identity-hiding gloom."[28] According to the perspective of both pastors and laypersons shaped by the culture of the sixties, the authoritative preacher and the passive hearers assumed in traditional preaching were no longer appropriate in the contemporary culture.[29]

The other serious criticism was provided for that traditional preaching is too idea-centered. In the traditional strategy of preaching, sermons are organized around ideas and points which are basically a schematic diagram of order and parts of the message. These sermons are mainly described as an argument which has linear logic. Don Wardlaw therefore summarizes the traditional preaching in general: "Preaching, *per se*, has meant marshalling an argument in logical sequence, coordinating and subordinating points by the canons of logic, all in a careful appeal to the reasonable hearer."[30] Then,

---

was published in 1870, it was widely in use for homiletical education till the twentieth century. This is one of the most influential books representing traditional preaching theory in the United States. See O. C. Edwards, *A History of Preaching* (Nashville: Abingdon Press, 2004), 664; Rose, 14.

26 Broadus and Weatherspoon, 157.
27 Howe, 25.
28 Ibid., 35.
29 In the area of biblical hermeneutics, the development of reader-response criticism which emphasizes active role of the reader in interpretation process began in the late 1960's and expanded throughout the late 1970's. The attention to the reader's role of the reader-response criticism must have somewhat influenced the attention to the listener's role of the New Homiletic. For the discussion, see Sarah Jane Smith, "Hearing Sermons: Reader-Response Theory as a Basis for a Listener-Response Homiletic" (Th.D. diss., University of Toronto, 2003).
30 Don M. Wardlaw, "The Need for New Shapes," in *Preaching Biblically*, ed. Don M. Wardlaw (Philadelphia: Westminster Press, 1983), 12. Also see Richard A. Jensen, *Telling the Story: Variety and Imagination in Preaching* (Minneapolis: Augsburg Pub., 1980), 27.

homileticians became suspicious and began to question to the traditional idea-centered approach to preaching.

In the first place, it is a reduction of the Bible, which is not merely a composition of ideas following a logical sequence. The Bible rather is comprised of a variety of genres, which not only deliver ideas or themes but also evocate rich experiences and feelings. It is an essential weakness that the idea-centered approach cannot reflect the biblical genres and eliminates rich and multilateral facts which could be provided by the biblical text. The traditional preachers only "boil" the texts "down"[31] to ideas or themes, which David Buttrick calls "distillation."[32] Thomas Long recapitulates this discontent as follows:

> Engaging a biblical text is at least as multifaceted as any of those encounters, and while ideas are surely uncovered in biblical interpretation, there are also moods, movements, conflicts, epiphanies, and other experiences that cannot be pressed into a strictly ideational mold. Sermons should be faithful to the full range of a text's power, and those preachers who carry away only main ideas, it was alleged, are traveling too light.[33]

It is necessary to note that this attention to the various effects and genres of the biblical text, which concluded to the discontent with traditional preaching, stemmed from that the foundation of biblical studies shifted in those days. In spite of going "behind" the biblical text to examine earlier source or historical references, scholars with the extensive agreement on the decline of the historical-critical method became interested in the final form of the biblical text, including rhetorical and aesthetic factors. Sidney Greidanus summarizes this shift: "The Bible is taken first and finally as a literary object."[34] This new understanding of viewing the biblical text as a

---

31 Thomas G. Long, *The Witness of Preaching* (Louisville: Westminster John Knox Press, 2005), 101.
32 David Buttrick, *Homiletic: Moves and Structures* (Philadelphia: Fortress Press, 1987), 265.
33 Long, 101.
34 Sidney Greidanus, *The Modern Preacher and the Ancient Text: Interpreting and Preaching Biblical Literature* (Grand Rapids: W. B. Eerdmans Pub., 1988), 50. Greidanus also writes, "For biblical studies has recently entered into the new world: it has undergone a paradigm shift from historical to literary studies so that scholarly interest today is focused not so much on history as on *genres* of biblical literature – with a concomitant shift in homiletics to *forms* of sermons." Greidanus, xi. Italics original.

45

literary work brought homileticians to reconsider the traditional sermons moving along a linear logic which is not able to echo the literary characteristics of the text.

In addition to the criticism that sermons along with the logical arrangement ignore the literary dynamics and genres of the biblical texts, homileticians also became critical of that the traditional sermon form does not consider the dynamics of the human listening process. The logical form of preaching does not seem to be as effective in a medium of oral communication, because it is inherently a form as a written organization of argument. Therefore, sermons with tight argumentation do not stand to gain a great hearing of the listeners on Sunday as it did in the days of literary preachers when sermons were more commonly made available in print.[35] Moreover, homileticians criticized that the traditional sermon form, which in general follows a deductive logic, is not appropriate to capture and maintain interest of hearer. With starting with the main idea in the beginning of the sermon and making divided categorical sub-points in the process, it cannot stimulate tension and suspense of the listeners; and then intrinsically tedious for the listeners. Regarding the deductive preaching as unnatural and ineffective mode of communication for the listeners, Fred Craddock writes, "The conclusion does not come first any more than a trip starts at its destination, a story prematurely reveals its own climax, or a joke begins with the punch line."[36] According to David Buttrick, "Categorical systems are easy, but *only* for the clergy. Because they are static and have no moving excitement will happen next? – they are hard to listen to in a congregation."[37]

A growing numbers of homileticians were united in their rejection of conventional homiletical approach. For them, the traditional preaching is too preacher-centered and too idea-centered. These features of traditional preaching were often mentioned in many homiletical books published in those days as the main culprit in the crisis of preaching. It is natural that the aspiration to escape from the weakness of traditional preaching became strong impetus for the appearance of the New Homiletic.

---

35 Fant, 114–115.
36 Craddock, *As One without Authority*, 52.
37 David Buttrick, *A Captive Voice: The Liberation of Preaching* (Louisville: Westminster John Knox Press, 1994), 84.

2.1.3. The New Hermeneutic

As mentioned above, it is evident to many that traditional preaching was in necessity of renewal. Among those who recognized the need of a renewal of preaching is David Randolph. Randolph, in his *The Renewal of Preaching*,[38] titled with his hope first introduced the new hermeneutic to the homiletical field.[39] After Randolph, the new hermeneutic was appropriated for North American homiletics and fundamentally contributed for the appearance and development of the New Homiletic.

Although many scholars in the United States and Germany have participated in the debate concerning the new hermeneutic, Ernst Fuchs and Gerhard Ebeling are commonly regarded as the leading figures in the theological approach.[40] It is also true that Fuchs and Ebeling were much influenced by their former teacher at Marburg University, Rudolf Bultmann.[41] Because of this, some scholars call the new hermeneutic the "post-Bultmannian."[42]

---

38 David James Randolph, *The Renewal of Preaching* (Philadelphia: Fortress Press, 1969).

39 See Scott M. Gibson, "Defining the New Homiletic," *The Journal of the Evangelical Homiletics Society* 5, no. 2 (2005): 21; James F. Kay, *Preaching and Theology* (Saint Louis: Chalice Press, 2008), 77–78; John S. McClure, *Preaching Words: 144 Key Terms in Homiletics* (Louisville: Westminster John Knox Press, 2007), 94–95; David James Randolph and Robert Stephen Reid, *The Renewal of Preaching in the Twenty-First Century: The Next Homiletics Commentary* (Eugene: Cascade Books, 2009), 113–115.

40 Paul J. Achtemeier, *An Introduction to the New Hermeneutic* (Philadelphia: Westminster Press, 1969), 85. Hendrik Krabbendam states, "Since the publication of the symposium The New Hermeneutic, edited by J. M. Robinson and J. B. Cobb, Jr., in 1994, the title of this work has become increasingly the standard designation of a theological approach of which E. Fuchs and G. Ebeling are the chief representatives." Hendrik Krabbendam, "The New Hermeneutic," in *Hermeneutics, Inerrancy, and the Bible: [Papers from ICBI Summit II]*, eds. Earl D. Radmacher and Robert D. Preus (Grand Rapids: Academie Books, 1984), 535.

41 Gerhard Ebeling and David James Randolph, *On Prayer: Nine Sermons* (Philadelphia: Fortress Press, 1966), 2; Werner G. Jeanrond, *Theological Hermeneutics: Development and Significance* (New York: Crossroad, 1991), 148; Richard N. Soulen, "Ernst Fuchs: New Testament Theologian," *Journal of the American Academy of Religion* 39, no. 4 (1971): 468.

42 Kay, 80.

Bultmann's chief concern was to interpret the Christian faith to his contemporaries in a "modern scientifically oriented culture."[43] According to Bultmann, the New Testament is profoundly imbued with a first-century worldview or cosmology that is no longer acceptable. To make the New Testament understandable to modern people, Bultmann initiated demythologization – the myth in the New Testament should be interpreted not to present "an objective world picture" but to show "how we human beings understand *ourselves* in our world."[44] The myth ought to be revealed in order to explore the "existential meaning" within.[45] Therefore, Bultmann's demythologization program is an existential interpretation of mythology in the New Testament.

Bultmann writes his existential interpretation as follows: "The 'most subjective' interpretation is the 'most objective,' because the only person who is able to hear the claim of the text is the person who is moved by the question of his or her own existence."[46] An interpreter cannot delve into a text with a neutral attitude, but only with a certain level of pre-understanding or even prejudice.[47] The interpreter's pre-understanding must concern the most fundamental questions of his or her own existence. In Bultmann's existential interpretation, it is absolutely impossible and even meaningless to discover the original and objective meaning of the text, which is traditionally understood as the task of the hermeneutics.

Fuchs and Ebeling utilized much of Bultmann's contributions. They were especially convinced that Bultmann's existential interpretation is a new breakthrough in the relationship with the traditional hermeneutics, to which there can be no return. Appropriating Martin Heidegger's reflection on language, however, Fuchs and Ebeling thought that Bultmann failed to

---

43 Morris Ashcraft, *Rudolf Bultmann*, Makers of the Modern Theological Mind (Waco: Word Books, 1972), 11–12.
44 Rudolf Karl Bultmann, "New Testament and Mythology," in *New Testament and Mythology and Other Basic Writings*, ed. Schubert Miles Ogden (Philadelphia: Fortress Press, 1984), 9. Italics added.
45 Raymond F. Surburg, "New Hermeneutic Versus the Old Hermeneutics in New Testament Interpretation," *Springfielder* 38, no. 1 (1974): 13.
46 Rudolf Karl Bultmann, "The Problem of Hermeneutics," in *New Testament and Mythology and Other Basic Writings*, ed. Schubert Miles Ogden (Philadelphia: Fortress Press, 1984), 86.
47 See Rudolf Karl Bultmann, "Is Exegesis without Presuppositions Possible?," in *Existence and Faith: Shorter Writings of Rudolf Bultmann*, ed. Schubert Miles Ogden (New York: Meridian Books, 1960).

properly consider the essential connection between human existence and language. According to Heidegger, language itself speaks or language is the voice of existence. Heidegger writes, "But the essence of language does not consist entirely in being a means of giving information. [...] Language is not a mere tool. [...] Rather it is that event which disposes of the supreme possibility of human existence."[48]

Following the idea of Heidegger, Fuchs and Ebeling stressed in hermeneutics the necessity of "eventfulness," which is an inherent capacity of language to reveal the existence in the present. Through the event occurred through language, in Fuchs' sense it is a "language-event" and in Ebeling's sense, it is a "Word-event;"[49] the existence finally can be discovered and interpreted. Ebeling writes, *"The primary phenomenon in the realm of understanding is not understanding OF language, but understanding THROUGH language."*[50] Like Bultmann, they no longer understood their hermeneutical task as the interpretation of biblical texts, but as the interpretation of existence. Fuchs clearly declares that the hermeneutical task is no more than *"the interpretation of our own existence."*[51] Transferring of the concern of Bultmann, however, they articulated that the interpretation of existence is possible only through language – the Word-event or language-event.

Notably, Fuchs and Ebeling's emphasis on the event-character of language elevates the spoken word, which transmits what they consider to be the Word-event or language-event in the present. Ebeling writes, "This transition from text to sermon is a transition from Scripture to the spoken word. Thus the task prescribed here consists in making what is written into spoken word or, as we can now also say, in letting text become God's Word again."[52] The spoken word is advanced as the Word of God but the text is degraded as a medium to recreate the Word of God in the present in proclamation. Thus, preaching as spoken word plays an essential role in the new hermeneutic.

---

48 Martin Heidegger, *Existence and Being* (London: Vision Press, 1949), 299–300.
49 Robinson believes that these two terms are synonyms. James M. Robinson, "Hermeneutic since Barth," in *The New Hermeneutic*, eds. James M. Robinson and John B. Cobb (New York: Harper & Row, 1964), 57.
50 Gerhard Ebeling, *Word and Faith* (Philadelphia: Fortress Press, 1963), 318. Italics original.
51 Ernst Fuchs, "The New Testament and the Hermeneutical Problem," in *The New Hermeneutic*, eds. James M. Robinson and John B. Cobb (New York: Harper & Row, 1964), 117. Italics original.
52 Ebeling, *Word and Faith*, 329.

When it comes to preaching, it is needed to note that the main concern of the new hermeneutic is what happens in the present to the listener through Word-event or language-event when the Scripture is proclaimed. Ebeling notes, "But the sermon as a sermon is not exposition of the text as past proclamation, but is itself proclamation in the present – and that means, then, that the sermon is EXECUTION of the text."[53] Randolph describes preaching from the new hermeneutic perspective: "The genius of preaching, as it is here understood, is its *eventfulness*. What is crucial for homiletic is not so much what the sermon 'is' as what the sermon 'does.'"[54] There is a fundamental shift from traditional preaching based on the original meaning of the text, to sermon as an event or experience disclosing its meaning through its relationship to the hearer.

Many homileticians in North America thought that the revision of preaching which the new hermeneutic made had potential to renew the preaching. The group of scholars has become widely influential in the homiletics and their approaches to preaching were known as the New Homiletic.

2.2. The Common Characteristics of the New Homiletic

2.2.1. The Elevation of the Listener's Role: Partner of Preaching

Though diversity is present among the approaches of the New Homiletic, it is also true that they represent a "common homiletical family" with "genetic link" and "apparent resemblances."[55] The New Homiletic, Lucy Rose states, "is a large umbrella under which stand a number of homiletical scholars."[56] There are the apparent resemblances tiding their approaches to a family.

The heart of the New Homiletic can be described as the "turn to the listener" as described by Ronald Allen, Thomas Long, and Wesley Allen.[57]

---

53 Ibid., 331. Emphasis in the original.
54 Randolph, *The Renewal of Preaching*, vii. Italics original.
55 Lowry, 12.
56 Rose, 59.
57 Ronald J. Allen, "The Turn to the Listener: A Selective Review of a Recent Trend in Preaching," *Encounter* 64, no. 2 (2003): 166–196; Thomas G. Long, "And How Shall

Although it is obvious that this turn toward the listener is not new in the history of the church,[58] its influence upon theories and practices in contemporary preaching is significant. Beverly Zink-Sawyer states, "This recent 'move toward the listeners,' as it is called, has been heralded as a new discovery and a valuable contribution to the shape of homiletics in North America."[59] For the main feature of the New Homiletic, Long describes, "One after another, homileticians have joined the choir, eager to sing the anthem that listener-oriented sermons are called for by the rhetoric of kerygma itself."[60]

It is to some extent an estimated scenario that the new direction of approaches to preaching in New Homiletic takes a bearing on emphasis on the role of listener in the preaching, because traditional preaching have been criticized as too preacher-centered, which is regarded as inappropriate for the era where the authority of preacher is questionable. With deemphasizing the authority of preacher, the New Homiletic opened the door for a listener-centered approach to preaching.

Fred Craddock expanded the homiletical concern for the hearer to such an extent that he has been described as "an innovator of listener-driven homiletics."[61] In his book, *As One without Authority*, which is regarded as one of the first homiletical texts to advocate for the authority of the listener,[62] proposes inductive preaching which includes inductive movement from particular experiences to general conclusion. Unlike as deductive preaching assuming "no dialogue, no listening by the speaker, no contributing by hearer,"[63] Craddock believes that the inductive preaching respects the hearer

---

They Hear?," in *Listening to the Word: Studies in Honor of Fred B. Craddock*, eds. Gail R. O'Day and Thomas G. Long (Nashville: Abingdon Press, 1993), 167–188. O. Wesley Allen, "Introduction: The Pillars of the New Homiletic," in *The Renewed Homiletic*, ed. O. Wesley Allen (Minneapolis: Fortress Press, 2010), 8.

58 Beverly Zink-Sawyer demonstrates that throughout the history of the church preaching has been shaped by the weight attributed to various elements in preaching, including the listeners. Beverly Zink-Sawyer, "The Word Purely Preached and Heard," *Interpretation* 51, no. 4 (1997).
59 Ibid.: 342.
60 Long, "And How Shall They Hear?," 172.
61 Ibid., 181.
62 Ronald J. Allen, Barbara Shires Blaisdell, and Scott Black Johnston, *Theology for Preaching: Authority, Truth, and Knowledge of God in a Postmodern Ethos* (Nashville: Abingdon Press, 1997), 51.
63 Craddock, *As One without Authority*, 46.

as a partner of preaching and consequently preaching is considered to be understood as the process of dialogue.

According to Craddock, the listener has "right" to participate in the inductive study process on the text of the preacher instead of only hearing the conclusion. The listener is no longer to absorb passively the conclusion of the sermon reached by preacher in the study. Rather, the listener in an actual preaching moment is to be invited to participate in the inductive movement which reflects the inductive study process. Craddock asks, "Why not on Sunday morning retrace the inductive trip he took earlier and see if the hearers come to that same conclusion?"[64]

The listener has also "right" to complete the inductive sermon. Craddock believes that inductive preaching expects the listeners to arrive at a conclusion that is their own, not just preacher's. The listeners can draw their conclusions and implications for their situations which are not only obvious but also personally inescapable. In this respect, "The listener completes the sermon."[65] For Craddock, preaching is characterized by open-endedness in order to permit the listeners to make their own conclusions.

It is natural that Craddock's attention to the right of the listener in preaching – participation and completion – elevates the position of the listener and restricts the role of the preacher traditionally assumed. The listener becomes "one with authority"; the preacher becomes "one without authority." For Craddock, the listener is not "the destination of the sermon"[66] but an active partner in preaching. Therefore, preaching cannot be described as a monologue but a dialogue.

To promote the participation of the listener in preaching, Eugene Lowry's strategy for preaching is also designed to produce movement replacing preacher's peremptory address of the preacher in the sermon. He contrives "the homiletical plot" composing of five stages which could create "the moving suspense of story from disequilibrium to resolution."[67]

---

64 Ibid., 48.
65 Ibid., 53.
66 Ibid., 52.
67 Eugene L. Lowry, *Doing Time in the Pulpit: The Relationship between Narrative and Preaching* (Nashville: Abingdon Press, 1985), 52. Lowry defines these stages as "(1) upsetting the equilibrium, (2) analyzing the discrepancy, (3) disclosing the clue to resolution, (4) experiencing the gospel, and (5) anticipating the consequences." Eugene L. Lowry, *The Homiletical Plot: The Sermon as Narrative Art Form* (Louisville: Westminster John Knox Press, 2001). Lowry, *The Homiletical Plot: The Sermon as Narrative Art Form*, 26.

According to Lowry, this suspense-driven plotting movement capturing listener's attention revitalizes the spontaneous participation of the listener in preaching. Instead of being given the conclusive answer of the preacher, the plot also invites the listener to the journey from "problematic itch" to "resolutional scratch."[68] The essential function of Lowry's plot is nothing but to provide the listener with an active role to participate in preaching. Lowry lucidly describes his understanding of preaching and the preacher's task: "We [preachers] are authorized to invite a new *conversation* may end in freedom to trust and courage to *relinquish*."[69] Like Craddock, Lowry also thinks that preaching is a dialogue and to embody this thought it is required for the preachers to relinquish their authority.

Rejecting the hierarchical distance between preacher and listener that she perceives in the other models of preaching, Lucy Rose proposes a conversational approach to preaching.[70] Her conversational approach to preaching is derived from her conviction that the relationship the preacher and the listener is one of equal partnership in the community of faith and therefore preaching should be a conversation between two. In Rose's method, the preacher does not declare but does make "tentative interpretations," "proposals," or "wagers,"[71] which means the preacher is not the authoritative figure. By suggestions rather than declaration, Rose believes that the listener can find space to re-interpret the message. In this way, further and ongoing conversations are possible.[72] Rose's approach to preaching places a greater emphasis on the role of the listener as an active partner in a dialogue of preaching.

By restricting the role of the preacher, the New Homiletic has much focused on the role of the listener as a participant in preaching. Under the great influence of the New Homiletic, the listener is not treated like "javelin catcher" any more to borrow Craddock's famous line, but an active partner in a dialogue. This new understanding of the listener's role in preaching has guided that much contemporary homiletical dialogue has

---

68 Lowry, *The Homiletical Plot: The Sermon as Narrative Art Form*, 19.
69 Lowry, *The Sermon: Dancing the Edge of Mystery*, 89. Italics added.
70 Rose. Although Rose herself distinguishes her conversational approach to preaching from the New Homiletic, which she calls "transformational preaching," Lowry includes her approach to preaching in the New Homiletic. See Lowry, *The Sermon: Dancing the Edge of Mystery*, 30.
71 Rose, 100–101.
72 Ibid., 107.

revolved around the elevated role of the listener. The "turn to the listener" therefore must be a catchword which illustrates one of the most important features of the New Homiletic.

2.2.2. Experience as the Primary Purpose of Preaching

The common emphasis of approaches to preaching within the New Homiletic is more on the evocation of an experience from the listener in preaching, rather than teaching or transmitting of knowledge from the biblical text. Jeffery Bullock observes:

> During the last quarter century, theorists of what is coming to be known as the New Homiletic have been engaged in a radical re-appraisal of preaching. […] Although each theorists appears to have a different technique for making this move, it appears that this new homiletical model is more focused on what a sermon may do and even undo in the *experience* of the receiving audience, than on pointedly conveying content. This renewed emphasis on the *experience* of the listener appears to be the most productive aspect of this emerging paradigm shift in homiletic method.[73]

This feature of the New Homiletic is dependent on their understanding of the purpose of preaching that appears to be different from traditional preaching. Scholars within the New Homiletic understand that the goal of traditional preaching is to teach the lesson of the biblical text and to transmit the proposition to the listener.[74] However, they found a limitation on the purpose of traditional preaching and began to set up a new purpose preaching as reflects in the following comment. "It wrestled tolerably well with the *idea* of transparency but conveyed the *experience* of transparency less ably."[75] Their primary purpose of preaching is to facilitate an experience in the preaching event.

The experience of the listener is very fundamental for Fred Craddock's homiletical approach. The starting point of his inductive sermon is with listener's particular experiences. Along with the process of the sermon, the

---

73 Jeffrey Francis Bullock, *Preaching with a Cupped Ear: Hans-Georg Gadamer's Philosophical Hermeneutics as Postmodern Wor(l)d* (New York: Peter Lang, 1999), 48. Italics original.
74 Jensen, 11.
75 Ronald J. Sider and Michael A. King, *Preaching About Life in a Threatening World* (Philadelphia: Westminster Press, 1987), 16. Italics original.

experiences of the listener are also an integral element to provide analogy and identification for the listener, who participates in preaching and finally draws his or her own conclusions. According to Craddock, therefore the sermon not only begins but also ends with experience in the listener:

> Because the particulars of life provide the place of beginning, there is the necessity of a ground of shared experience. [...] these common experiences, provided they are meaningful in nature and are reflected upon with insight and judgment, are for the inductive method essential to the preaching experience.[76]

The inductive movement is also designed not to deliver ideas or propositions from the study of preacher but to carry the very inductive process experienced by the preacher throughout the interpretation. Thus the sermon, Craddock maintains, should be patterned along with the very inductive procedure of discovery the preacher goes trough in the text study. The inductive movement itself in preaching becomes an experiential bridge from the text to the listener. Thomas Long pinpoints, "Craddock wanted the eventfulness of exegesis to become the eventfulness of the sermon."[77] Craddock's inductive preaching seeks to allow the listener to participate in an experience the preacher reenacts.

What the listener effectively experience in preaching is also at the center of David Buttrick's homiletical approach. He also rejects to deliver ideas in preaching. The purpose of sermon, argues Buttrick, "cannot be stated in some clear single sentence as older homiletic texts suggested."[78] Instead, preaching is transformational in his thought. A sermon must be structured to shape the "faith consciousness" of the listeners.[79] Therefore, his approach is founded on "what happens" in human consciousness during the preaching event.

Like Buttrick, the basic agenda of Eugene Lowry's homiletical method is the creation of an experience in the listener. Lowry believes that preaching is the experiential event[80] and thus experience is the foundation for his homiletical method. For Lowry, the sermon is to be an ordering of experience rather than an ordering of ideas. To embody the process of ordering of experience in an actual sermon, he contrives the homiletical plot. In

---

76 Craddock, *As One without Authority*, 49.
77 Long, *The Witness of Preaching*, 103.
78 David Buttrick, "Interpretation and Preaching," *Interpretation* 35, no. 1 (1981): 58.
79 Buttrick, *Homiletic: Moves and Structures*, 301.
80 Lowry, *The Homiletical Plot: The Sermon as Narrative Art Form*, xx. Italics original.

the homiletical plot, a clue to resolution is uncovered as he described it as "one piece which allows the whole puzzle to come into sharp focus" is essential.[81] The clue is to be experienced as a surprise to the listeners. He claims, "Such a revelatory clue is *experienced* by the congregation rather than simply *known*."[82] With the plot, he believes that the preacher maximizes the possibilities of evoking or creating an experience for the listener. It is evident that Lowry's goal of preaching is to evoke an experience in the listener. He finally writes, "Evocation is key."[83]

A central point of Henry Mitchell's approach to preaching is also in his insistence that the purpose of preaching is the recreation of a meaningful experience.[84] Since the "intuitive consciousness" is affected directly by "experiential encounter," Mitchell claims the creation of such an encounter to be the purpose of preaching.[85] Therefore, it is not an overstatement that the terms most often associated with approach to preaching of the New Homiletic are "experience," "event" and "experiential encounter."

It is essential to note that the shift from transmission of ideas to evocation of experience in homiletical approaches of the New Homiletic is comprehensively influenced by the new hermeneutic. As explored above, the new hermeneutic claims that language is much more than a mean to deliver information but is inherently powerful – eventfulness. The insistence helped advocators of the New Homiletic view the sermon as an event or experience and redefine the task of preaching as evocation of the listener via the sermon. David Randolph formalized the work of the new hermeneutic in his book *The Renewal of Preaching*, as seen in the title of the first chapter in the book, "Preaching and the New Hermeneutic: Toward a New Homiletic." He defines his new homiletic thus: "*Preaching is the event in which the biblical text is interpreted in order that its meaning will come to expression in the concrete situation of the hearers.*"[86]

The importance of this characteristic of the New Homiletic leads Robert Reid to note, "it is fair to claim that a central, if not *the* central,

---

81 Ibid., 54.
82 Ibid. Italics original.
83 Lowry, *The Sermon: Dancing the Edge of Mystery*, 31.
84 Henry H. Mitchell, *The Recovery of Preaching* (San Francisco: Harper & Row, 1977), 33.
85 Henry H. Mitchell, *Celebration and Experience in Preaching* (Nashville: Abingdon Press, 1990), 25.
86 Randolph, *The Renewal of Preaching*, 1. Italics original.

unifying thread in the New Homiletic is the variety of ways in which each of the theorists are intent on creating an experience for an audience."[87] The New Homiletic has redefined the task of preaching as the creation of an affective experience for the listener.

2.2.3. Attention to Alternative Sermon Forms

The New Homiletic gives special attention to alternative sermon forms to idea-centered sermon forms traditionally used. The scholars within the New Homiletic have devoted themselves to invent new homiletical methods to design sermons and sermon form and considered it to be an important issue in their homiletic literature. Thus, Eugene Lowry calls attention to the sermon form of the New Homiletic "the revolution of sermonic shape."[88] In evaluating the influence of the New Homiletic Thomas Long also notes, "Indeed, it would not stray far from the truth to say that the one issue that has most occupied books and articles about preaching over the last few decades has been sermon form."[89]

Proponents of the New Homiletic normally believe that the logical sermon form traditionally used originated from Aristotelian rhetoric, which therefore is foreign to the Bible. For example, Fred Craddock critiques how traditional sermons are divided into parts and points as "the gospel [...] be [is] impaled upon the frame of Aristotelian logic,"[90] and objects that the sermon should be subsumed into rhetoric. Thus, Lowry describes a significant commonality of the New Homiletic as the move away from "the older paradigm of preaching which grew out of rhetorical principles and structures."[91]

As explained above, the growth of literary criticism in biblical studies stoked their searching for alternative sermon forms, which are not unfamiliar with the biblical text. An obvious example is Henry Davis' book,

---

87 Robert Stephen Reid, "Postmodernism and the Function of the New Homiletic in Post-Christendom Congregations," *Homiletic* 20, no. 2 (1995): 8. Italics original.
88 Eugene L. Lowry, "The Revolution of Sermonic Shape," in *Listening to the Word: Studies in Honor of Fred B. Craddock*, eds. Gail R. O'Day and Thomas G. Long (Nashville: Abingdon Press, 1993), 93.
89 Long, *The Witness of Preaching*, 122.
90 Craddock, *As One without Authority*, 38.
91 Lowry, "The Revolution of Sermonic Shape," 100.

Design for Preaching, which initiated the evolutionary process to sermon form. Davis was concerned with the function of the biblical text, which determines sermonic form. He asserts that a sermon should be "a living organism," "like a tree."[92] To Davis, a sermon structure is a living unity, an organism with "parts or members in structural and functional relation to one another and to the whole."[93] He suggested that sermon form is not constructed by dividing the main idea into its sub-parts; instead, the main idea of a sermon (biblical text) grows into a sermon form, like a seed producing a tree. Davis's argument was well received by other scholars within the New Homiletic, and then they become interested in the rhetorical dimension or the genre of the biblical text.[94] Homileticians realized that the Bible is not only the source for what is preached but also how one preaches. Gail O'Day and Thomas Long describe this feature of the New Homiletic as "Turning to the Text."[95]

To invent alternative sermon forms, scholars within the New Homiletic have been apt to prefer narrative genre to other biblical genres. Emphasizing the narrative texts, the attention paid to narrative preaching has become the most influential and popular movement in the New Homiletic. Therefore, "Turning to the Narrative Text" is a more accurate expression to describe the characteristic of the New Homiletic than "Turning to the Text." Their passion for narrative preaching cannot be explained only by the truth that the largest portion of the Bible is composed of narrative. It is closely related to other characteristics addressed above – the elevated position of the listener as a partner of preaching and the emphasis on experience as the purpose of preaching.

---

92   Henry Grady Davis, *Design for Preaching* (Philadelphia: Muhlenberg Press, 1958), 15.
93   Ibid., 23.
94   Eugene Lowry shows an apparent effort to extend the scope of the New Homiletic with including Henry Grady Davis. Lowry writes, "Perhaps the beginning of what Richard Eslinger called the 'Copernican Revolution' in North Americans homiletics could be dated with an earlier publication: *Design for Preaching* (1958), by H. Grady Davis." Lowry, *The Sermon: Dancing the Edge of Mystery*, 12. Lowry also writes, "Long after I had ceased using H. Grady Davis's *Design for Preaching* as a course text, it finally dawned on me that an underlying prciple of his, quietly named in the middle of the book, acually is central to all preaching." Eugene L. Lowry, *The Homiletical Beat: Why All Sermons Are Narrative* (Nashville: Abingdon Press, 2012), xi.
95   Gail R. O'Day and Thomas G. Long, "Introduction," in *Listening to the Word: Studies in Honor of Fred B. Craddock*, eds. Gail R. O'Day and Thomas G. Long (Nashville: Abingdon Press, 1993), 11–12.

Narrative preaching fits with the methodology of the New Homiletic because it does not demand high level of authority on the side of the preacher. Narrative approaches to preaching have advised the preacher not to be overly concerned about direct guidance or application. Narrative preaching assumes the use of indirect rather than direct address. Advocates of the New Homiletic believe that the indirect method does not threaten the listener rather it invigorate the voluntary participation and involvement of the listener in preaching. The listener in the indirect address even can complete the sermon. Richard Jensen notes, "The open-endedness of story preaching is inevitable if participation and involvement of the listener is a fundamental goal."[96] Narrative preaching is the natural choice of the New Homiletic because it permits the listener to the responsible for the own formulation and advances their position during the preaching.

Homileticians of the New Homiletic also promote narrative preaching because they believe that it is an effective way to achieve their goal of preaching – experience. Narrative preaching, although it takes a variety of shape, is generally considered as a sermon which includes narrative movement or plot, whose ingredients are opening discrepancy and final resolution.[97] The essential movement in narrative preaching maximizes the expectation of the listener and then finally culminates into the listener experiencing the sermon. Therefore, Eugene Lowry writes, "The purpose [of narrative movement] is singular – namely, to provide the context of heightened expectation in preparation for the evocation of the sermon's experiential meaning."[98] Charles Campbell aptly observes, "Narrative preaching seeks to touch the hearer at the level of experience. [...] Narrative is valued for its distinctive ability to produce or evoke experience."[99] Scholars within the New Homiletic normally have a preference for narrative preaching because a narrative sermon form is very efficient to provide experience for the listener, which is their purpose of preaching.

It should be emphasized that the growing attention to sermon form in the New Homiletic is based not only on the recognition that the biblical

---

96 Jensen, 145.
97 Lowry, *The Sermon: Dancing the Edge of Mystery*, 25.
98 Eugene L. Lowry, "Narrative Preaching," in *Concise Encyclopedia of Preaching*, eds. William H. Willimon and Richard Lischer (Louisville: Westminster John Knox Press, 1995), 342.
99 Charles L. Campbell, *Preaching Jesus: New Directions for Homiletics in Hans Frei's Postliberal Theology* (Grand Rapids: W. B. Eerdmans Pub., 1997), 122.

text has literary features but also on *the way in which the listeners listen*. Since other homileticians also have attempted to reflect the studies in literary criticism,[100] it could be said that the focus on the dynamic of the listening process is more exclusive characteristic of the New Homiletic. Regarding the issue of sermon form, Fred Craddock suggests that preachers must not only consider the literary dimension of the biblical text but also how the listeners listen. Thus, he builds his inductive preaching on his "psychology of listening" – an assumption that "people think and pattern their experiences inductively."[101] After Craddock, homiletical approach to sermon form of the New Homiletic crosses over to a new stage – attention to the patterns of human listening. Scott Johnston notes, "For, in directing our attention toward the way people listen, *As One without Authority* lays the foundation for the methodological predilection that has consumed homiletics for the last two decades."[102] Craddock's work on sermon form has spawned much interest among those who embrace the New Homiletic and try to invent new sermon forms that mindful of the consciousness of the listener.[103]

The attention to sermon form is an essential characteristic of the New Homiletic. Proponents of the New Homiletic who were not satisfied with traditional sermonic form have taken an interest in literary elements of the biblical text in particular narrative nature of the text, and created narrative sermon forms. They have also produced various other types of sermon forms that give special consideration on how listeners receive the sermon. Their solid interest on alternative sermon forms achieved "the Copernican Revolution in homiletic."[104]

---

[100] For a typical example, see Thomas G. Long, *Preaching and the Literary Forms of the Bible* (Philadelphia: Fortress Press, 1989). In North America, since 1980s there has been also a resurgence of interest in expository preaching homiletics, sensitive to literary characteristics of the biblical text. See Greidanus; Haddon W. Robinson, *Biblical Preaching: The Development and Delivery of Expository Messages* (Grand Rapids: Baker Book House, 1980).

[101] Thomas G. Long, "Form," in *Concise Encyclopedia of Preaching*, eds. William H. Willimon and Richard Lischer (Louisville: Westminster John Knox Press, 1995), 149.

[102] Scott Black Johnston, "Who Listens to Stories?: Cautions and Challenges for Narrative Preaching," *Insights* 111, no. 2 (1996): 4.

[103] Lowry, *The Homiletical Plot: The Sermon as Narrative Art Form*, 130.

[104] Richard L. Eslinger, *A New Hearing: Living Options in Homiletic Methods* (Nashville: Abingdon Press, 1987), 65.

2.3. A Critical Reflection on the New Homiletic

2.3.1. Critique against the Elevation of the Listener's Role

Since the birth of the New Homiletic, the homiletical world has witnessed both the proliferation of homiletical literature and the greater formation of new sermon forms. The New Homiletic has enjoyed a high level of prominence in homiletical conversations especially in North America. However, it is conceded that the New Homiletic did not overcome all of its weakness it hoped to correct. There are criticisms towards the New Homiletic.

Though homileticians of the New Homiletic have brought about preachers' recognition on the role of the listener and the necessity of partnership with the listener, their increased attention to the listener reduces the authority of the biblical text in preaching. Approaches elevating the status of the listener within the New Homiletic normally began with the conviction that the preachers can assume neither their authority nor the authority of the Bible in the anti-authority ethos of the contemporary postmodern culture. For example, Fred Craddock clearly claims, "No longer can the preacher presuppose the general recognition of her authority as clergy; or the authority of her institution, or the authority of scripture."[105] Based on this conviction, proponents of the New Homiletic attempt to appeal by having the listeners participate in the sermon and allowing them to deducing their own conclusions, rather than relying on the biblical text and message which are no longer authoritative enough. It could result in the sermon where the voice of God cannot be heard over the gab of the listeners. In such a sermon that is full of the voice of the listener, it becomes difficult for listener to hear the transcended voice over their own. As a result, the authority of the sermon shifts from biblical text to the listener. Though they intend to introduce the listener as a partner of preaching, they consequently raise the listener as a top decision maker of preaching.

Homileticians of the New Homiletic also have elevated the role of the listener to such heights that the role and authority of the preacher is diminished. As described in the title of Craddock's seminal work *As One without Authority*, they continually argue that preachers are not viewed as authoritative figures. It is no exaggeration to say that the New Homiletic

---

105 Craddock, *As One without Authority*, 14.

has developed as it takes away authority from the preachers. However, they seems to forget that the preacher go to the pulpit with the authority which resides not in him or her but in the biblical revelation and authority. If God has spoken through the Bible, then the preacher from the biblical text is actually speaking a divine message to the congregation. Any authority that the preacher occupies is not his or her own; instead, the authority depends on God who has spoken. John Stott illustrates a portrait of the preacher as a steward, not a prophet and not an apostle, which shows the nature of the preacher's authority. He writes, "True, it is indirect authority. It is not direct like that of the prophets, nor like that of the apostles, who issued commands and expected obedience, but it is still the authority of God."[106] Though preachers should not require the same degree of authority as prophets and apostles who were given direct authority from God, it is evident that they also have some amount of authority – indirect authority. In the anti-authority ethos of postmodernism, it might be an easier option for preachers to shy away from preaching with authority as many homileticians of the New Homiletic advocate than to assert authority. However, preachers must resist the temptation to give up their God-given authority. This authority which the preacher is given from God cannot be transferred.

The elevated perspective on the listener finally brought about an attempt to completely eliminate the unique nature of the preacher. As stated previously, Lucy Rose has tried to remove separation between the preacher and the congregation and her attention to equality between the two triggered her to come up with conversational preaching with a high level of dialogue between equal participants.[107] While the preacher needs enough time to sit at the roundtable having a dialogue with the listeners to hear their voices and opinions, the role of the preacher however cannot be identified with the role of the congregation. Thomas Long rightly describes the distinctiveness of the preacher's role: "But finally the preacher, even the pastor, is set apart, called to the one who must get up from the roundtable, stand in the preaching spot, and prayerfully say, 'Let the words of my mouth be acceptable in thy sight, O God. Hear now the word of God.'"[108] Rose also seems not to consider that all people are not all equal in their gift and their roles in the church. It is God's will that people are gifted in

---

106 John R. W. Stott, *The Preacher's Portrait: Some New Testament Word Studies* (Grand Rapids: W. B. Eerdmans Pub., 1979), 29–30.
107 Rose, 4.
108 Long, *The Witness of Preaching*, 35.

different ways to build the Christian community. Moreover, the difference in gifts and roles in the church does not mean that one is superior to others. All gifts and roles in the church community have same value in the eyes of God. Just as uniformity does not mean equality, diversity does not mean inequality.

2.3.2. Critique against the Primacy of the Experience

Advocates of the New Homiletic have replaced sermons of teaching and delivering the contents in the biblical text to the listener with sermons of creating an experience in the listener. They generally believe that the crafting of an experience in preaching is the best way to have a meaningful communication with listeners who has sufficient knowledge of the Bible. Though the Christendom collapsed in the United States, Fred Craddock believed that American people in general still had certain amount of biblical knowledge and general understanding of Christian theology because the culture had just escaped from the Christendom.[109] Therefore, Craddock and others within the New Homiletic were confident that what is necessary for the listeners is not to inform them about the contents of the biblical text; but to help them overcome their boredom. They attempted to appeal the listener in a new way which evocates an experience. The problem, however, is that the current listeners are not considered to be knowledgeable about the Bible. Many scholars concur that the United States has *completed* its change into a post-Christian society. David Randolph, in his thirtieth anniversary edition of *The Renewal of Preaching*, writes, "The Church of Christendom is past. The day when the Christian church enjoyed a privileged position is long gone. The culture no longer supports Christianity and its values. […] We live in a post Christian church."[110] In the post-Christian society, preachers are not preaching a well-known message to knowledgeable listeners. Craig Loscalzo thus claims: "Biblical knowledge, Christian doctrine and theological reflection must be presented and re-presented from America's

---

[109] Craddock writes, "I do not wish to argue here that Christendom still prevails in this country as a whole. Nevertheless, the basic presuppositions can values of that portion of society to which I expose the gospel are traditionally Christian." Fred B. Craddock, *Overhearing the Gospel* (St. Louis: Chalice Press, 2002), 17.

[110] Randolph and Reid, *The Renewal of Preaching in the Twenty-First Century: The Next Homiletics Commentary*, 4.

pulpits – yes, even to American Christians."[111] Therefore, homileticians of the New Homiletic again need to reconsider their purpose of preaching in this new environment of non-Christendom.

For advocates of the New Homiletic, the experience of the listener is not only their purpose of preaching but also the source of preaching. Since the biblical text and the preacher no longer possess the authority that they did before, the experience of the listener is a source which both the preacher and the listener concede. The experience in preaching, not the Bible, becomes a shared source between the preacher and the listeners. The preaching now becomes too dependent on listener's experience; and this dependency is quite similar to the assumption made by liberal theology, which argues that essential source for Christian faith and theology lies in human experience. Charles Campbell argues that Craddock and others within the New Homiletic follow the fault of Friedrich Schleiermacher and Paul Tillich fell into, which bases Christian faith primarily on human experience. He complains, "What Craddock's inductive method finally preaches is not the identity of Jesus Christ rendered in the gospel narratives, but rather a liberal theology of human experience."[112]

Their solid reliance upon experience in preaching could also form Christianity which is experientially oriented with little or no emphasis on cognitive, reflective dimensions of the faith. Though experience is essential to preaching, it needs proper interpretation in the light of the Christian faith. Christians also need to be familiar with something about the words, categories, and claims of the Christian tradition in other to mature their faith.[113] Because Christian faith seeks understanding, it is true that preaching should be the occasion for deep teaching in the faith. The approaches within the New Homiletic have ignored the essential task of preaching.

Proponents of the New Homiletic genuinely presume that the postmodern congregation prefers a sermon that evokes an experience to one teaching the biblical text. They write, "Regardless what people may say, what they appear to want is an *experience* that moves them. Thus, regardless of theological stripe, that is the rhetorical strategy of preaching that is

---

111 Craig A. Loscalzo, *Apologetic Preaching: Proclaiming Christ to a Postmodern World* (Downers Grove: InterVarsity Press, 2000), 24.
112 Campbell, 156.
113 Thomas G. Long, "When the Preacher Is a Teacher," *Journal for Preachers* 16, no. 2 (1993): 22–23.

increasingly commensurate with the emerging postmodern sensibility."[114] Homileticians of the New Homiletic have believed that not only their strategy of preaching is useful in the post-modern society but it is very timely and adequate. Some of them think that the New Homiletic and postmodernism homiletic to be synonyms.[115] Ironically, however, recent studies about contemporary listeners in preaching show that the listeners expect the sermon to be based on the Bible.[116] A number of listeners also believe that teaching is still a major purpose of preaching.[117] Moreover, it would be inaccurate to conclude that the New Homiletic clearly presents postmodernism. It must be noted that postmodern scholars tend to refuse the presumed resemblances in all people – in this case, postmodern people prefer a sermon that creates an experience. It is debatable whether the New Homiletic approach is perfectly appropriate for postmodern listeners and postmodernism as much as they are convinced.

2.3.3. Critique against the Attention to the Sermon Forms and Narrative Preaching

Through the development of the New Homiletic, Preaching has shifted toward obtaining a hearing by the form, the "how" of sermons. This shift toward the technique of preaching resulted in a variety of sermon forms to attract the listener and served to overcome the criticism that preaching became an old trivia. However, there is no denying that the immoderate emphasis on the "how" of preaching in the New Homiletic minimizes the "what," or the content of the preaching. "It is possible to focus so thoroughly on the *way* as sermon says something as to pay no heed to *what* is being said," David Greenhaw notes in response to "many reform

---

114 Reid, "Postmodernism and the Function of the New Homiletic in Post-Christendom Congregations," 11.
115 Paul Scott Wilson, *Preaching and Homiletical Theory* (Saint Louis: Chalice Press, 2004), 136–137.
116 Lori Carrell, *The Great American Sermon Survey* (Wheaton: Mainstay Church Resources, 2000), 27; Mary Alice Mulligan and others, *Believing in Preaching: What Listeners Hear in Sermons* (St. Louis: Chalice Press, 2005), 21ff.
117 Mulligan and others, 7. Two-thirds of the listeners interviewed by the researchers indicate that they believe teaching was a major purpose of preaching.

movements" of preaching.[118] "What is underplayed" in the development of homiletical forms given by the New Homiletic, Thomas Long also states, "is exactly what was emphasized in the traditional model" – biblical "content and didactic purpose."[119] Preachers become more interested in utility of alternative sermon design to appeal the listener an evocate an experience in the listener rather than teach biblical content.

Moreover, many homileticians of the New Homiletic have preferred narrative preaching as primary form for preaching. Since narrative preaching tends to be reluctant to directly teach the biblical content, the popularity of narrative preaching may also result in biblical illiteracy for contemporary listeners. Contemporary approaches to narrative preaching have ignored "the voice of teacher."[120] Calvin Miller argues that excessive use of narrative preaching results in "the loss of didache (or teaching) in the church," to the point that "many theologians are growing concerned that the church is losing the ability to define and defend its faith."[121] It is evident that the general decline in biblical literacy nowadays is partly due to excessive interest in the various sermon forms that appeal to the listener and narrative preaching, and the lack of interest in the substance of the preaching. Contemporary listeners lack biblical knowledge and thus the capacity of listeners to utilize theological language has been damaged. Thomas Long describes the biblical literacy of the contemporary listeners as follows: "Many people in the pews simply lack enough biblical knowledge to place the biblical text into any meaningful context and, thus, listen to Scripture episodically."[122] The listeners need some background knowledge about the literary and historical contexts of the biblical text and even the big framework of the whole Bible more than a piece of story line and the experience of narrative if they are to engage in a meaningful dialogue with the text and to attempt spiritual mature.

As narrative preaching has become a dominant form of sermon in the New Homiletic, other biblical genres were put away. Adding an emphasis

---

118 David M. Greenhaw, "As One with Authority," in *Intersections: Post-Critical Studies in Preaching*, ed. Richard L. Eslinger (Grand Rapids: W. B. Eerdmans Pub., 1994), 107.
119 Long, "Form," 151.
120 Thomas G. Long, *Preaching from Memory to Hope* (Louisville: Westminster John Knox Press, 2009), 16.
121 Calvin Miller, "Narrative Preaching," in *Handbook of Contemporary Preaching*, ed. Michael Duduit (Nashville: Broadman Press, 1992), 108.
122 Long, "When the Preacher Is a Teacher," 25.

on the narrative texts, homileticians within the New Homiletic seek means to reform other biblical genres into narrative sermons. For example, Eugene Lowry suggests that a sermon can have a narrative shape without dependence on any narrative text. The purpose of his homiletical plot is to make "any sermon – life situational, doctrinal, or expository – a narrative event."[123] Exclusive reliance on narrative preaching, which ignores other biblical genres, is rather ironic because homileticians of the New Homiletic had complaint on traditional approach of "one type fits all" and thus became interested in alternative sermon forms like narrative sermon to reflect diverse biblical genres. Narrative preaching of the New Homiletic now has becomes "one type fits all" approach. In particular, as narrative preaching increased in popularity in the New Homiletic, many started to regard Paul's preaching as an unlikely model for the contemporary listeners. Along with the enthusiastic acceptance of narrative preaching, Paul and his letters have become "the missing dimension" in the current homiletical dialogue.[124]

Many homileticians of the New Homiletic placed the foundation of their preference on narrative or story preaching in the parables of Jesus. They insist that the preacher have to preach like Jesus and thus have to preach narrative sermons.[125] However, there is room for doubt about their belief that the parables of Jesus should be the primary model for contemporary preaching. What is worthy of attention is the fact that apostles did not copy Jesus' parable-preaching. The apostles, including Paul, did not preach like Jesus but they preached Jesus the Messiah in a more direct way. David Allen challenges those who advocate the parables of Jesus as the biblical model for preaching: "If the parables as a genre or as a foundation for the church's teaching was God intended, why does it not show up in the apostolic preaching of Acts or in the canonical writings of Paul, Peter, John, James, Jude and the author of Hebrew?"[126] It is hardly logical to argue that Jesus' parables are the archetype of biblical preaching when the apostles never preached in such a way. It must be also noted that the parables are not the only preaching or teaching method of Jesus. Instead

---

123 Lowry, *The Homiletical Plot: The Sermon as Narrative Art Form*, 91.
124 James Thompson, *Preaching Like Paul: Homiletical Wisdom for Today* (Louisville: Westminster John Knox Press, 2001), 14.
125 Campbell, 272.
126 David L. Allen, "A Tale of Two Roads: Homiletics and Biblical Authority," *Journal of the Evangelical Theological Society* 43, no. 3 (2000): 500.

of using a parable, Jesus also *explained* what was said in the Scripture concerning himself (Luke 24:27). Jesus did not exclusively use parables. Moisés Silva points out, "Although the use of parables was the most distinctive feature in Jesus' method of teaching, it was hardly the only one."[127] The biblical rationale for Jesus' parables as the primary model of preaching is not complete.

2.3.4. Critique against the Turn to the Individual Listener

As has been demonstrated, the New Homiletic has gone through substantial critique. Many of the critiques considered the common features of the New Homiletic. At this juncture, it must be noted that these critiques are relevant to the individualistic approach of the New Homiletic both directly and indirectly. The individualistic orientation would produce their understanding of preaching ministry lacking the presence of the Christian community, more than just individuals. In the Christian tradition, however, the intimate relationship between preaching and the community is strongly emphasized. For example, reformer John Calvin claims, "Whenever we see the Word of God purely preached and heard, and the sacraments administered according to Christ's institution, there, it is not to be doubted, a church of God exists."[128] Surely that connection has not been lost in the history of the church. Though one might attempt to equate "the turn to the listener" of it with "the turn to the church,"[129] it is necessary to reconsider whether the homileticians have paid adequate attention to the listener as collective entity. Recognizing the influence of the New Homiletic emphasis on an expanded understanding of the listener, the questions about corporate sense of the listener – the listeners as the Christian community or the church – disclose serious limitations in the approaches of the New Homiletic.

---

127 Walter C. Kaiser and Moisés Silva, *An Introduction to Biblical Hermeneutics: The Search for Meaning* (Grand Rapids: Zondervan, 2007), 167.
128 John Calvin, *Institutes of the Christian Religion* (Philadelphia: Westminster Press, 1960), 1023.
129 For example, see Christian David Eichorn, "Ecclesial Preaching: The Homiletical Theology of Vatican II and Its Influence Upon Protestant Homiletics of the Twentieth Century" (Ph.D. diss., Drew University, 2001), 208–209.

It is hard to argue against the criticism that the excessive elevation of the listener's role and authority in preaching of the New Homiletic stresses an individualistic approach to preaching. The preaching as an open-ended dialogue in which the listener actively participates ends up permitting listeners the right to experience the sermon for themselves, to feel their own feelings, and to think their own thought. Each listener is responsible to draw his or her own conclusions. In the words of Richard Lischer, "The individual hearer – and not the church – 'make' the sermon."[130] With this concept of the New Homiletic, the listeners are naturally treated as a loosely connected group of individuals who have the right to make their own decisions, rather than the church as being one body.

It is necessary to note that their idea that the hearer has the right or freedom to make their own conclusions reflects the individualistic culture of North America. William Willimon comments about the freedom that the New Homiletic emphasizes:

> Freedom is not freedom to obey God or the result of a well-formed character. Freedom is the individual's 'room to choose.' Freedom is not freedom to choose or to reject Christ, or the freedom of all the baptized to wrestle together over the implication of the gospel. Freedom, in *As One without Authority*, is freedom of the individual, apart from Scripture or community, to draw his or her own democratic conclusions.[131]

Focusing on extension of the freedom of individual listener, therefore, Charles Campbell argues that the New Homiletic has submitted itself to the "tyranny" of contemporary culture and particularly to the "tyranny" of individualism in North America.[132] It would not be an overstatement if we say that this American individualism has given a birth to the New Homiletic's concept of listener, the one with individual authority to make his or her own judgment and make conclusion about sermon.

Craddock, Rose, and others within the New Homiletic claim that giving the listener the right to decide and come up with their individual conclusion is actually a practical application of the doctrine of the priesthood of all believers. However, theologian Robert Brown notes that the doctrine is meant to serve as a "corrective to understanding of grace focused on individual 'religious experience.'" According to the theologian, the doctrine

---

130 Richard Lischer, "The Interrupted Sermon," *Interpretation* 50, no. 2 (1996): 173.
131 William H. Willimon, *Peculiar Speech: Preaching to the Baptized* (Grand Rapids: W. B. Eerdmans Pub., 1992), 48–49.
132 Campbell, 144.

of the priesthood of all believers means that every person is to be a priest to every other person, not to serve oneself as priest. Their perspective on the doctrine represents what Brown identifies as a "widespread misunderstanding of the doctrine"[133] and ironically confirms the individualistic approach inherent in their homiletical theories.

That the New Homiletic heavily relies on the new hermeneutic is a conclusive evidence that its concept of listener processes individualistic characteristic than corporate characteristic. As explored in the above, the concept of the word-event or the language event in the new hermeneutic, which is a fundamental foundation of the New Homiletic, stemmed from an existential approach which primarily focuses on the self-understanding of the listener. Therefore, the event in preaching is a calling to evoke an experience on individual hearer's part. With the de-emphasis on the content of the biblical text, their emphasis now appears to be on experience in preaching that allow little concern for the community of faith. Charles Campbell criticizes Craddock's limited understanding of community underlying individualism:

> Craddock's linguistic community exists primarily in the moment of preaching; it is an "event," which is not surprising in light of Craddock's reliance on the new hermeneutic. [...] Craddock's "community" is finally little more than a collection of individuals who share no distinctive discourse or practices and who draw their own conclusions about the meaning of the gospel apart from any recognition of communal authority or any process of communal decision making.[134]

This criticism not only pertains to Craddock but also to general homileticians within the New Homiletic whose purpose of preaching is the experiential event. The experience highlighted within the New Homiletic results in an individualistic orientation to their homiletical theories. Their focus of preaching is primarily the individual listener.

Their ongoing concern for how to preach sermon that evokes individual listener with experiential events has widely ignored the larger context of preaching, the Christian community where preaching is enacted. It is not an overstatement that technical elements have received a disproportionate attention in the New Homiletic. The reason for their attention to the

---

133 Robert MacAfee Brown, *The Spirit of Protestantism* (New York: Oxford University Press, 1965), 94–95.
134 Campbell, 134.

listener has usually been pragmatic.[135] Criticizing the excessive discussion of the homiletical technique that is pragmatically driven within the New Homiletic, James Thompson points out, "The advocates of the New Homiletic have said little about how this kind of preaching will create a communal identity with its own ethical norms and mission."[136] When it comes to the approach of narrative in their homiletical theories, their attention is limited in technical use of narrative forms to appeal the listener with experience and is indisposed toward the bigger role of narratives in the biblical text such as to construct the communal identity of listeners. In fact, it is no wonder that some scholars reflect that contemporary "homiletics is often tempted to follow its own interests rather than the needs of the church."[137] Giving too much focus on pragmatic skills designed to appeal to the individual listener, they have not given sufficient attention to the collective listener, the Christian community.

It must be noted that the homiletical approaches which respect the authority of individual hearer are naturally reluctant to challenge the fundamental convictions of the hearers. As perceived in narrative preaching, proponents of the New Homiletic avoid demanding any change in the lives of the listeners. They even do not preach against the forces of American individualism and pop-culture entertainment, which listeners subconsciously are saturated with. John Wright describes the current situation of preachers as follows: "Preachers constantly feel pressure to make market forces their friends, thus conserving the culture's deepest narrative."[138] Richard Lischer also writes, "The critical evaluation of our sermon entails […] analysis of the many ways our pulpit stories have been transparent to the needs of the ego but opaque to the claims of God's righteousness."[139] In the New Homiletic, especially in North America, the convictions of listeners including individualism remain intact, encouraged and even strengthened.

In summary, the critical assessment of the "turn to the listener" within the New Homiletic has proved that their approaches inherently have an individualistic orientation and thus give little attention to the cooperative

---

135 Zink-Sawyer: 351.
136 Thompson, 14.
137 Richard Lischer and William H. Willimon, "Interview with Richard Lischer & William Willimon," *Homiletic* 20, no. 2 (1995): 15.
138 John W. Wright, *Telling God's Story: Narrative Preaching for Christian Formation* (Downers Grove: IVP Academic, 2007), 48.
139 Richard Lischer, "The Limits of Story," *Interpretation* 38, no. 1 (1984): 36.

identity of listener in the community of faith. Desiring to be effective and relevant to the listener, it is also demonstrated that they avoid challenging the ways of the American culture represented by individualism. Their chief attention is to appeal for the individual listener, not communal identity of the listener or prosperity of the Christian community. Therefore, in order to accurately capture what it means by the "turn to the listener" of the New Homiletic, the catchphrase should be rephrased as the "turn to the individual listener," not "turn to the church."

2.4. Conclusion

The particular culture of North America in the 1960s has shown greater interest in the homiletical enterprise of the New Homiletic than any other homileticians. Proponents of the New Homiletic strongly argue that traditional preaching is neither attractive nor effective for contemporary listeners because it is too preacher-centered with authoritative role of preacher and too-idea centered without reflecting any literary dimensions of the biblical text and human listening process. Rather than employing traditional attempt to teach the content of the biblical text to listeners, scholars in the New Homiletic have focused on listeners' experience and participation in preaching and sermons. With the help of the new hermeneutic, their goal of preaching is to preach something to be heard, which means something to be experienced with. To insure that the sermon is heard, they have focused on inventing various sermon forms designed for the listener. Though their homiletical approaches based on their new and extended understanding of the listener have given a novel perspective to the contemporary preaching, their radical orientation to individual listener ended up neglecting the collective listener and overlooking the Christian community which have been the centerpiece of the Christian tradition.

Chapter Three
Paul's Main Intention of Preaching in 1 Thessalonians: Community Formation

This chapter, by thoroughly examining the situation and characteristics of the Thessalonian community, will argue that one of the most important intentions of Paul's preaching in 1 Thessalonians was to maintain and reinforce the fledgling community in the face of challenge of the larger pagan society. First, this chapter will introduce the pagan context of the city of Thessalonica, which dominated the life of the Thessalonians. The chapter next will focus on the Thessalonian community, which was formed a short time before the letter was written and whose members were mainly Gentiles, the former pagans of the city. The chapter then will show that the suffering of the community described in the letter was a result of the conflict with other pagan compatriots due to the converts' disapproval of certain cultic practices. With the inevitable difficulties caused by the suffering and the conflict within the Thessalonian community, Paul in 1 Thessalonians needed to put the process of community formation into effect for the continuing well-being of the community. This chapter, which demonstrates that Paul's intention in 1 Thessalonians was to carry out the process of the community formation, will legitimize the main focus of this overall study to delve into Paul's preaching for community formation in 1 Thessalonians.

3.1. The Pagan City of Thessalonica: The Cults

When Paul arrived in Thessalonica he was not entering into a religious vacuum. In Thessalonica the pagan cults thoroughly permeated and dominated the life of the Thessalonians. The challenges posed by religious and civic cults of Thessalonica, therefore, are reflected in the specific content of 1 Thessalonians. Karl Donfried writes, "The cults in Thessalonica were closely interrelated and that is a fact which is important to stress."[1]

Because the modern city of Thessalonica is built over the ancient city, archaeological work on the city is limited. In spite of the limited archaeological, epigraphic, and numismatic evidence on Thessalonica, the existing evidence indicates the presence of a number of cults. The primary gods traditionally worshipped in Thessalonica were mostly the members of the Greek pantheon such as Zeus, Athena, Heracles, Aphrodite among others.[2]

The Egyptian gods, Dionysus and Cabirus, also enjoyed special prominence in Thessalonica. The cult of the Egyptian gods, such as Serapis and Isis, might even date to as early as the third century B.C.[3] The worshippers of these gods held public celebrations of the cult and also gathered for common meals.[4] Though the precise characteristics of the cult of Isis are unknown, the worshippers of Isis believed that the cult provided healing, salvation and immortality.[5]

The worship of Dionysus, the god of wine and drunkenness, was established when the city was first founded.[6] The cult emphasized the hope of joyous afterlife, which was symbolized by the shape of a phallus.[7] During the cult ceremony, the phallus was revealed and carried to the god with hymns.[8] The sexual symbols of the cult were more than just representations of the hope of a joyous afterlife. Donfried notes, "They [the sexual symbols] were also sensually provocative. The fact that the god Dionysus was the god of wine and joy often gave allowance for a strong emphasis on noisy revelry of all sorts."[9]

---

1 Karl P. Donfried, *Paul, Thessalonica, and Early Christianity* (Grand Rapids: W. B. Eerdmans Pub., 2002), 22.
2 Holland L. Hendrix, "Thessalonica," in *Anchor Bible Dictionary Vol. 6*, ed. David Noel Freedman (New York: Doubleday, 1992). For details, see Charles Edson, "Cults of Thessalonica," *Harvard Theological Review* 41, no. 3 (1948).
3 Apostolos E. Vakalopoulos, *A History of Thessaloniki* (Thessalonike: Institute for Balkan Studies, 1963), 8.
4 Edson: 184.
5 Donfried, 23.
6 Vakalopoulos, 5–6.
7 Martin P. Nilsson, *The Dionysiac Mysteries of the Hellenistic and Roman Age* (New York: Arno Press, 1975), 44.
8 Ibid., 44–45.
9 Donfried, 24.

The cult of Cabirus is thought to have been established in Thessalonica in the first century B.C. Over time, Cabirus held the position of titular deity in the city.[10] The cult became the most important religious cult in Thessalonica during Paul's visit.[11] Rex Witt writes, "Without any doubt, this was the cult that during the Empire held the field at Tessalonike [...] on numismatic evidence, [Thessalonica] was addicted to the cult of what may perhaps be termed Kaberic monotheism."[12] In spite of diverse legendary narratives, Cabirus was basically described as a hero who suffered a martyr's death and was expected to return to help individuals and especially the city of Thessalonica.[13] The phallic symbol in the Cabirus cult had an important role in the celebration. Thus, Witt concludes that "the core of the mystery was a phallic ritual" and that "the stress during the initiation ceremony fell [...] on sex."[14]

Not only were religious cults prominent; political cults were also prevalent through Thessalonica. The Hellenistic ruler cult had a long history in Thessalonica, like other cities east of the Roman Empire, which is said to have begun with Alexander the Great.[15] Whether the cult was

---

10   Edson: 188–200.
11   Donfried, 25.
12   Rex E. Witt, "The Kabeiroi in Ancient Macedonia," in *Ancient Macedonia Vol. 2* (Thessaloniki: Institute for Balkan Studies, 1977), 78. Craig de Vos, however, argues that such a claim seems to be an overstatement, for it ignores the fact that other gods were also found on coins and in inscriptions during the same period. Craig de Vos, *Church and Community Conflicts: The Relationships of the Thessalonian, Corinthian, and Philippian Churches with Their Wider Civic Communities* (Atlanta: Scholars Press, 1999), 141.
13   Robert Jewett, *The Thessalonian Correspondence: Pauline Rhetoric and Millenarian Piety* (Philadelphia: Fortress Press, 1986), 128. Jewett suggests that the Cabirus cult was influential in the development of the Thessalonian church. Although the cult had originally been popular among the lower classes, it was incorporated into the purview of civic cult for high classes at Paul's time. This left laborers of the low classes receptive to Christ, with their recognition of the similarities between Cabirus and Christ. Jewett, 126–132, 165. However, Jewett's speculation that the Cabirus cult influenced the development of Thessalonian community has been called into question. For the skeptical description on the parallels between Christianity and the Cabirus cults, see Stephen C. Barton, "Review of Jewett 1986," *Expository Times* 99, no. 3 (1987): 90. For a critique on Jewett's understanding of the "hijacking" of the cult, see John M. G. Barclay, "Conflict in Thessalonica," *Catholic Biblical Quarterly* 55, no. 3 (1993): 519 n. 24.
14   Witt, 72–73.
15   E. A. Fredricksmeyer, "On the Background of the Ruler Cult," in *Ancient Macedonian Studies in Honor of Charles F. Edson*, ed. Harry J. Dell (Thessaloniki: Institute for Balkan Studies, 1981), 145.

demanded by him or his followers is still debated, but it is certain that the ruler cult was to be an important factor in the life of Thessalonians from the beginning.[16] The Greeks took a pragmatic stance in their view of religion or divinity. They believed that gods were worshipped because they had ability to benefit or harm humans. From their pragmatic perspective on divinity, it was just a small further step to deifying and worshiping a great ruler such as Alexander the Great.

The cult of Roman benefactors and the emperor cult were well-received in Thessalonica. In addition to the long history of the Hellenistic ruler cult, the cults prevailed in Thessalonica because of the close ties with the political situation of Thessalonica. When Macedonia became a Roman province in the middle of the second century B.C., Thessalonica, which had a strategic importance for the Roman Empire, was made the capital and the center of Roman administration. Thessalonica held a more favorable position as the city allied itself with the victor of the Roman civil war.[17] After Octavian's victory in 42 B.C., Thessalonica's "cooperation with the victor resulted in the declaration of its status as a free city, which meant that a measure of local autonomy, freedom from military occupation, the right to mint coins, and an advantageous tax situation could be enjoyed."[18]

To sustain and increase the commitments and favors of Romans who had the ability to determine their fortunes, the Thessalonians, especially the provincial elites, were willing to develop ways to honor their Roman benefactors.[19] The patronage relationship between the Roman benefactors and the Thessalonian elites accelerated and reinforced the cult of Roman benefactors and later the emperor cult in Thessalonica.[20] So, the Roman

---

16   Ibid., 148.
17   Donfried, 35–36.
18   Jewett, 123.
19   Holland L. Hendrix, "Thessalonicans Honor Romans" (1984), 253. About the rapid spread of the imperial cult through competition among cities and local elites, see Paul Zanker, "The Power of Image," in *Paul and Empire: Religion and Power in Roman Imperial Society*, ed. Richard A. Horsley (Harrisburg: Trinity Press International, 1997), 76–82.
20   About the intimate relation between the patron-client relationship and the imperial cult, see Peter Garnsey and Richard Saller, "Patronal Power Relations," in *Paul and Empire: Religion and Power in Roman Imperial Society*, ed. Richard A. Horsley (Harrisburg: Trinity Press International, 1997); Andrew Wallace-Hadrill, "Patronage in Roman Society: From Republic to Empire," in *Patronage in Ancient Society* (London: Routledge, 1989).

benefactors included objects to be honored next to the gods. Holland Hendrix dates this development to about 95 B.C. and writes that while "'the gods' of the city were due honors as the source of Thessalonica's continued well-being, important foreign agents of its immediate interests were acknowledged in concert with its divine sustainers. [...] Honors for the gods and Roman benefactors expressed a hierarchy of benefaction extending from the divine sphere into human affairs."[21] The cult of Roman benefactors was finally established and included a special priesthood, the "priest of Rome and of Roman Benefactors."[22]

The temple of Julius Caesar, the adoptive father of Augustus, shows that the development of the emperor cult in Thessalonica definitely reached a whole new level. The temple was built during the reign of Augustus as an expression of the loyalty to Augustus. For the emperor cult, a "priest and agonothete of the Imperator" Augustus, the "son of god," was appointed and attached to the temple. The priest apparently took priority over the other priesthoods.[23] The coins that were minted at that time in Thessalonica also confirm that Julius Caesar was regarded as a god and also implies that Augustus was given the status of *divi filius* – the deified son. It is also the deification of the emperor that that caused the image of Augustus to displace the image of Zeus on the coins in Thessalonica. The practice of honoring the Roman emperor continued with Tiberius and Gaius in Thessalonica.[24] It is clear that the imperial power in Thessalonica was construed in religious forms such as a temple, images, honorific inscriptions, sacrifices, and festivals. To gain the favor and protection of the Roman Empire, the aristocratic class of Thessalonica "demanded superior attention."[25]

In Thessalonica the prominent cults were not simply a private, but a communal affair. The worshipers of the same god often made a religious association to celebrate the cult and organize funeral rites.[26] The associations also organized common meals for the members.[27] Therefore, participation

---

21 Hendrix, "Thessalonicans Honor Romans," 336.
22 Vakalopoulos, 14.
23 Karl P. Donfried, "The Imperial Cults and Political Conflict in 1 Thessalonians," in *Paul and Empire: Religion and Power in Roman Imperial Society*, ed. Richard A. Horsley (Harrisburg: Trinity Press International, 1997), 218.
24 Hendrix, "Thessalonicans Honor Romans," 310.
25 Ibid., 312.
26 Edson: 154–160.
27 Hendrix, "Thessalonica," 525.

in the pagan cults would provide a sense of belonging.[28] The traditional cults were also incorporated to civic cult for the welfare of the city, which demonstrates that religion was linked with the political sphere. An extreme case of the amalgamation of religion and politics was the imperial cult. The cults in Thessalonica were thoroughly interrelated with the larger society of Thessalonica. In this completely pagan setting, Paul sought to evangelize the Thessalonians and form them into a community of faith.[29]

3.2. The Thessalonian Community: A Newly Born Gentile Community

Though scholars still debate Paul's strategies for founding a community in Thessalonica,[30] Paul's ministry to found a believing community in the city, where the pagan cults were prominent, seems successful as he was

---

[28] Everett Ferguson, *Backgrounds of Early Christianity* (Grand Rapids: W. B. Eerdmans Pub., 1993), 136.

[29] The purpose of Paul's ministry was not only to evangelize individuals but also to establish believing communities. Eckhard Schnabel writes, "The communication process of Paul's missionary work did not end with the oral proclamation of the good news of Jesus Christ and the conversion of individuals: the apostle established churches, communities of men and women who had come to faith in Jesus the Messiah and Savior and who had been baptized in the name of Jesus Christ." Eckhard J. Schnabel, *Early Christian Mission* (Downers Grove: InterVarsity Press, 2004), 1370. Derek Tidball also claims, "Paul's primary interest was not in the conversion of individuals but in the formation of Christian communities." Derek Tidball, "Social Setting of Maission Churches," in *Dictionary of Paul and His Letters*, eds. Gerald F. Hawthorne, Ralph P. Martin, and Daniel G. Reid (Downers Grove: InterVarsity Press, 1993), 885.

[30] For example, Ronald Hock suggests that Paul, as an artisan, worked and preached among the artisan in his workplace. Ronald F. Hock, *The Social Context of Paul's Ministry: Tentmaking and Apostleship* (Philadelphia: Fortress Press, 1980). Wayne Meeks thinks that Paul created and used house-church network for the missionary work. Wayne A. Meeks, *The First Urban Christians: The Social World of the Apostle Paul* (New Haven: Yale University Press, 1983). Abraham Malherbe suggests that, for his missionary work, Paul used pastoral methods of itinerant philosophers in his day. Abraham J. Malherbe, *Paul and the Thessalonians: The Philosophic Tradition of Pastoral Care* (Philadelphia: Fortress Press, 1987).

able to establish the "church of the Thessalonians" (1:1). Paul's ministry in Thessalonica definitely has resulted in the formation of a community.[31]

The Thessalonian community was a newly born community.[32] The fact that the Thessalonian community was newly born could be attested by two things: – the short duration of Paul's ministry in Thessalonica, and the short interim period between Paul's departure from the city and his writing of the letter. With his mention of three Sabbaths (Acts 17:2), Luke gives us the impression that the whole ministry of Paul in Thessalonica lasted no more than twenty seven days – less than one month.[33] Because of Paul's success in preaching in the synagogue, the Jews were jealous and caused a riot in their attempt to seize Paul. The description in Acts gives the impression that these events happened rapidly and within a short period of time. Some scholars assume this to be the natural understanding of Luke's description of the duration of Paul's stay in Thessalonica.[34] However, there is nothing intrinsic in the account of Acts that demands all incidents to happen within three weeks. I. Howard Marshall, therefore, points out that the

---

31 Paul, unlike the contemporary wandering preachers, did not mainly deliver an individualistic message to give up vice but instead intended as the formation of a community of those who responded to his preaching. Stanley K. Stowers, "Social Status, Public Speaking and Private Teaching: The Circumstances of Paul's Preaching Activity," *Novum testamentum* 26, no. 1 (1984): 80.

32 This study discusses two characteristics of the Thessalonian community: (1) It was a newly born community. (2) It consisted mostly of Gentiles. With application of sociological perspectives to the study of the New Testament, scholars also have been interested in the social status of the Thessalonian converts. For example, Robert Jewett suggests that the Thessalonian congregation came from the poor non-elite people, living in tenements. Robert Jewett, "Tenement Churches and Communal Meals in the Early Church: The Implications of a Form-Critical Analysis of 2 Thessalonians 3:10," *Biblical Research* 38 (1993). Craig de Vos thinks that the converts in Thessalonica were "free-born artisans and manual workers." de Vos, 154.

33 Whether Acts is used as a primary source of information about the founding of Pauline churches continues to be controversial. About this issue, see F. F. Bruce, "Is the Paul of Acts the Real Paul?," *Bullentin John Rylands Library* 58, no. 2 (1976). For an overview of some of the positions about the Thessalonian church, in particular among scholars, see Jewett, *The Thessalonian Correspondence: Pauline Rhetoric and Millenarian Piety*, 114–118.

34 For example, Gerd Lüdemann takes Acts 17:2 to mean that Paul stayed for three weeks in Thessalonica. See Gerd Lüdemann, *Paul, Apostle to the Gentiles: Studies in Chronology* (Philadelphia: Fortress Press, 1984), 177. Also see James E. Frame, *A Critical and Exegetical Commentary on the Epistles of St. Paul to the Thessalonians* (New York: C. Scribner's Sons, 1912), 7.

three Sabbaths "may well refer just to the period of Paul's initial mission in the synagogue."[35] Abraham Malherbe also writes, "A period of evangelizing outside the synagogue should therefore be assumed, but Luke does not mention it."[36]

1 Thessalonians itself does not give any obvious indication about how long Paul stayed in Thessalonica. The only verse that reveals a subtle hint is 2:9, where Paul mentions that he worked night and day. While Paul does not state the nature of his work in 1 Thessalonians or elsewhere, Acts 18:3 suggests that Paul was a "tentmaker."[37] It could have taken several days to find a place to stay and settle down for work in a workshop.[38] It is also reasonable that Paul would have needed to work hard for at least a few weeks in order for his statement in 2:9 to be meaningful. According to Philippians 4:16, Paul was financially supported more than once by the believers in Philippi while working in Thessalonica. However, Paul describes himself as working long hours, even into night, to meet his own financial need. Paul's description could also imply that Paul stayed in Thessalonica as long as he had pressing financial need in spite of the financial aid. When all the things above are taken into consideration, it is difficult to conclude that Paul only stayed for three weeks in Thessalonica. The overall positive nature of Paul's comments on the faith of the Thessalonian community also would not support the assumption that the community was established by only three-week ministry of Paul. Gordon Fee and Douglas Stuart aptly write, "Our letter indicates a church of much greater stability, Christian instruction, and renown than two or three weeks would have produced."[39]

It, however, does not mean that Paul stayed a considerable length of time in Thessalonica. If that were the case, Luke would have indicated so, as he did in Acts 18:11 and 19:10. In Luke's account of Paul's ministry in Thessalonica, Paul's stay was not long enough to be worth mentioning. Paul in 1 Thessalonians 2:15–16 also indicates that there was most likely hostile reaction that resulted in Paul's untimely departure. The image of

---

35   I. Howard Marshall, *1 and 2 Thessalonians: Based on the Revised Standard Version* (Grand Rapids: W. B. Eerdmans Pub., 1983), 5.
36   Malherbe, 13.
37   According to Hock, the "tentmaker" could indicate that Paul was more generally a leather worker since tents were mainly made of leather. Hock, 20–21.
38   For a description of the life of a tentmaker in antiquity, see Ibid., 31–37.
39   Gordon D. Fee and Douglas K. Stuart, *How to Read the Bible Book by Book: A Guided Tour* (Grand Rapids: Zondervan, 2002), 365.

"being made orphans," which Paul uses in 1 Thessalonians 2:17 suggests that Paul was forced to leave before he wanted to.[40] Though Paul stayed longer than three weeks, neither Acts nor 1 Thessalonians suggests Paul's long stay in Thessalonica.[41]

1 Thessalonians also appears to have been written soon after Paul's departure from the city. While there is no agreement on the details, most scholars believe that Paul's expulsion from Thessalonica occurred in A.D. 49. After leaving the city, Paul traveled to Athens and sent Timothy back to Thessalonica. Paul traveled to Corinth, from where he wrote 1 Thessalonians around A.D. 50 after receiving Timothy's report on the Thessalonian community.[42] This timeline indicates that the letter was written only a few months after Paul's departure from Thessalonica.[43] No other Pauline letter was written so soon after the formation of the community as is the case with 1 Thessalonians. Considering the short duration of Paul's ministry and the short period between his departure and his writing of the letter, Paul wrote to the Thessalonian community when the community was still young.

The Thessalonian community was primarily composed of Gentiles who were former pagans. The clear reference to the identity of converts in Thessalonica can be founded in 1:9, where Paul identifies the recipients of the Thessalonian correspondence as converts who have "turned to God from idols to serve the living and true God." Some scholars propose

---

40   Ernest Best, *A Commentary on the First and Second Epistles to the Thessalonians* (New York: Harper & Row, 1972), 124.

41   Malherbe suggests that Paul's ministry in Thessalonica must have lasted as long as two to three months. Abraham J. Malherbe, *The Letters to the Thessalonians: A New Translation with Introduction and Commentary* (New York: Doubleday, 2000), 61.

42   See G. K. Beale, *1–2 Thessalonians* (Downers Grove: InterVarsity Press, 2003), 14; Best, 11; F. F. Bruce, *1 and 2 Thessalonians* (Waco: Word Books, 1982), xxxiv–xxv; Victor Paul Furnish, *1 Thessalonians, 2 Thessalonians* (Nashville: Abingdon Press, 2007), 30; Malherbe, *The Letters to the Thessalonians: A New Translation with Introduction and Commentary*, 71–74; Marshall, 20–22; Leon Morris, *The First and Second Epistles to the Thessalonians* (Grand Rapids: W. B. Eerdmans Pub., 1991), 13. A few scholars suggest an earlier date. For example, Karl Donfried considers the date of 1 Thessalonians about A.D. 43. Donfried, *Paul, Thessalonica, and Early Christianity*, 76. For an argument against Donfried, see Ben Witherington, *1 and 2 Thessalonians: A Socio-Rhetorical Commentary* (Grand Rapids: W. B. Eerdmans Pub., 2006), 10.

43   The period scholars calculate is generally in the range of two or three months to six months. For a more extensive discussion, see Malherbe, *The Letters to the Thessalonians: A New Translation with Introduction and Commentary*, 71–74.

that the statement of 1:9–10 includes a pre-Pauline formulation, which is different from typical terms of Paul. Ernest Best, for example, argues that this unit contains a pre-Pauline source originated from Hellenistic Jewish missionaries in order to be preached to Gentiles.[44] If so, chances are that the terms were not written by Paul and the reference to the recipients of the letter also does not accurately reflect the Thessalonians' own situation. However, it is not necessary to conclude that the terms were originated from pre-Pauline elements based on some similarities to the terms of Hellenistic Jewish missionaries. Paul's likeness to the language of Jewish missionaries is not surprising since Paul have been a Jewish missionary before he became an apostle of Christ.[45] Moreover, the presence of terms found only here also does not suffice to prove a pre-Pauline formulation. It is more likely that Paul himself composed this statement making use of current missionary terms derived from scriptural concepts and idioms[46] and reflecting the Thessalonians' situation in Paul's initial ministry. Though it might be admitted that there is a commonly acknowledged formula in this statement, Paul must have advertently selected the formulation to echo the situation of the Thessalonian community because Paul claimed this statement to be the report of the faith of the Thessalonians. Whether Paul composed this statement or used a concrete formulation, therefore, this statement yields essential clues to the content of Paul's own missionary preaching especially in Thessalonica, and in this statement Paul presupposed that the Thessalonian converts would recognize their own experience.

Paul's expression to identify the Thessalonian converts could not have been a description of Jews.[47] Jews used the term "idol" to refer to representations of gods, which is prohibited by the Decalogue.[48] Therefore,

---

[44] Best, 82. Best argues that Paul whenever he uses the term "serve," he does it in relation to Jesus not to God.

[45] Charles A. Wanamaker, *The Epistles to the Thessalonians: A Commentary on the Greek Text* (Grand Rapids: W. B. Eerdmans Pub., 1990), 85.

[46] Furnish, 48.

[47] See Raymond F. Collins, *Studies on the First Letter to the Thessalonians* (Leuven: University Press, 1984), 287; Gordon D. Fee, *The First and Second Letters to the Thessalonians* (Grand Rapids: W. B. Eerdmans Pub., 2009), 46; Jewett, *The Thessalonian Correspondence: Pauline Rhetoric and Millenarian Piety*, 118–119; Marshall, 82; Wanamaker, 85.

[48] Raymond F. Collins, *The Birth of the New Testament: The Origin and Development of the First Christian Generation* (New York: Crossroad, 1993), 53.

the term was used to identify characters and practices of non-Jews. In the same vein, Paul, as a Jew himself, would not have depicted Jews as idol worshippers. Ernst Best observes, "Obviously the Thessalonians were Gentiles before they became Christians for Jews would not have been described as turning from idolatry."[49] The term identifies the Thessalonian converts as former pagans ruled by idolatry widespread in Thessalonica.

I. Howard Marshall suggests that the verb ἐπεστρέψατε in 1:9 refer to either Jews or Gentile as "In the case of Jews conversion is from a false attitude to God to a true one, but in the case of Gentile it is from the worship of false gods to worship of the true God."[50] However, it is necessary to consider that their turning was from "idols." This expression indicates that, prior to their conversion, the Thessalonians must have taken part in the pagan cultic activities. Therefore, it is more appropriate to refer to non-Jews as being involved in the practices of idol worship. Gene Green properly concludes, "The implication of this verse is that the converts to the faith in Thessalonica were not Jewish but Gentiles, or at least that the vast majority of the church was Gentile."[51]

Another clue that reveals the identity of the community in Thessalonica can be found in 2:14. In the verse, Paul makes a comparison between the Thessalonian community and the Judean churches in terms of the hostility they encountered. According to Paul, the Thessalonian community was suffering from its own countrymen, just as the Jewish believers in Judaea had suffered from some of their fellow Jews. The English word "countrymen" does not necessarily imply people of same ethnos; it embraces all who share the same locality. It could lead one to conclude that it was not only Gentiles but also Jews who continued to oppress the Thessalonian community.[52] However, the Greek word συμφυλετῶν means "one who is a member of the same tribe or people group."[53] This verse therefore can be understood to mean that the Gentile community was suffering from the compatriots in Thessalonica. One might think that this contradicts with the

---

49 Best, 82.
50 Marshall, 57.
51 Gene L. Green, *The Letters to the Thessalonians* (Grand Rapids: W. B. Eerdmans Pub., 2002), 107–108.
52 See Marshall, 78–79; D. Michael Martin, *1, 2 Thessalonians* (Nashville: Broadman & Holman, 1995), 89–90.
53 Walter Bauer, *A Greek-English Lexicon of the New Testament and Other Early Christian Literature* (Chicago: University of Chicago Press, 2000), 960.

account of Luke. In Acts 15:5, Luke states that opposition originated from Jews, not Gentiles. F. F. Bruce's comment may better reflect the meaning of 2:14 when he notes, "According to Acts 17:5 the opposition to the missionaries in Thessalonica was fomented by members of the local Jewish community, but from the present reference it appears that the persecution of the converts was the work of their fellow-Thessalonians."[54] Gentiles became the perpetrators of the persecution that was originally initiated by Jews in the synagogue.

It is also necessary to consider that Paul in 1 Thessalonians does not give special attention to Jewish characters or practices and there is little use of the Old Testament. It is certain that Paul, who was familiar with the language of the LXX, often deliberately quoted or adapted it to his own purpose in his letters. When compared with other Pauline letters, the cases where Paul used words and phrases from the LXX in 1 Thessalonians are rare; in addition, the possible cases have been questioned about whether Paul deliberately used them. "Although, consciously or unconsciously," Alfred Plummer concludes that Paul "sometimes uses the language of the LXX, yet he nowhere quotes the Old Testament, which would have little interest for imperfectly instructed Macedonian converts."[55] This suggests that the letter was written to Gentile believers for whom the Old Testament was an unknown and foreign text.

Paul, also in the ethical admonitions, warns that the Thessalonians should move away from the "lustful passion" of those "Gentiles who do not know God" with contracting the Thessalonians to whom he writes are Gentiles who know God (4:5).[56] In particular, Paul addresses the sexual matters seriously. It was obviously connected with the widespread pagan cults in Thessalonica. As explored above, a number of religious cults in the city had a strong sexual character and incorporated sexual activity as part of their cultic practices. The cults actually promoted a lifestyle that would have been viewed as immoral from a Christian view. Paul's emphasis against sexual immorality indicates that the recipients of 1 Thessalonians were non-Jews who had recently converted from such practices.

---

54 Bruce, *1 and 2 Thessalonians*, 46.
55 Alfred Plummer, *A Commentary on St. Paul's Second Epistle to the Thessalonians* (London: Robert Scott, 1918), xiv.
56 Beverly R. Gaventa, *First and Second Thessalonians* (Louisville: Westminster John Knox Press, 1998), 3. See also Furnish, 29.

The account of Acts 17:4, describing the results of Paul's ministry in Thessalonica, however, seems to propose a presence of Jews in the Thessalonian community. "Some" of the Jews who attended the synagogue where Paul preached became believers. Nevertheless, Luke also explains that the Jewish converts were fewer in number compared to "a large number of" Gentile converts. Considering the account of Luke, there might have been some existence of Jewish converts among the community in Thessalonica,[57] but the number was so small that Paul did not need to give them any special attention in 1 Thessalonians.

Not only was the Thessalonian community established during the short duration of Paul's ministry, the community was a newly born one when it received Paul's letter soon after he departed from the city. Moreover, the majority of its members were Gentiles who used to participate in the regional cults. Though the Gentile converts had turned from the cults in their response to Paul's ministry and had formed themselves into a community of faith, the larger society of Thessalonica still remained a pagan setting in which the converts took part not long ago. The newly formed community was enclosed by the influence of the larger pagan society. William Barclay describes the situation the community was facing as follows:

> Paul's converts did not have centuries of Christian tradition behind them; they were so short a distance from the life which they had once lived. They did not live in a society permeated by Christian ideals and ideas, even when it has abandoned Christian belief. They were, as it has been put, a little island of Christianity surrounded by a sea of paganism.[58]

It must have been difficult for the fledgling community to endure the heavy influence of paganism.

---

57 Raymond Brown notes, "Many reject the Acts information that some converts were Jews. Yet it is difficult to conceive that at least some would not have been and so it is overly precise to argue from 1 Thess. that all the Christian had to be Gentiles." Raymond E. Brown, *An Introduction to the New Testament* (New York: Doubleday, 1997), 458.

58 William Barclay, "A Comparision of Paul's Missionary Preaching and Preaching to the Church," in *Apostolic History and the Gospel: Biblical and Historical Essays Presented to F.F. Bruce on His 60th Birthday*, eds. W. Ward Gasque and Ralph P. Martin (Grand Rapids: Eerdmans, 1970), 170.

3.3. The Suffering of the Community: Conflict with the Larger Pagan Society

Although some scholars suggest that the converts in Thessalonica were not suffering when 1 Thessalonians written,[59] in fact, their suffering provides a base for understanding Paul's concern in the letter. Much is made of Paul's use of the term "θλῖψις," which in one form or another occurs in 1 Thessalonians. The occurrences in 1:6 (θλίψει) and 3:3 (θλίψεσιν), along with the presence of the term ἐπάθετε in 2:14, are used to describe the suffering faced by the Thessalonian community.

Focusing on the context of 1:6, Abraham Malherbe emphasizes that the suffering must be understood in light of the Thessalonians' reception and acceptance of the gospel. According to Malherbe, the suffering was "the distress and anguish of heart experienced by persons who broke with their past as they received the gospel."[60] He writes, "Like other converts, these new Christians in Thessalonica continued to be distressed."[61] He gives examples of converts who suffered spiritual and mental distress. For Malherbe, the suffering indicates that the converts experienced internal distress. It is natural for the converts to experience much distress as they all had to leave behind their former ways of life.

It is, however, questionable that the suffering of the Thessalonians only referred to internal distress. In 1:6, Paul recommends his converts to become imitators of the missionaries and the Lord through their suffering. It is certain that Paul and Jesus Christ experienced much greater suffering than mental distress. Moreover, Paul in 1:7 claims that, as a consequence of the suffering, the community "became an example to all the believers in Macedonia and in Achaia." This statement "implies very strongly that

---

[59] For example, Thomas Manson argues that the persecutions described in 1 Thessalonians were part of the community's past experience, whereas those of 2 Thessalonians were a present reality when the letter was written. Based on this argument, he concludes that 2 Thessalonians was written earlier than 1 Thessalonians. See Thomas Walter Manson, *Studies in the Gospels and Epistles* (Philadelphia: Westminster Press, 1962), 259–278. Also see Wanamaker, 37–45. For an argument against the view of Manson and Wanamaker, see Green, 64–69. So rightly, Barclay, "Conflict in Thessalonica," 514 n. 5; Todd D. Still, *Conflict at Thessalonica: A Pauline Church and Its Neighbours* (Sheffield: Sheffield Academic Press, 1999), 268–269.

[60] Malherbe, *Paul and the Thessalonians: The Philosophic Tradition of Pastoral Care*, 48.

[61] Ibid.

in v. 6 Paul was speaking about more than mere 'distress and anguish of heart.'"[62] In 2:14 Paul maintains that the Thessalonians experienced "the same suffering" as the churches in Judea did. This comparison suggests that the Judean and the Thessalonian believers shared similar types of external afflictions.[63] Additionally, Paul in 3:3 uses θλίψεσιν for the external oppression the Thessalonian community endured. It, therefore, can be concluded that the suffering of the Thessalonians was more serious than only internal turmoil.[64]

A strong indication of the nature of the suffering in Thessalonica can be inferred from 2:14.[65] There Paul states that, as a result of their conversion, the Thessalonians were subject to suffering from their fellow Gentiles. Pheme Perkins remarks, "Conversion implied a break, a separation with one's fast and social environment, which frequently led to hostility."[66] This suffering is understood as external oppression from Gentile opposition.[67] The ubiquitous pagan cults in Thessalonica explain the extent and presence of suffering. Todd Still notes, "Presumably, the believers' decision to abandon their former gods (viewed by Paul as 'idols') in order 'to serve a living and true God' (1:9) sparked an ongoing controversy with their Gentile compatriots."[68]

The Thessalonian converts' rejection of the pagan cults and the exclusivity of their claim to worship God would have left the fellow citizens feeling offended and even betrayed. Family members would have considered a refusal of pagan gods they ancestrally worshipped as evidence of dereliction of family responsibilities.[69] The fellow citizens might have perceived the converts' denial of the cults as ungrateful attitude toward

---

62   Wanamaker, 81.
63   Still, 211.
64   Todd Still suspects the influence of the Western individualistic interpretation of Malherbe's proposal: "It may be, however, that Malherbe's proposal of psychological affliction for Paul's Thessalonian converts is more attuned to the Western individualistic interpretive tradition than to a Mediterranean cultural milieu." Ibid., 210.
65   Still states, "In fact, it seems best to view the affliction mentioned in 1:6 and 3:3–4 in light of the suffering spoken of in 2:14." Ibid., 212.
66   Pheme Perkins, "1 Thessalonians and Hellenistic Religious Practices," in *To Touch the Text: Biblical and Related Studies in Honor of Joseph A. Fitzmyer*, eds. Maurya P. Horgan and Paul J. Kobelski (New York: Crossroad, 1989), 326.
67   Barclay, "Conflict in Thessalonica," 514; de Vos, 155.
68   Still, 229.
69   Barclay, "Conflict in Thessalonica," 515.

the gods. The peace of the city, the success of agriculture, and freedom from natural disasters were generally thought to lie in the hands of gods. Therefore, withdrawing from the cults was regarded as a threat to the civic community, inviting the wrath of the gods. The ancient sources confirm that if anything went wrong, the believers could be blamed.[70]

Since the pagan cultic activities permeated every aspect of life in the city, strict avoidance of participation in the cults also meant that the converts would need to remove themselves from much of the public life of the city. Ramsey MacMullen observes, "There existed […] no form of social life […] that was entirely secular. Small wonder, then, that Jews and Christians, holding themselves aloof from anything the gods touched, suffered under the reputation of misanthropy."[71] Moreover, the believers' rejection of their traditional religious practices would have tagged them as "atheists." The charge of atheism was more dangerous since one who denies the reality of gods would be ostracized, even stoned in the streets.[72]

Given the incorporation between religion and politics, it is likely that the converts' abandonment of the cults would have been understood as being politically subversive.[73] As explored above, Thessalonica especially had a long history of devotion to the Roman emperor.[74] Participation in the imperial cults was a focal expression of gratitude toward those who were identified to be the benefactors of the city. In the imperial cult, Thessalonians would also meet their obligations as clients by wishing for the empire's peace and the emperor's security (εἰρήνη καὶ ἀσφάλεια; 5:3). As long as their patron was strong and his clients were loyal, peace and prosperity of the city would remain. The rejection of the imperial cults meant withdrawal from cultic display of gratitude and clients' duty to the most influential benefactor of the city, which must have exerted a harmful influence upon the welfare of the city. It should be not surprising, therefore, that the Thessalonian converts who withdrew from the emperor cult were suspected of being a subversive element in the society.

---

70 Ibid. Also see David A. deSilva, *Honor, Patronage, Kinship & Purity: Unlocking New Testament Culture* (Downers Grove: InterVarsity Press, 2000), 38–39.
71 Ramsey MacMullen, *Paganism in the Roman Empire* (New Haven: Yale University Press, 1981), 40.
72 Ibid., 62.
73 de Vos, 156.
74 See § 3.1.

The Thessalonians' turning away from idols, therefore, was more than what it literally means; it was not only replacing one set of loyalties with another, but also challenging the system and conviction sustaining the larger society. David DeSilva writes,

> Participation in the cults of Rome, the emperor, and the traditional pantheon showed one's *pietas* or *eusebeia*, one's reliability, in effect, to fulfill one's obligations to family, patron, city, province, and empire. Participation showed one's support of the social body, one's desire to do what was necessary to secure the welfare the city, and one's commitment to the stability and ongoing life of the city.[75]

Thus, it is not difficult to imagine how their refusal to participate in the social and cultic activities under such circumstances would have resulted in conflict with the larger society. The larger society would have tried to amend the deviants – the Thessalonian converts – and pressure would have been applied to make them return to the approved way of life within the context of the larger society. The Thessalonian community experienced marginalization and oppression in a hostile society.

Paul does not specify what kind of oppression the Thessalonian community experienced. Karl Donfried emphasizes very real physical persecution that the Thessalonian converts faced in the political setting related with imperial worship. For him, "this situation of affliction and suffering" was "produced in all likelihood by political opposition."[76] In this vein, Donfried suggests that Paul in 4:13 may imply the martyrdom of a few converts.[77] In 1 Thessalonians, however, Paul does not specifically link these deaths with martyrdom in the letter. If there were martyrs in the Thessalonian community, Paul would have celebrated the deceased as martyrs.[78] The image of falling asleep, which Paul used to describe the deaths, is also "a rather passive image for such a violent departure from this life."[79] It is also necessary to consider that there is no evidence that the believers anywhere during a half-century suffered organized physical

---

75 David A. DeSilva, *The Hope of Glory Honor Discourse and New Testament Interpretation* (Collegeville: Liturgical Press, 1999), 92. Italics original.
76 Donfried, "The Imperial Cults and Political Conflict in 1 Thessalonians," 220.
77 Ibid., 223. Also see John S. Pobee, *Persecution and Martyrdom in the Theology of Paul* (Sheffield: JSOT Press, 1985), 113.
78 Barclay, "Conflict in Thessalonica," 514.
79 David A. deSilva, "Worthy of His Kingdom: Honor Discourse and Social Engineering in 1 Thessalonians," *Journal for the Study of the New Testament* 19, no. 64 (1996): 62 n. 25.

persecution from the Roman Empire.[80] Nevertheless, it cannot be completely excluded that few converts in the Thessalonian community died as a result of persecution.[81] Thus, Raymond Collins notes, "Sporadic outbreaks of violence or oppression would have been sufficient to lead Paul to write about the persecution of his beloved Thessalonian Christian. The violence may even have led to the deaths of some Christians."[82]

If the oppression was not physical attack or abuse, it was at least some kind of social pressure. John Barclay is cautious when he speaks of the oppression of the Thessalonian community, "Although the deaths of some of the converts cannot be directly attributed to θλῖψις [...] it would certainly be easy for non-Christians to mock those whose faith in a 'savior' appeared so ineffective."[83] Carol Schlueter suggests that, instead of violent persecution, the Thessalonians would have suffered from "public insults, social ostracism and other kinds of non-violent opposition."[84] The converts in the Thessalonian community could have experienced social pressure of all kinds – verbal harassment, social exclusion, and possible political sanctions – from the larger group, such as their family, friends, and associates. Even if there were only social pressure without any physical violence in Thessalonica, the converts would still have experienced considerable suffering, considering the strong group-oriented culture of those days.[85] In the first-century Mediterranean culture, it was essential for a person to gain the approval and to avoid the disapproval of his or her larger group. No matter what kind of social pressure the converts faced, therefore, it must have been severe and intolerable suffering.

---

80   Donfried also admits the point. He writes, "We certainly do not wish to imply any systematic persecution." Donfried, "The Imperial Cults and Political Conflict in 1 Thessalonians," 222 n. 24.
81   Collins, *The Birth of the New Testament: The Origin and Development of the First Christian Generation*, 112; de Vos, 160; Still, 216–217.
82   Collins, *The Birth of the New Testament: The Origin and Development of the First Christian Generation*, 112.
83   John M. G. Barclay, "Thessalonica and Corinth: Social Contrasts in Pauline Christianity," *Journal for the Study of the New Testament* 15, no. 47 (1992): 53.
84   Carol J. Schlueter, *Filling up the Measure: Polemical Hyperbole in 1 Thessalonians 2:14–16* (Sheffield: JSOT Press, 1994), 52.
85   Bruce Malina, among others, contends that Mediterranean culture both past and present is characterized by "dyadism" not "individualism." Bruce J. Malina, *The New Testament World: Insights from Cultural Anthropology* (Louisville: Westminster John Knox Press, 1993), 67.

At this point, it is necessary to consider the opinion about Paul's internal opponents in the Thessalonian community. Some scholars have argued that Paul was attacked by opponents within the community, such as Judaizers,[86] Gnostics[87] and Millenarianists.[88] In 1 Thessalonians Paul apologetically responded to their accusations, particularly in 2:1–12. However, there seems to be no solid evidence for the formation of parties of opposition within the community. First, Paul did not clearly mention the presence of his opponents in the Thessalonian community. There is no clear consensus about the presence of Paul's opponents and to their specific identity.[89] Second, Paul does not begin the letter by mentioning his apostolic status. In the portion of epistolary prescript in other letters, he identified himself as an apostle of Christ (Rom. 1:1; 1 Cor. 1:1; 2 Cor. 1:1; Gal. 1:1). In the case of the communities of Romans, Corinthians, and Galatians, Paul's authority and status were thought to be questionable to some degree. However, Paul does not seem to feel the need to defend his status with the Thessalonian converts. The absence of Paul's mention of his apostolic status in 1 Thessalonians suggests that there is very little change of the presence of Paul's opponents in the community. Third, Paul's relationship with the Thessalonian community in the letter appears to have been a positive one rather than one in which he had to defend himself against accusations. In 1 Thessalonians, it is not difficult to find Paul's positive statements about the community. He states that the community was well founded and following his example and serving as an example to other communities (1:3; 1:6–7; 2:14; 4:9). The Thessalonians' attitude toward Paul is also apparently positive, as exemplified by Timothy's report (3:6). Compared to Galatians and 2 Corinthians where Paul's apostolic authority is overtly challenged (Gal. 1:6; 2 Cor. 11:4; 12:20–21), the tone in 1 Thessalonians is friendly and suggests a good relationship between Paul and the Thessalonians.[90] Finally, the antithetical style used in 2:1–12 does not necessary assume that the function of the passage was purely

---

86 Frame, 9–10; William Neil, *The Epistle of Paul to the Thessalonians* (New York: Harper & Brothers, 1950), xv–xvi.
87 Walter Schmithals, *Paul and the Gnostics* (Nashville: Abingdon Press, 1972), 128–318.
88 Jewett, *The Thessalonian Correspondence: Pauline Rhetoric and Millenarian Piety*, 159–178.
89 George Lyons, "Modeling the Holiness Ethos: A Study Based on First Thessalonians," *Wesleyan Theological Journal* 30, no. 1 (1995): 208.
90 Judith L. Hill, "Establishing the Church in Thessalonica" (Ph.D. diss., Duke University, 1990), 87–88.

apologetic. Abraham Malherbe has demonstrated the similarities between the passage and Dio Chrysostom's *Discourses 32*. Malherbe argues that the Cynic philosopher used an antithetical style to teach about himself, claiming that the style was appropriate to the parenetic use, not apologetic.[91] Even assuming the apologetic function of the passage, it still does not mean that Paul in this passage was defending against actual accusations and that opponents existed. One should not exclude a possibility that Paul was responding to potential charges that he feared might be made. In light of the above considerations, it is unlikely that Paul was facing attack within the Thessalonian community.

The hardship of the Thessalonian community mainly came from external opponents, and not internal opponents of Paul. It seems certain that there is no officially organized persecution of converts to whom Paul sent his first letter in Thessalonica. However, it does not mean that the Thessalonian community would not be exposed to unofficial acts of hostility. The converts' refusal of social and cultic practices in which they had formerly participated was regarded as a negligence or failure to perform the suitable responsibilities toward family, city, province, and empire. Therefore, their disapproval of the cults could have been viewed a challenge to the *status quo* of the larger society. In such a case, the conflict between the converts and the larger society was inevitable, which resulted in oppression of the Thessalonian community.

3.4. Paul's Writing of the Letter: Community Formation in the Face of Challenge

Being aware of the suffering and the conflict between the Thessalonian community and the larger pagan society, Paul was deeply concerned that the Thessalonian converts facing external pressure might abandon their

---

91 Abraham J. Malherbe, "'Gentle as a Nurse': The Cynic Background to I Thess II," *Novum testamentum* 12, no. 2 (1970): 203–217. Due to Malherbe's influential work, many contemporary scholars consider the function of the passage to be parenetic. See deSilva: 69; Gaventa, 25–26; Lyons: 207; Steve Walton, "What Has Aristotle to Do with Paul? Rhetorical Criticism and 1 Thessalonians," *Tyndale Bulletin* 46, no. 2 (1995): 244; Wanamaker, 91.

new faith and turn back to their previous way of life, so that the fledgling community might collapse. Paul was obviously not sure that the new converts could well deal with the challenges facing them. Therefore, Paul sent Timothy back to visit the Thessalonian community to learn the state of their faith. Paul's sending of Timothy was his response to the pastoral needs of the community.[92] Though unable to visit himself, Paul did not want the suffering community to be left without any pastoral support. The emissary finally returned with the positive news that the Thessalonians still had good memories of Paul and longed to see him. Nevertheless, Paul wrote as if the wave of suffering still crashed against them: "We sent Timothy […] to strengthen and encourage you in your faith, so that no one would be unsettled by these trials. You know quite well that we were destined for them. In fact, when we were with you, we kept telling you that we would be persecuted. And it turned out that way, as you well know" (3:2–4). Paul did not want the Thessalonian community to be "disturbed" or "shaken" by the suffering they endured perpetrated by the surrounding society. Therefore, his primary concern in 1 Thessalonians was the well-being of the newly born community in the face of formidable challenge of the surrounding society.

It is true that the occasion of 1 Thessalonians could be only partially discovered in the circumstances that led to the sending of Timothy to Thessalonica. Paul certainly kept up with the situation of the Thessalonian community only after Timothy's return and subsequent report, though he had been informed about the situation of the community (1:8–9). News of the community delivered by Timothy would have been a newly updated description of the situation there, and Paul may have reflected upon it when he later wrote the letter. In spite of Timothy's positive report of the Thessalonians' faith, Paul in 3:10 says that he may meet the believers in Thessalonica face to face and "supply what is lacking in your faith." Just as Paul intended his letter to serve as a substitute for his actual presence,[93] Paul wanted to address the deficiencies of their faith through the letter. Along with the circumstances that required Timothy's visit, this statement also reflects the occasion of the letter. In addition to the suffering and external conflict they were facing, the Thessalonian community's immaturity in faith must have provided essential motivation for Paul to write the letter.

---

92 Malherbe, *Paul and the Thessalonians: The Philosophic Tradition of Pastoral Care*, 61.
93 See § 1.3.

This statement, however, does not seem to mean that some aspect of the community's faith has been lost or neglected. As mentioned above, Paul's comments on the faith of the community are positive. There is no strong criticism of the community either. Paul rather encouraged the Thessalonians along a path they were already pursuing (4:1, 10). Moreover, widespread paraenetic section (4:1–5:22) of the letter does not change the impression that the community was still doing well. Paraenesis is exhortation about which the audience was already familiar.[94] Using the paraenesis, Paul reminds the converts of what he has already taught them and exhorts them to behave according to his earlier teaching.[95] Paul's paraenesis is not a response to their neglect of faith, nor is it concerned with rebuking or newly advising the community. Paul's paraenetic style of the letter demonstrates that the community was firmly committed to the faith that Paul had taught them.

Paul's statement in 3:10 therefore describes for the need to maturate their faith by having them deeply understand their faith and behaving in ways that fit their faith.[96] Gene Green states that the verb καταρτίσαι was commonly used in educational contexts to refer to training and completing education, and thus Paul's usage of the verb intends for not repairing that which needs restoration but "to make complete."[97] Just as a teacher has the responsibility of completing his teaching so that his pupil can live as an adult, Paul as a pastor[98] had the responsibility of completing what he had begun during his initial ministry in Thessalonica so that the community could mature and prosper. Given his unwanted departure from Thessalonica, it is

---

[94] Stanley K. Stowers, *Letter Writing in Greco-Roman Antiquity* (Philadelphia: Westminster Press, 1986), 91–92. Stowers distinguishes between "protrepsis," which urges the audience to adopt a new way of life, and "paraenesis," which encourages and exhorts the audience to continue a certain way of life. Based on this distinction, Paul's missionary preaching is protrepsis but the letter is paraenesis.

[95] Malherbe, *The Letters to the Thessalonians: A New Translation with Introduction and Commentary*, 81–86.

[96] See Fee, *The First and Second Letters to the Thessalonians*, 127; Furnish, 80–81; Wanamaker, 139.

[97] Green, 174.

[98] While Paul does not describe himself as a pastor in his letters, Paul's portrait described in his letters is of a very skilled pastor. Derek Tidball writes, "His theology arises out of the questions thrown up by pastoral and everyday situations in the churches. And his writings constantly reveal his pastoral heart, his pastoral ambitions, his pastoral techniques, his pastoral advice, and his pastoral frustrations." Derek Tidball, *Ministry by the Book: New Testament Patterns for Pastoral Leadership* (Downers Grove: IVP Academic, 2008), 108.

natural that Paul did not consider his task of the community formation complete. He believed that formation and development of the young community was not yet sufficiently completed.[99] Therefore, Bengt Holmberg suggests 3:10 means that Paul "builds upon the foundation he laid on his first visit" through the letter.[100] By the means of the letter, Paul sought to continue the process of community formation that he had begun during his foundation visit to Thessalonica.

The external pressure that resulted in converts' suffering demonstrates that the continuing process of the community formation, which Paul anticipated through his letter, is not only essential but also urgent. As observed above, the Thessalonians were alienated from their larger society which provided social networks and sense of belonging, leaving them with a sense of social dislocation. The Thessalonians experienced isolation and estrangement from communities of which they were previously a part. Mikael Tellbe properly remarks,

> The need for identity would have been especially pressing for gentile Christians, who were socially dislocated after they had converted from pagan gods to the Christian faith and dissociated themselves from their ancestral religious practices. [...] Who were they then, and where did they belong?[101]

As a result, they would have found themselves in need of a strong alternative community to fill the vacuum. It is not surprising that in 1 Thessalonians Paul reminds the converts that they belong to a new family as Craig de Vos mentions, "Paul is trying to 'nature a new, fictive kinship' among the Christian there."[102] In the ancient Mediterranean world, family or household was the basic social group to which individuals belonged. The family provided its members with a sense of security and identity that other larger groups were unable to give.[103] According to Abraham Malherbe, the unusual beginning

---

99 Earl Richard, *First and Second Thessalonians* (Collegeville: Liturgical Press, 1995), 171. Also similarly, Marshall, 98.
100 Bengt Holmberg, *Paul and Power: The Structure of Authority in the Primitive Church as Reflected in the Pauline Epistles* (Philadelphia: Fortress Press, 1980), 80–81.
101 Mikael Tellbe, *Paul between Synagogue and State: Christians, Jews, and Civic Authorities in 1 Thessalonians, Romans, and Philippians* (Stockholm: Almqvist & Wiksell, 2001), 69.
102 de Vos, 173.
103 Philip H. Towner, "Household and Household Codes," in *Dictionary of Paul and His Letters*, eds. Gerald F. Hawthorne, Ralph P. Martin, and Daniel G. Reid (Downers Grove: InterVarsity Press, 1993), 417.

of 1 Thessalonians in which Paul uses the phrase ἐν θεῷ πατρὶ to emphasize God's initiative demonstrates how this community was "brought into being by God the Father."[104] This expression, together with the description of the Thessalonians as "sons" (υἱοὶφωτόςἐστε καὶ υἱοὶἡμέρας; 5:5), shows "the God of creation as calling Gentiles into a new relationship with himself in which he would be their father and they his beloved children."[105] To counter their sense of dislocation and alienation, Paul intended to form the community into "God's new family in Thessalonica."[106]

Though Paul, by using kinship language, usually depicts his believing communities as family groups, this strategy is particularly conspicuous in 1 Thessalonians. For example, Paul uses the term ἀδελφοὶ[107] to address his congregation fourteen times in the letter,[108] more than he does in other Pauline letters. Only in 1 Corinthians does Paul use the term more often, namely twenty-two times. Given that 1 Corinthians is much longer than 1 Thessalonians, the term is used by Paul with greater frequency in 1 Thessalonians. Moreover, he portrays himself as a "nursing mother" (τροφὸς; 2:7) to the Thessalonians whom he describes as his "children" (τέκνα; 2:7, 11). Paul even appears to reverse the parent-child relationship by referring to himself as an "infant" (νήπιοι; 2:7) and an "orphan" (ἀπορφανισθέντες; 2:17).[109] Family language is pervasive in this letter.

---

104 Malherbe understands the function of the preposition instrumentally. Malherbe, *The Letters to the Thessalonians: A New Translation with Introduction and Commentary*, 99. Also see Best, 62. However, others understand the preposition in a locative manner. For example, Bruce, *1 and 2 Thessalonians*, 7; Fee, *The First and Second Letters to the Thessalonians*, 15–16.
105 Abraham J. Malherbe, "God's New Family in Thessalonica," in *The Social World of the First Christians: Essays in Honor of Wayne A. Meeks*, eds. L. Michael White and O. Larry Yarbrough (Minneapolis: Fortress Press, 1995), 118.
106 Ibid., 116.
107 This term is inclusive of the whole community, men and women. In terms of current English usage, the NRSV's paraphrase "brothers and sisters" seems to be more accurate. For a discussion on the membership of women in the Thessalonian community, see Lone Fatum, "Brotherhood in Christ: A Gender Hermeneutical Reading of 1 Thessalonians," in *Constructing Early Christian Families: Family as Social Reality and Metaphor*, ed. Halvor Moxnes (New York: Routledge, 1997), 192–194.
108 In 1:4; 2:1, 9, 14, 17; 3:7; 4:1, 10, 13; 5:1, 4, 12, 14, 25.
109 Though Paul's parental roles for his Thessalonian "children" are obvious, Paul's role of "infant" is disputed. For the possibility of his role as "infant," see Jeffrey A. D. Weima, "'But We Became Infants among You': The Case of NHITIOI in 1 Thess 2.7," *New Testament Studies* 46, no. 4 (2000): 547–564.

Paul's effort to shape the community into a fictitious family is not limited to his usage of the kinship language. He also provides the community with a way to think about themselves as a family by demanding a set of attitudes and behaviors that follows naturally from the view. It is especially demonstrated in Paul's instructions to do φιλαδελφία known as "brotherly love,"[110] prominent in 1 Thessalonians (4:9–12). By the instructions based on the sense of kinship, Paul sought to maintain "the appropriateness of kinship patterns,"[111] which will be treated in more detail in the following chapter. The conclusion of the letter also provides a clear illustration of Paul's appeal to family members: "Greet all the brethren with a holy kiss" (5:26). In Greco-Roman society, a kiss was exchanged by family members or friends as an expression of their reciprocal affection. Therefore, Michael Penn concludes that "the kiss's performance is a way to define Christianity as family."[112] The kiss serves to symbolize the solidarity of the Thessalonian community as a family and so Paul issues the order to the Thessalonians to "perform family."[113]

For the Thessalonians who have experienced conflict with family and friends, it is evident that Paul's use of family language and his appeal to family norms in the letter serve to create a new family in place of the old. Wayne Meeks writes, "The natural kinship structure into which the person has been born and which previously defined his place and connections with the society are here supplanted by a new set of relationships."[114] It is urgent for Paul that he continues to form the Thessalonians into an alternative community that is able to substitute for the social groups to which they previously belonged.

Although external conflict caused the crisis in the community, if responded to appropriately, the conflict could provide an opportunity for the community to resume its formation, which was suspended by Paul's unwanted departure. It has been argued among sociologists that conflict can

---

110 The word includes the entire community, not just male members.
111 Philip F. Esler, "'Keeping It in the Family': Culture, Kinship and Identity in 1 Thessalonians and Galatians," in *Families and Family Relations as Represented in Early Judaisms and Early Christianities: Texts and Fictions*, eds. Jan Willem van Henten and Athalya Brenner (Leiden: Deo, 2000), 171.
112 Michael P. Penn, "Performing Family: Ritual Kissing and the Construction of Early Christian Kinship," *Journal of Early Christian Studies* 10, no. 2 (2002): 158.
113 Ibid.: 175.
114 Meeks, 88.

aid a group in establishing its identity and maintaining internal cohesion.[115] Especially, conflict with an external group increases the formation of in-group/out-group stereotypes and creates the "them versus us" attitude that can solidify members' identification with their group. Derek Tidball notes,

> The existence of conflict can strengthen a group by defining its boundaries, disciplining its members, bonding them together in more intense relationships against a common enemy, demanding total adherence and heightening the sense members have of belonging.[116]

1 Thessalonians shows that Paul makes an effort to reinforce the distinctive identity of the community and to maintain the community in the midst of conflict. Paul does not avoid describing that the community is in a state of conflict with the surrounding environment. He instead confirms the "agonistic" nature of the larger society, and develops the collective identity of the believers in "conflict-oriented differentiation" from the surrounding society.[117] When Paul refers to the beginning of the community, for example, he sharply separates his converts from their non-believing follow citizens by referring to the former as those who "turned to God from idols" (1:9). This division between in-group and out-group, "between us and them," is repeated throughout the letter. The converts are regarded as "beloved and chosen by God" (1:4), "called by God" (2:12), and "sons of the light and the day" (5:5); the remainder are those "who do not know God" (4:5), "outsiders," (ἔξω; 4:11–12), and "who belong to the night or darkness" (4:5). Based on contemporary models of religious sects, scholars have suggested that this language represents social context.[118] Most pertinent, however, for the present concerns, is that this language plays a role in the construction of identity. It is evident that Paul's dualism of language sets a limit between those who are members of the community and those who are outside the community, thereby strengthening the collective identity among members of the community.

---

115 Among others, see Lewis A. Coser, *The Functions of Social Conflict* (Glencoe: Free Press, 1956), 87–95; Georg Simmel, *Conflict and the Web of Group-Affiliations* (New York: Free Press, 1955), 92–93.
116 Tidball, "Social Setting of Maission Churches," 886.
117 Esler, 163.
118 For example, see Robin Scroggs, "The Earliest Christian Communities as Sectarian Movement: Studies for Morton Smith at Sixty," in *Christianity, Judaism and Other Greco-Roman Cults*, ed. Jacob Neusner (Leiden: Brill, 1975).

In addition to the distinction between insiders and outsiders, Paul utilizes suffering itself originated from conflict as an essential element in the identity construction of the Thessalonian community. Although Paul intends to comfort and encourage his suffering converts, he makes no attempt to eliminate their suffering. Instead, Paul argues that the suffering confirms their faith because it is to be expected. He also affirms that there is a commonality in their suffering (1:6; 2:14–16). The experience of suffering is not unique to the Thessalonians; they are walking in the footsteps of Paul, the Lord, and the other believing communities in Judea. Their suffering therefore serves to reinforce in the community not only the collective identity, which is the identical pattern founded in their Lord, their founder, and even other believers transcending regional boundaries, but also the distinctive identity over the surrounding society. It is certain that Paul presents suffering as an identity maker for the community.[119] Elizabeth Castelli writes the relationship between persecution and identity of the Thessalonian community:

> The suffering, for which they are praised by Paul [...] ties their experience to that of everyone else in the mimetic system: Paul, the Lord, and the other persecuted communities. In becoming imitators of others' sufferings, their experience is structurally linked to that of all these other persecuted ones. Their sufferings become a way of establishing identity within the group and in the face of "outsiders," a way for Paul both to praise them and to claim them.[120]

The suffering at the hands of their previous associates would have served to strengthen the collective identity, which was totally separated from outsiders of the community. The distinctive identity of the community must have contributed to Paul's community formation in Thessalonica.

Though suffering caused by conflict with the larger society might have threatened the survival of the Thessalonian community, Paul in 1 Thessalonians turned it to his advantage and an opportunity for community formation, which he could not complete in his initial ministry. For the Thessalonians who experienced isolation from their family and associates, Paul continually attempted to form an alternative community

---

119 Wayne A. Meeks, "Social Functions of Apocalyptic Language in Pauline Christianity," in *Apocalypticism in the Mediterranean World and the near East*, ed. David Hellholm (Tübingen: J. C. B. Mohr, 1983), 692.
120 Elizabeth A. Castelli, *Imitating Paul: A Discourse of Power* (Louisville: Westminster John Knox Press, 1991), 94.

to offset the sense of loss and imbue the sense of belonging and security. God's new family that Paul intended to shape substituted its old kinship relationships and provided a new foundation of belonging. Through his usage of language, Paul also sought to fortify the collective identity of the Thessalonian community by creating in-group/out-group differentiation. Paul even identified their experience of suffering as an essential identity maker, manifesting that they well followed an example of Paul and consequently of Christ, and this is one of things that separated the Thessalonians from outsiders. In the midst of the conflict with the surrounding society, therefore, Paul continually executes the process of formation of the Thessalonian community.

3.5. Conclusion

Thessalonica was a pagan city where cults were pervasive in all spheres of life. Many religious and civic cults in Thessalonica were interrelated with each other and incorporated various roles, from providing entertainment, and a sense of belonging, and a hope for afterlife, to wishing for and maintaining the welfare of the city. In spite of the pagan context of the city, Paul's initial ministry resulted in founding a believing community of Gentiles who had previously participated in the cults in Thessalonica. The Gentiles abandoned their former gods and join the believing community in order to serve God. From the viewpoint of the compatriots of the Gentiles, the believers' disapproval of the religious and civic practices of the cults could have been regarded as a failure to perform the latter's duty toward the larger community of which they were a part, and even a challenge to the well-being of the larger society. This led the newly formed community into conflict with other citizens and the new converts were suffered the oppression of the larger society. This crisis could have caused the young community to collapse. Therefore, Paul wrote 1 Thessalonians to sustain and reinforce the Thessalonian community, for its well-being. As the continuation of his initial ministry and the pastoral response of the challenge threatening the survival of the community, 1 Thessalonians aims at the formation of community.

Chapter Four
Paul's Preaching for Community Formation: The Creation and Maintenance of Symbolic Boundaries

This chapter explores Paul's preaching for community formation in 1 Thessalonians by drawing on the sociological concept of "symbolic boundaries." This chapter will first investigate the concept of symbolic boundaries to provide the background for the rest of the chapter. The chapter will then focus on three symbolic resources Paul uses in his preaching to create boundaries for the Thessalonians: the kerygmatic narrative, the local narratives, and the ethical norms. The resources will be examined based on how Paul incorporates them into his preaching and how they function as the symbolic boundary to create a collective identity of the community and to distinguish the Thessalonians from the outside world. The chapter thereby will demonstrate that Paul's adept usage of the kerygmatic narrative, the local narratives, and the ethical norms essentially contributes to the construction of the Thessalonian community.

4.1. Symbolic Boundaries and Community Formation

In recent years, the concept of symbolic boundaries has received much attention in the social sciences. According to Michèle Lamont and Virág Molnár, symbolic boundaries are "conceptual distinctions made by social actors to categorize objects, people, practices, and even time and space."[1] They are intangible lines that include some people and things while excluding others. They become tools for individuals and groups to make symbolic distinctions between themselves and others.

---

1 Michèle Lamont and Virág Molnár, "The Study of Boundaries in the Social Sciences," *Annual Review of Sociology* 28, no. (2002): 168.

The concept of boundaries is not novel in sociology. It is rooted in the well-established tradition of sociology and elaborated by Émile Durkheim, Karl Marx, and Max Weber, illustrating the dynamics among boundaries marked by religion, class, and ethnic groups. For Durkheim, it was the overriding distinction between the sacred and the profane that guided his research.[2] Marx argued that a social class objectively shares a common relationship with the means of production, and subjectively has some consciousness of the similarity, presenting the dynamics among several class boundaries.[3] Weber argued that innate competition among mankind over scarce resources inevitably discriminates toward groups on the basis of their characteristics such as language, education, religion, and ethnicity.[4]

Contemporary researchers have further developed the classic concept of boundaries by making a distinction between symbolic and social boundaries. When symbolic boundaries are widely recognized and received in a society, they become social boundaries as "objective forms of social differences."[5] With this distinction, the study of boundaries focuses on how they are contoured by cultural repertories, resources, and narratives that individuals can appropriate.[6] By widely recognizing and accepting the function of symbolic boundaries, – both inclusion and exclusion, scholars have applied the concept of symbolic boundaries to various fields of social studies. Symbolic boundaries drawn along the lines of race, gender, or social class are researched in terms of social exclusion and social inequality of marginalized groups.[7] In contrary, religious boundaries are often considered as a basis for inclusion, shaping meaningful subcultures within a society.[8]

---

2 Émile Durkheim, *The Elementary Forms of the Religious Life* (New York: Free Press, 1965).
3 Karl Marx, *The Eighteenth Brumaire of Louis Napoleon* (New York: International Publishers, 1963).
4 Max Weber, *Economy and Society Vol. 1* (Berkeley: University of California, 1978).
5 Lamont and Molnár: 169.
6 For example, see Margaret R. Somers, "Reclaiming the Epistemological 'Other': Narrative and the Social Constitution of Identity," in *Social Theory and the Politics of Identity*, ed. Craig J. Calhoun (Cambridge: Blackwell, 1994); Ann Swidler, *Talk of Love: How Culture Matters* (Chicago: University of Chicago Press, 2001).
7 See Michèle Lamont and Marcel Fournier, *Cultivating Differences: Symbolic Boundaries and the Making of Inequality* (Chicago: University of Chicago Press, 1992).
8 See R. Stephen Warner, "Work in Progress toward a New Paradigm for the Sociological Study of Religion in the United States," *American Journal of Sociology* 98, no. 5 (1993).

As the concept of symbolic boundaries has gained analytical prominence across various disciplines, the emergent literature on identity construction and group formation has received its due diligence. In particular, social psychologists have become interested in the concept of social identity of groups to which individuals belong. According to Henri Tajfel, social identity is "that *part* of an individual's self-concept which derives from his knowledge of his membership of a social group (or groups) together with the value and emotional significance attached to that membership."[9] Based on the presupposition that one's identity is profoundly influenced by the groups to which he or she belongs, scholars seek to provide a comprehensive explanation about how identity is related to "group membership, group process, and intergroup relations."[10]

In contrast to the characterizations of personal identity, the concept of social identity naturally assumes the presence of some commonality among its members within the group. Individuals in a same group share a collective identity. In the same group, individuals evaluate themselves in the same way and share a common definition of who they are and what their characteristics are. This similarity intrinsically implies difference. That members of one group are similar in a particular way implies that the members of the group differ from other groups. Therefore, the members in a same group recognize their common identity more clearly by comparing and contrasting with people outside their group. Communal identity of a group emerges from the comparison between in-group and out-group.

---

9   Henri Tajfel, "Social Categorization, Social Identity and Social Comparison," in *Differentiation between Social Groups: Studies in the Social Psychology of Intergroup Relations*, ed. Henri Tajfel (London: Academic Press, 1978), 63. Italics original. The work of Tajfel and his colleagues developed social identity theory, which some scholars have found helpful for understanding the development of identity of Christ-followers. Philip Esler has made the most detailed application of Tajfel's theory in New Testament studies thus far. See Philip F. Esler, "Group Boundaries and Intergroup Conflict in Galatians: A New Reading of Galatians 5:13–6:10," in *Ethnicity and the Bible*, ed. Mark G. Brett (Leiden: E. J. Brill, 1996); Philip F. Esler, *Galatians* (London: Routledge, 1998); Philip F. Esler, "Jesus and the Reduction of Intergroup Conflict: The Parable of the Good Samaritan Jesus and the Reduction of Intergroup in the Light of Social Identity Theory," *Biblical Interpretation* 8, no. 4 (2000).

10   Michael A. Hogg, "Social Identity Theory," in *Contemporary Social Psychological Theories*, ed. Peter J. Burke (Stanford: Stanford Social Sciences, 2006), 111.

Michael Hogg thus claims, "Group membership is a matter of collective self-construal – 'we' and 'us' versus 'them'"[11] W. A. Elliot also suggests,

> Group consciousness [...] imports a sense of *us* [...] with a corresponding sense of distinctiveness from others regarded as *them*. [...] People only display attitudes of us due to an acquired sense of *we-ness* determined largely by a sense of *they-ness* in relation to others. So-called ingroup and outgroup behavior therefore merely reflect the two sides of group consciousness.[12]

To strengthen the collective identity of a group, it is indispensable to provide the members with a clear description of the similarities within the group and the differences with other groups. The clearer that description of similarities and differences is provided for the members, the stronger the communal identity of the group is created. Thus, members of the group tend to exaggerate differences between groups, and at the same time minimize differences and highlight similarities within their group.[13] While members of a group sharply distinguish themselves from others, they are described in ways that accentuate their similarities and diminish the differences, the features that bind them together and produce the collective identity of the group. Common identity of a group is produced from "the interplay of similarity and difference."[14]

Boundaries are very critical to the sense of similarity and difference within a group. Delineating the boundaries of collective "we" requires the identification of "them." By clearly drawing a line between us and them, boundaries provide the members with a heightened sense of who are similar to us and who are not. Therefore, boundaries function as a medium for the distinction between in-group and out-group, as criteria for which members are included and excluded. Richard Jenkins writes, "To define the criteria for membership of any set of object is, at the same time, also

---

11   Ibid., 115.
12   W. A. Elliott, *Us and Them: A Study of Group Consciousness* (Aberdeen: Aberdeen University Press, 1986), 6, 8. Italics original.
13   Michael A. Hogg and Deborah J. Terry, *Social Identity Processes in Organizational Contexts* (Philadelphia: Psychology Press, 2001), 5. Scholars name this process "accentuation and assimilation." See Rupert Brown, "Tajfel's Contribution to the Reduction of Intergroup Conflict," in *Social Groups and Identities: Developing the Legacy of Henri Tajfel*, ed. William Robinson (Oxford: Butterworth-Heinemann, 1996), 170.
14   Richard Jenkins, *Social Identity* (London: Routledge, 2008), 37–38.

to create a boundary, everything beyond which does not belong."[15] The essential role of symbolic boundaries is to "separate people into groups and generate feelings of similarity and group membership."[16] As Penny Edgell, Joseph Gerteis, and Douglas Hartmann has shown:

> Symbolic boundaries are effective […] in promoting a sense of solidarity and identity by virtue of imagining an 'other' who does not share the core characteristics imagined to be held by those who are legitimate participants in the moral order; the imagined community must have outsiders as well as insiders.[17]

Symbolic boundaries demarcate, distinguish, and exclude "others"; and, in so doing, they function to construct a semblance of identity among those who fall within the established boundaries of a given formation. The creation of symbolic boundaries for distinction between insiders and outsiders has a central constitutive role in the production of shared identity within a group.

In addition to serving as criteria for which members of a group include insiders and exclude outsiders, the drawing of boundaries acts as a means of establishing and maintaining a hierarchical group status between groups. Thomas Gieryn describes this process of inter-group hierarchy creation via the phenomenon in which scientific explanations, rather than metaphysical and religious explanations, became well received. For him, boundary building is "an ideological style found in scientists' attempts to create a public image for science by contrasting it favorably to non-scientific intellectual or technical activities."[18] According to Gieryn, this process of differentiation of science from non-science allowed a hierarchical status to appear. No longer were non-scientific explanations of religion or meta-physics equivalent to the explanations provided by the practice of the scientific method. Scientific explanations of phenomena became superior to non-scientific ones. Gieryn states that this formation of hierarchical status was the result of successful boundary building accomplished by the scientific community.

---

15   Ibid., 102.
16   Lamont and Molnár, "The Study of Boundaries in the Social Sciences," 168.
17   Penny Edgell, Joseph Gerteis, and Douglas Hartmann, "Atheists as 'Other': Moral Boundaries and Cultural Membership in American Society," *American Sociological Review* 71, no. 2 (2006): 231.
18   Thomas F. Gieryn, "Boundary-Work and the Demarcation of Science from Non-Science: Strains and Interests in Professional Ideologies of Scientists," *American Sociological Review* 48, no. 6 (1983): 781.

Boundaries usually create hierarchies among groups. By drawing boundaries, members of a group position themselves above those with whom they draw distinctions. Boundaries provide the members with a sense of the positive distinctiveness of their group, which successfully convinces them that the in-group is better than the out-group. This in-group conviction then contributes to the creation and maintenance of collective identity and the solidification of the group cohesion.

It is necessary to note the significance of the symbolic boundaries for peripheral or marginal groups in the process of boundary building. Symbolic boundaries are frequently considered to be one of the only dimensions the members of marginal groups can place for themselves against those groups with more tangible social capital. For example, marginal groups often draw boundaries on moral grounds.[19] Ethics in these groups normally function as a "badge of distinction,"[20] which the groups use to construct a distinctive identity and emphasize differences with others. Moral discourse provides them with a sense of righteousness, which helps them strengthen their sense of worthiness in the face of perceived marginality. In this way, symbolic boundaries provide them with an alternative definition of hierarchies of value, creating positive identity of the group against the common idea of the surroundings.

Symbolic boundaries create not only a common consciousness of its own distinctiveness from other groups but also of the superiority over other groups. The creation of boundary can be viewed as a central process to construct common identity and group solidarity; thus, it is a key to group formation. In communities in the early period of Christian origins, it cannot be denied that boundary building was a powerful group process. Symbolic boundaries had a central function in shaping and developing a distinctive "Christian" identity.[21] Though the movement of Christ-followers

---

19 See Michèle Lamont, *Money, Morals, and Manners: The Culture of the French and American Upper-Middle Class* (Chicago: University of Chicago Press, 1992); Lois Weis, Amira Proweller, and Craig Centrie, "Re-Examining 'a Moment in History': Loss of Privilege inside White Working-Class Masculinity in the 1990s," in *Off White: Readings on Race, Power, and Society*, eds. Michelle Fine et al. (New York: Routledge, 1997); Amy C. Wilkins, *Wannabes, Goths, and Christians: The Boundaries of Sex, Style, and Status* (Chicago: University of Chicago Press, 2008).
20 Wilkins, 11.
21 The term "Christian" does not emerge as a self-definition until around the end of the first-century. Thus, the word is not used by Paul. To avoid an anachronistic use of the term, the members of the Thessalonian community in this study as seen in previous

was initially known as a part of Judaism, before long it expanded to include non-Jews. In the new age inaugurated by the death and resurrection of Jesus Christ, Paul and other leaders of the movement claimed that there is "no distinction" (Rom. 3:22; 10:12, NASB) between Jews and gentiles. Therefore, the previous concept of boundaries to protect the identity of the Jews was no longer appreciated, and new boundaries needed to be updated to reflect the new identity, which included both the Jews and Gentiles "in Christ."[22] When social boundaries such as ethnicity, class, and gender were removed (Gal. 3:27–28), the role of symbolic boundaries became certainly more important for the boundary building for the construction of the Christian identity.

Given the situation and profile of the Thessalonian community as explored in chapter 3, the making of symbolic boundaries plays a central role in Paul's formation of the Thessalonian community, compared to other Christ-following communities that he served. A clear distinction between who belonged to the Thessalonian community and who did not was essential because most of the members were recently converted gentiles unaccustomed to the criteria for the membership in the Christ-following community. In the conflict with the surrounding society, moreover, the formation of communal identity of the Thessalonian community was mainly accomplished by drawing the symbolic group differentiation against the larger society. Paul's drawing of symbolic boundaries created a strong sense of in-group similarity and out-group contrast, constructing communal identity of the Thessalonian community. Furthermore, the suffering community in Thessalonica needed to maintain and solidify its positive distinction against the negative appraisals of the larger society. The symbolic boundaries of the Thessalonian community created a perception of in-group superiority over the larger pagan society. Paul drew symbolic boundaries to distinguish the converted gentiles from their surrounding

---

chapters are identified as "believers," "converts," or "Christ-followers." For the term as a label, see David G. Horrell, "'Becoming Christian': Solidfifying Christian Identity and Content," in *Handbook of Early Christianity: Social Science Approaches*, eds. Anthony J. Blasi, Jean Duhaime, and Paul-André Turcotte (Walnut Creek: AltaMira Press, 2002), 327–328.

22 The expression of "in-Christ" functions as the boundary that distinguishes insider from outsider, articulating the essential common identity of the Christian communities. For further description, see David. G. Horrell, "Models and Methods in Social-Scientific Interpretation: A Response to Philip Esler," *Journal for the Study of the New Testament* 22, no. 78 (2000).

pagan society and to justify their superiority over the larger society, and constructed an alternative collective identity for community formation. Charles Wanamaker writes,

> Perhaps the most important contribution of Paul to the formation of the Christian community in Thessalonica was that he gave converts a new sense of identity as Christians. This was accomplished at *a symbolic level* by what Meeks terms "the language of separation," that is symbolic annihilation of the previous worldview, and "the language of belonging."[23]

Though Wanamaker at this point mentions the language as only the resource for Paul to draw the distinction between in-group and out-group, Paul's use of symbolic markers to create the boundaries of the community cannot be restricted to the language.[24] Paul, especially in 1 Thessalonians, skillfully exploits the kerygmatic narrative, the local narratives, and ethical norms to make the symbolic distinction and so to contribute to the formation of the Thessalonian community.

4.2. Preaching of the Kerygmatic Narrative to Create Boundaries

4.2.1. The Kerygmatic Narrative Incorporated

Though 1 Thessalonians is not regarded as a narrative genre like other Pauline letters, it cannot be denied that Paul weaves the elements of narratives into his preaching in the letter. According to Michael Gorman, the narratives that Paul intertwines in his preaching can be categorized into three kinds: "stories of the crucified, risen, and coming Lord Jesus; the

---

23 Charles A. Wanamaker, *The Epistles to the Thessalonians: A Commentary on the Greek Text* (Grand Rapids: W. B. Eerdmans Pub., 1990), 16. Italics added.
24 Wayne Meeks outlines five indicators of group boundaries that Paul uses in Pauline letters: (1) language of separation; (2) rules and rituals of purity; (3) membership sanctions; (4) autonomous institutions; and (5) interaction with macro-society. Wayne A. Meeks, "Since Then You Would Need to Go out of the World: Group Boundaries in Pauline Christianity," in *Critical History and Biblical Faith: New Testament Perspectives*, ed. Thomas J. Ryan (Villanova: Horizons, 1979), 4–29.

cruciform apostolic team headed by Paul; and the persecuted Thessalonians."[25] His categorization is not wrong, but it is not enough to reveal all main characters of the stories that Paul exploits in 1 Thessalonians. Paul in the epistolary prescript of the letter appears to introduce major characters of all narratives: "Paul, Silas and Timothy, To the church of the Thessalonians in God the Father and the Lord Jesus Christ: Grace and peace to you" (1:1). His intention to present the characters of the narratives makes the prescript of the letter more extended than what was typical for his times.[26] John Simpson notes,

> Paul wanted to name at the outset the principal players in the kerygmatic drama as it intersected with the lives of his addresses. So he extended the typical epistolary prescript to name his missionary associates, God, and Jesus as well as himself and his addressees.[27]

The narratives that Paul presents in 1 Thessalonians are stories of God and Jesus, the missionaries,[28] and the Thessalonian converts.

Paul labels the kerygmatic narrative to the Thessalonians, "the gospel of God" (2:2, 8, 9). The genitival phrase τοῦ θεοῦ could be either subjective or objective. If taken as a subjective genitive, God is the initiator or origin of the gospel. If viewed as objective, it emphasizes the nuance of which God is the content of the gospel Paul proclaimed. In this case, nevertheless, the sense of subjective genitive to refer to God as the gospel's origin is preferred, because the content of the kerygma Paul preached in Thessalonica also includes the action of Christ, as 1:9–10 demonstrates.[29]

---

25 Michael J. Gorman, *Apostle of the Crucified Lord: A Theological Introduction to Paul and His Letters* (Grand Rapids: W. B. Eerdmans Pub., 2004), 151.
26 For example, the prescript of Michigan Papyrus 513, a typical letter, is: "Chairemon to Sepapion, greeting." See E. Randolph Richards, *Paul and First-Century Letter Writing: Secretaries, Composition, and Collection* (Downers Grove: InterVarsity Press, 2004), 128.
27 John W. Simpson, "Shaped by the Stories: Narrative in 1 Thessalonians," *Asbury Theological Journal* 53, no. 2 (1998): 17.
28 In the light of Paul's headship of the missionary work in Thessalonica and writing of 1 Thessalonians, the story of the missionaries is in this study alternately used with the story of Paul.
29 Judith L. Hill, "Establishing the Church in Thessalonica" (Ph.D. diss., Duke University, 1990), 125. Many scholars view the phrase subjective genitive. See Ernest Best, *A Commentary on the First and Second Epistles to the Thessalonians* (New York: Harper & Row, 1972), 91; F. F. Bruce, *1 and 2 Thessalonians* (Waco: Word Books, 1982), 25; Gordon D. Fee, *The First and Second Letters to the Thessalonians* (Grand Rapids:

Paul later calls the gospel, "the gospel of Christ" (3:2), which in this case can be an objective genitive, meaning "the gospel that is all about Christ, and what he has done."[30] Whichever the grammatical sense of the genitives is, it is nevertheless necessary to emphasize that both titles of the gospel as used by Paul are very appropriate because God and Christ are "the two main characters" of the kerygmatic narrative.[31]

While the other stories that Paul uses in his preaching are about the past and thus are told retrospectively, the kerygmatic narrative includes events in the past as well as the future. When Paul tells the past and future parts of the kerygmatic narrative in 1 Thessalonians, he does not tell the full range of the content or the outline of the narrative. Instead, he alludes to the kerygmatic narrative by mainly using compact references and brief formulations.[32]

Paul's allusions to the past portion of the kerygmatic narrative are primarily concerning Jesus, in particular, his death and resurrection. First, Paul alludes that Jesus is the one whom God "raised from the dead" (1:10). Paul arranges this allusion to Jesus' death and resurrection right after describing the way in which the Thessalonian converts had received the missionaries and responded to their initial missionary work. This arrangement implies that the story about Jesus' death and resurrection is at the heart of the kerygmatic narrative preached during Paul's initial ministry. Nevertheless, Paul does not forget that the primary agent in the death and resurrection of Jesus is ultimately God, as he describes that God raised his Son from the dead.

W. B. Eerdmans Pub., 2009), 58; Abraham J. Malherbe, *The Letters to the Thessalonians: A New Translation with Introduction and Commentary* (New York: Doubleday, 2000), 137; Wanamaker, 93.

30 Fee, 58.

31 Margaret M. Mitchell, "1 and 2 Thessalonians," in *The Cambridge Companion to St. Paul*, ed. James D. G. Dunn (Cambridge: Cambridge University Press, 2003), 52.

32 Richard Hays cogently argues that we find in clipped references such as Galatians 3:13–14 and 4:3–6 "the presence and shape of a gospel story to which Paul alludes and appeals." Richard Hays, *The Faith of Jesus Christ: The Narrative Substructure of Galatians 3:1–4:11* (Grand Rapids: W. B. Eerdmans Pub., 2002), 116. Hay's another work is the well-known overview on the detection of allusion and echo of Pauline letters. See Richard Hays, *Echoes of Scripture in the Letters of Paul* (New Haven: Yale University Press, 1989). In this work, Hays distinguishes between allusion and echo: "*allusion* is used of obvious intertextual references, *echo* of subtler ones." Hays, *Echoes of Scripture in the Letters of Paul*, 29. Italics original. In this study, however, allusion is only used for any case.

Paul inserts another allusion to the past part of the kerygmatic narrative into 4:14, "We believe that Jesus died and rose again." This insinuating element also spells out the essence of the kerygmatic narrative – the death and resurrection of Jesus. Prior to the kerygmatic allusion, Paul put the phrase "We believe." This first-person plural includes not only Paul and his colleagues but also the Thessalonian believers. With this phrase, Paul emphasizes that the story of Jesus' death and resurrection is the common foundation of faith between Paul and the Thessalonians. According to Ivan Havener, the phrase πιστεύομεν ὅτι is a typical introduction of a creed that had been handed over to the church. This allusion to the kerygmatic narrative is regarded as part of a creedal formula.[33] If he is correct, the kerygmatic narrative can be a common denominator of the faith of Paul and the Thessalonian community as well as of all other Christ-following communities.

Paul in 5:10 also interfuses an allusion to the story of Christ's death. Unlike in the two previously mentioned allusions, he particularly stresses the purpose of the death; he states, "He died for us." This is the only place in 1 Thessalonians where the purpose of the death of Jesus is described. Here, however, Paul does not elaborate any more on the significance of Christ's death. The absence of a fuller elaboration of Christ's death may imply that Paul already preached about the story of Christ's death in his founding ministry and the believers also understand what Paul preached. F. F. Bruce therefore writes, "It is mentioned as something known to the readers; it had doubtless been emphasized as the gospel was first preached to them."[34]

While the past part of the kerygmatic narrative focuses on the death and resurrection of Jesus, the future portion of it is primarily about the coming of Jesus. Paul in 1:10, where he alludes to the story of Christ's death and resurrection also insinuates an allusion to the future story, the coming of God's Son from the heavens. By tightly connecting the stories of the past and the future, Paul demonstrates that the past story is closely linked with the future story in God's redemptive narrative. The coming of Jesus would have been impossible without his death and resurrection.

---

33   Ivan Havener, "The Pre-Pauline Christological Credal Formulae of 1 Thessalonians," *Society of Biblical Literature Seminar Papers* 20 (1981): 111. On this statement as part of a creedal statement of the early church, also see Best, 187–188; Richard N. Longenecker, "The Nature of Paul's Early Eschatology," *New Testament Studies* 31, no. 1 (1985): 90; Wanamaker, 168–169.
34   Bruce, 114.

Paul repeatedly makes allusions to the future part of the kerygmatic narrative by using the word παρουσία, which refers to the coming of Jesus (2:19, 3:13, 4:15, 5:23). The word literally means "coming" or "presence."[35] In those days, the word had a more technical sense of divine or political visitation. The term in Hellenistic religions could describe the coming of a hidden divinity whose presence was celebrated in the cult. In the realm of politics, the term was used to describe a visit to a region by a dignitary. In the context of the prevailing amalgamation between religion and politics in Thessalonica,[36] the Thessalonians might have understood the word in terms of the visits by the imperial rulers regarded as the manifestations of deities, which required ceremonies to honor them. In addition to the use of the technical term, in all four occasions when Paul speaks of the coming of Jesus, he designates Jesus as "Lord." This title also shows that Jesus was regarded to be an authority figure in the future story of kerygma.[37] Jesus would come as the divine ruler to bring judgment for godless sinners.

For the future event of judgment of the kerygmatic narrative, Paul takes over the concept of "the day of the Lord" (5:2)[38] from the prophets of the Old Testament. The day of the Lord was used for the eschatological event when the Lord comes to judge God's opponents and Israel's enemies, and to pour out his wrath on them (Isa. 13:6–13; Obad. 15; Joel 1:13–15). For the people of God, however, the day of the Lord will be a day of deliverance (Joel 2:31–32; Zech. 14:1–21; Mal. 4:5). This same double emphasis on judgment and deliverance at the day of the Lord is seen throughout the prophetic literature of the Old Testament. This idea of the day of the Lord can be also found in Jewish pseudepigraphal documents such as 4 Ezra, 1 Enoch, and 2 Baruch, and in selected Qumran documents.[39] It is worth noting that Paul expands and revises the inherited

---

[35] Paul expresses his gratitude for the παρουσία of Stephanas, Fortunatus, Achaicus (1 Cor. 16:17), and Titus (2 Cor. 7:6). He also speaks of his own presence (2 Cor. 10:10; Phil. 1:26; 2:12).
[36] See § 3.2.
[37] Raymond F. Collins, *The Birth of the New Testament: The Origin and Development of the First Christian Generation* (New York: Crossroad, 1993), 68.
[38] Paul in 5:4 uses "the day."
[39] L. Joseph Kreitzer, "Eschatology," in *Dictionary of Paul and His Letters*, eds. Gerald F. Hawthorne, Ralph P. Martin, and Daniel G. Reid (Downers Grove: InterVarsity Press, 1993), 259.

concept by transferring the day of the Lord to Christ, whom he identifies as the Lord.[40] Margret Mitchell thus notes,

> The gospel story Paul offered the Thessalonian pagans is an updated version of Jewish apocalyptic narratives, known to us from a range of extant writings, both biblical [...] and apocryphal [...], which forecast dramatic divine intervention in human history to exact final judgment on the god and evil.[41]

As to when the eschatological event will occur, Paul acknowledges that there is nothing more he can add to it, since the Thessalonians already knew "very well" about the progressing manner of the future story: "The day of the Lord will come like a thief in the night"[42] (5:2). The eschatological event will unexpectedly come and threaten those who are unprepared at the time of judgment. However, the converts will "receive salvation through our Lord Jesus Christ" (5:9) and "be with the Lord forever" (4:17) because Jesus is the one "who rescues us from the coming wrath (1:10)." Therefore, Paul's basic plot of the future narrative is that Jesus Christ, as Lord in the day of the Lord, would come to judge the opponents of God and deliver the people of God.

On the fundamental story of the future, Paul adds a detailed description presumably to respond to a concern about the dead in Christ raised by the Thessalonian converts (4:13–18).[43] It is the portion in which Paul most elaborately tells the future story in 1 Thessalonians. Paul firstly speaks of

---

40   See Paul refers to "the day of Christ (Phil. 1:10, 2:16)," "the day of Jesus Christ (Phil. 1:6)," "the day of our Lord Jesus Christ (1 Cor. 1:8)," and "the day of our Lord Jesus (2 Cor. 1:14)." According to N. T. Wright, Paul "subverts" the Jewish story and thus reconstructs his grand narrative. He normally evokes the rethought grand narrative by "his use of the very world *Christ*." N. T. Wright, *The New Testament and the People of God* (Minneapolis: Fortress Press, 1992), 405–407. Italics original.
41   Mitchell, 52.
42   Many scholars think this image of the coming of Jesus indicates that Paul is well acquainted with the teaching of Jesus (Matt. 24:44; Luke 22:40). Among them, see David Wenham, *Paul and Jesus: The True Story* (Grand Rapids: W. B. Eerdmans Pub., 2002), 96–107. He concludes, "What is important is the strong evidence of Paul's knowledge of Jesus' teaching about the Lord's return, and the strong evidence that Jesus' teaching had been passed on to the Thessalonians."
43   Scholars have attempted to determine why the Thessalonian converts were not informed regarding the destiny of the dead converts, but no agreement has been reached. For a description of the various scholarly proposals, see I. Howard Marshall, *1 and 2 Thessalonians: Based on the Revised Standard Version* (Grand Rapids: W. B. Eerdmans Pub., 1983), 120–122.

the destiny of the converted dead: "God will bring with Jesus those who have fallen asleep in him" (4:14).[44] While Paul does not explicitly refer to the resurrection of those who have died prior to the coming of Jesus, he grounds this statement in the crux of the kerygmatic narrative, "Jesus died and rose again," which demonstrates that even as God raised Jesus, so also God will raise the Thessalonian dead and bring them with Jesus when he comes.[45] Paul confirms that the resurrection of Jesus is put forward as the guarantee of the resurrection of believers. Therefore, those who have died will not be in an inferior position relative to the living converts (4:15). The dead in Christ will not be disadvantaged at the coming of Jesus nor be deprived of their place at the climax of God's grand narrative. And, Paul further elaborates the content of the future story by using poetic style and vivid imagery (4:16–17). However, he does not attempt to describe some finely comprehensive calendar or to formulate some scenario of eschatological events.[46] Instead, Paul's presentation of the "dramatic, poetically structured, image-filled vision" of the end story seems intended to appeal to the listeners' emotions so that they can indeed "encourage each other with these words" (4:18), rather than being primarily informative.[47]

4.2.2. The Kerygmatic Narrative Functioned as Symbolic Boundaries

The kerygmatic narrative that Paul intertwines with his preaching in 1 Thessalonians plays a significant role in reminding the converts about who belongs to the in-group and who does not, thereby creating a collective identity of the community and delineating distinction between them and outside world.

The role as the symbolic boundary is not incidental but intrinsic to the kerygmatic narrative. It is clear that, in the founding ministry, Paul's

---

44 About Paul's depiction of death for the believers as sleep, see Best, 185.
45 On the important role of God in Paul's eschatology in 1 Thessalonians, see Jerome H. Neyrey, "Eschatology in 1 Thessalonians: The Theological Factor in 1:9–10; 2:4–5; 3:11–13; 4:6 and 4:13–18," *Society of Biblical Literature Seminar Papers* 19 (1980): 219–231.
46 Todd D. Still, "Eschatology in the Thessalonian Letters," *Review and Expositor* 96, no. 2 (1999): 197.
47 Gary S. Selby, "'Blameless at His Coming': The Discursive Construction of Eschatological Reality in 1 Thessalonians," *Rhetorica* 17, no. 4 (1999): 402.

kerygmatic preaching was the means by which he converted the Thessalonians. Though conversion is a theological matter, it also engages a social dimension – people are called out of their previous social world and invited into a new community sharing a foundation and boundaries, a conversion that Peter Berger and Thomas Luckmann refer to as a process of "re-socialization."[48] Also, the Thessalonians not only turned away from idols but transformed themselves into a believing community that responded to and received the kerygmatic narrative by Paul. In the process of re-socialization, therefore, full reception of the kerygmatic narrative was the prerequisite for entering the community, and their knowledge of the kerygmatic narrative was the essential feature for all members of the community. Thus, Georgia Keightley writes, "Christian identity is immediately attributable to the gospel; as a result of Paul's preaching, the Thessalonians now find themselves to be members of a new society."[49] Their common group identity was fundamentally shaped by the kerygmatic narrative. At the same time, the people in Thessalonica responded differently to the kerygmatic narrative by Paul and ended up dividing into two groups. Some became converts and entered the community, while others continued to identify themselves primarily in terms of their allegiance to the ancient gods. The reception to the kerygmatic narrative served as an invisible demarcation between the in-group and outside world. In Paul's initial ministry, therefore, the kerygmatic narrative intrinsically functioned as the symbolic boundary by providing the converts with the common group identity and separating them from the larger society.

The boundary created by the kerygmatic narrative, however, appeared to be in jeopardy and led to the collapse of the community as the larger society maintained pressure on the community.[50] In this critical situation, Paul retells the kerygmatic narrative, which the converts already know. Paul's main intention for telling it is not to teach something the listeners do not know but to provide a rhetorical effect for them. Undoubtedly, Paul's repetition of the kerygmatic narrative, which called the community into existence, reminds the converts of the shared foundation of the membership. Communal identity is created and sustained by retelling of the

---

48 Peter L. Berger and Thomas Luckmann, *The Social Construction of Reality: A Treatise in the Sociology of Knowledge* (New York: Anchor Books, 1967), 157–158.
49 Georgia M. Keightley, "The Church's Memory of Jesus: A Social Science Analysis of 1 Thessalonians," *Biblical Theology Bulletin* 17, no. 4 (1987): 155.
50 See § 3.3.

founding narrative. James Thompson writes, "For Paul's original converts, the recitation of the facts of the gospel served as a needed reminder of the conviction that brought a diverse group together as a community."[51] Paul treats them as a unit with the founding narrative and strengthens their communal identity shaped by the kerygmatic narrative.

Paul's retelling of the kerygmatic narrative also allows the believers to re-experience a sense of distinctiveness as members of the community formed by the narrative and to re-confirm their in-group membership. It is clear that Paul intends to buttress the separation between the in-group and the out-group by retelling the kerygmatic narrative. The distinction is reinforced by the dualistic perspective embedded in the kerygmatic narrative itself.[52] The sharp distinction between the converts who worship the living and true God and others who continue to worship idols has dualistic consequences: the former group, destined to be saved by Jesus at his coming, and the latter group, destined for divine wrath.[53] The repetition of the kerygmatic narrative emphasizes and legitimates the dualistic distinction between the Christ-following and pagan communities in Thessalonica.

As far as Paul's technique for telling the kerygmatic narrative goes, he does not tell it in detail. As discussed in the above section, Paul's telling of the kerygmatic narrative is fundamentally based on the allusions to the narrative rather than the depiction of it. This allusive way of telling indicates that Paul already shared the kerygmatic narrative in common with his listeners and the knowledge of it is shared among the listeners. It

---

51 James Thompson, *Preaching Like Paul: Homiletical Wisdom for Today* (Louisville: Westminster John Knox Press, 2001), 145.
52 Scholars in general think the dualism of 1 Thessalonians is a characteristic of apocalyptic discourse. See Wayne A. Meeks, "Social Functions of Apocalyptic Language in Pauline Christianity," in *Apocalypticism in the Mediterranean World and the near East*, ed. David Hellholm (Tübingen: J. C. B. Mohr, 1983); Charles A. Wanamaker, "Apocalyptic Discourse, Paraenesis and Identity Maintenance in 1 Thessalonians," *Neotestamentica* 36, no. 1 (2002); Duane Waston, "Paul's Appropriation of Apocalyptic Discourse: The Rhetorical Strategy of 1 Thessalonians," in *Vision and Persuasion: Rhetorical Dimensions of Apocalyptic Discourse*, eds. Greg Carey and L. Gregory Bloomquist (St. Louis: Chalice Press, 1999).
53 Wanamaker, "Apocalyptic Discourse, Paraenesis and Identity Maintenance in 1 Thessalonians," 135. Wayne Meeks states that three main categories of dualities are presented in 1 Thessalonians: (1) a cosmic duality – heaven/earth, (2) the temporal duality – this age/the age to come, and (3) social duality – those who know/do not know God, insiders/outsiders, and the children of light/the children of darkness. See Meeks, "Social Functions of Apocalyptic Language in Pauline Christianity," 689.

presupposes not only a sense of fellowship between Paul and the listeners but also some degree of solidarity and social consensus within the community. Through the use of allusions, Paul appeals to and stimulates the shared knowledge among the converts, thereby maintaining the collective identity of the community.

Paul's allusive telling of the kerygmatic narrative also creates a distinction between the in-group and the out-group, based on whether or not they understand the allusions. James Dunn aptly states, "It is one's knowledge of the tradition which enables one to recognize the allusions and which thus attests one's membership of the community. Those who do not recognize the allusions thereby demonstrate that they are still outside the community."[54] Paul's way of telling the kerygmatic narrative separates those who recognize the allusions from those who fail to do it.

In addition to internal cohesion and external separation, Paul's telling of the kerygmatic narrative also serves as criteria to assure the members' conviction that belonging to the community is superior to not belonging. The kerygmatic narrative confirms the higher status of the members. The main characters of the kerygmatic narrative that the members share are the living and true God and his raised Son, who are qualitatively different from the dead and false idols that the rest of their compatriots worship. N. T. Wright summarizes the shared knowledge shaped by the kerygmatic narrative among Thessalonians:

> The creator God was the true God, now made known in Jesus the Messiah, his son, who would come as judge of all things; in this light, pagan deities, their shrines, temples, status and hierarchies, were a bunch of shames, unreal gods who could still enslave people but had no power to save them.[55]

It is evident that their knowledge in relativizing other gods strengthens the confidence that their community is better than any other group in the larger society. The kerygmatic narrative's function justifying their superiority over the rest of Thessalonians is perhaps at its most obvious in the future story about the contrasted fates of the believers and non-believers. Philip Esler writes, "The focus in 1 Thessalonians on future events provides an important means of differentiating the positively valued ingroup

---

54 James D. G. Dunn, *The Theology of Paul the Apostle* (Grand Rapids: W. B. Eerdmans Pub., 1998), 652.
55 N. T. Wright, *Paul in Fresh Perspective* (Minneapolis: Fortress Press, 2009), 103.

from negatively valued outsiders."[56] The kerygmatic narrative predicts that the other pagan Thessalonians who think they are at "peace and safety" (εἰρήνη καὶ ἀσφάλεια; 5:3)[57] will experience inescapable destruction, whereas the believers who suffer will inherit a salvation. The affirmative denouement of the kerygmatic narrative that Paul reminds his audience of provides the converts with a positive distinctiveness of their community, which naturally convinces them that their community is superior to the rest of the Thessalonians who are destined to the negative ending.

4.3. Preaching of Local Narratives to Create Boundaries

4.3.1. Local Narratives Incorporated

In addition to the kerygmatic narrative, Paul also weaves the local narratives into his preaching in 1 Thessalonians, which embrace stories of Paul with his fellow missionaries and of the Thessalonian believers. While the kerygmatic narrative is divided into the past and the future, Paul's story can temporally be divided into the events while Paul was in Thessalonica and events after his departure from the city. Regarding the events of the missionary work, Paul allusively tells his own story: "You know how we lived among you for your sake" (1:5). This allusion reflects on the missionaries' character and conduct, which the Thessalonians witnessed. The believers could testify that the lives of the missionaries matched the gospel they preached. Paul and his missionary fellows presented the gospel not only in their words but also in their lives. Paul proves this story to be true

---

[56] Philip F. Esler, "'Keeping It in the Family': Culture, Kinship and Identity in 1 Thessalonians and Galatians," in *Families and Family Relations as Represented in Early Judaisms and Early Christianities: Texts and Fictions*, eds. Jan Willem van Henten and Athalya Brenner (Leiden: Deo, 2000), 165.

[57] The formulation, which is not typical of Paul, seems to be related to the political context of the Roman Empire. *pax et securitas* was a popular slogan of the Roman propaganda. On Paul's language of challenge to the imperial cults, see Karl P. Donfried, "The Theology of 1 Thessalonians," in *The Theology of the Shorter Pauline Letters*, eds. Karl P. Donfried and I. Howard Marshall (Cambridge: Cambridge University Press, 1993), 15–18; Todd D. Still, *Conflict at Thessalonica: A Pauline Church and Its Neighbours* (Sheffield: Sheffield Academic Press, 1999), 260–266.

by appealing to the Thessalonians' memory of what they "know" about the initial visit of the missionary team.

The story of how Paul and his colleagues did their missionary work in Thessalonica is more elaborately told in 2:1–2 and 2:5–12. Paul in 2:1–2 states that the result of his founding ministry was "not a failure."[58] This positive result of his ministry is not just evaluated by himself; there must have also been wide agreement among the Thessalonian converts. By using the expression "You know" (οἴδατε; 2:1), Paul prompts the Thessalonians to verify what he says from their own experience. This effective result is not produced without any difficulty but accomplished despite the hostility experienced in Philippi. Here, Paul seems to allude to the incident described in Acts 16:12–40. Though Paul does not provide a detailed story in Philippi, the phrase "as you know" (καθὼς οἴδατε; 2:2) indicates that the Thessalonians clearly knew the missionaries' experience in the city. Despite the harsh experience, with God's help, Paul and his coworkers risked preaching the gospel encountering strong opposition in Thessalonica, with positive results.

In 2:5–12, Paul tells his story with more focus on the missionaries' character and conduct during the initial visit. Because they eschewed the use of flattery, Paul and his fellow missionaries were not seeking human approval, did not seek to promote their own financial interest, and did not look for fame (2:5–6). Instead, they were gentle,[59] caring, and loving among the Thessalonians (2:7–8). Also, they earned their own living while in Thessalonica (2:9) and conducted themselves honorably (2:10) with father-like devotion (2:11–12). It is true that Paul provides a more detailed description of his story in 1 Thessalonians. However, it is also true that Paul does not depict thoroughly what he and his coworkers did in Thessalonica.

---

58 The word κενὴ alternatively could be rendered "empty," which means that the content of Paul's preaching was not empty of truth. However, the meaning of "not a failure" or "without results" is more typical of Paul's use of this word elsewhere (1 Thess. 3:5; 1 Cor. 15:10; 15:58; 2 Cor. 6:1) and also fits well with 1:9–10, which emphasizes the results of Paul's preaching ministry. See G. K. Beale, *1–2 Thessalonians* (Downers Grove: InterVarsity Press, 2003), 64.

59 Though the reading "gentle" has been challenged in recent years, it is still the preferred reading among commentators. See Bruce, 31; Gene L. Green, *The Letters to the Thessalonians* (Grand Rapids: W. B. Eerdmans Pub., 2002), 126; Wanamaker, *The Epistles to the Thessalonians: A Commentary on the Greek Text*, 100; Ben Witherington, *1 and 2 Thessalonians: A Socio-Rhetorical Commentary* (Grand Rapids: W. B. Eerdmans Pub., 2006), 80.

Just as in other parts where Paul tells his story, this part of Paul's story is also told based on the Thessalonians' knowledge of what Paul did in the city, rather than Paul's exhaustive description. In this portion, Paul's use of the formulas for "recall motif" is frequent.[60] In the use of the expression "You know" in the starting point of this portion, Paul reminds the Thessalonians of what they themselves saw in Paul's behavior (2:5). Paul also calls on the Thessalonians to "remember"[61] what he did (2:9). He continues to invoke the Thessalonians as "witnesses" (2:10). Closing his story and using the phrase "For you know," Paul again appeals to the Thessalonians' experience of his initial ministry (2:11). These overt appeals to the Thessalonians' memory of the missionaries' character and behavior are amplified in the portion of Paul's story.

Different from Paul's story during his stay in Thessalonica, his story after his departure is not told based on the recollection of the Thessalonians. There is no reason for the Thessalonians' memory to be in Paul's telling of this story, because the converts cannot see what has happened with Paul since his departure. Considering that the story after Paul's departure is not based on the recall motif, unlike the story about his founding visit, John Simpson concludes that the converts "do not already know what is being narrated and so are being told about it for the first time."[62] Though it is correct that Paul himself has not told the story to the converts, it is possible that Timothy already told the story to them while he returned to Thessalonica. Moreover, due to Timothy's visit, new information acquired from Paul's story after his departure seems to become minimal. Most of the story after Paul's unwanted departure is actually related to Timothy's revisit mission: Paul repeatedly attempted to return to Thessalonica, but these endeavors failed (2:17–18). So a decision was made that Timothy should return as Paul's representative (3:1–3). In the strict sense, it is only new to the coverts that the events that happened after Timothy's revisit. Paul tells this new portion of his story: Paul felt the sense of relief with Timothy's positive report of their faith and good memories of Paul and his colleagues (3:6–8). This portion includes a report about the converts and does not also contain much new information delivered to the converts.

---

60 Collins, 11.
61 The reason Paul use the term instead of "you know" might be for the sake of "stylistic variation." Wanamaker, *The Epistles to the Thessalonians: A Commentary on the Greek Text*, 102.
62 Simpson: 16.

The story of the Thessalonians that Paul tells is mainly about their response to his missionary work. Paul's telling of their conversion story can be found in the portion that preserves his missionary proclamation among the Thessalonians and contains many allusions to the kerygmatic narrative (1:9–10). Overlapping of the stories of the kerygmatic and the Thessalonians is not surprising since the story of the Thessalonians is nothing but their response to the kerygmatic narrative.[63] With their receptive response to the kerygmatic story, the Thessalonians turned toward God and away from the idols of their pagan heritage. And, they served God and waited for his Son, Jesus, described as the risen and delivering one. In addition to their conversion story, Paul tells the story about their suffering situation which came from their external conflict, as discussed in the previous chapter. In terms of suffering, they became imitators of both Paul and the Lord (1:6, 2:13–14).

4.3.2. Local Narratives Functioned as Symbolic Boundaries

The local narratives, stories of the missionaries headed by Paul and of the Thessalonian converts, function as a boundary including those who are in the community and excluding those who are not. The central focus on Paul's way of telling the local narratives facilitates the converts to derive a common identity from the community to which they belong and differentiate their community from the outside world.

The function of the symbolic boundary can be found in Paul's telling of his story concerning his work among the Thessalonians. As explored in the above section, Paul assumes that the listeners are familiar with his story of the founding visit and thus he primarily tells the story based on the recollection of the believers as seen in his repeated use of the recall motif. Therefore, it is clear that Paul's intention of telling his story is beyond simply transmitting information to the converts. Paul's reliance on the memory of the converts indicates that his story is truthful. Paul does not have to make any superfluous arguments for the story since the listeners themselves witnessed it. Paul's appeal to the recollection also provides a sense of intimate relationship between him and the converts by recognizing and reiterating the shared memory.

---

63   Witherington, 74.

Perhaps most importantly for the topic of this study, Paul's reminders of the collective memory among the converts create and support the communal identity of the community. The common identity of a group is grounded in the shared memory of the group. Group memory is the means by which a group identifies with its common past.[64] Georgia Keightley notes,

> Recollections associated with the period of origins as well as those subsequently recognized as having significance for the shared life are particular to it and make the community what it is. In truth, procession of a select body of memory serves to distinguish one community from another.[65]

Collective memory is certainly essential to the articulation of the corporate identity of a community. The same is true of the Thessalonian community. Paul constantly recalls the converts' collective memory in his way of telling of his story so that they can construct and strengthen their collective identity.

It should be noted that Paul reminds the converts about his story to give an example to imitate.[66] Paul invites the converts to remember his own witness, in particular the manner in which he lived and worked, and

---

[64] Sociologist, Maurice Halbwachs was a pioneer in a new approach to social or collective memory. He has argued that memory is socially determined; it is a social and collective phenomenon: "It is in society that people normally acquire their memories. It is also in society that they recall, recognize and localize their memories." Maurice Halbwachs, *On Collective Memory* (Chicago: University of Chicago Press, 1992), 38.

[65] Keightley: 152. In the article, Keightley applies Halbwachs' theory of the collective memory to her analysis of 1 Thessalonians. For a succint but encompassing explanation of the social-scientific concept of social memory, see Ernest van Eck, "Social Memory and Identity: Luke 19:12b–24 and 27," *Biblical Theology Bulletin* 41, no. 4 (2011): 201–205.

[66] This argument is based on the assumption that Paul's autobiographical sections are parenetic rather than apologetic in nature. See § 3.3. The concept of imitation is not uncommon not only in 1 Thessalonians but also other Pauline letters. See Stephen E. Fowl, *The Story of Christ in the Ethics of Paul: An Analysis of the Function of the Hymnic Material in the Pauline Corpus* (Sheffield: JSOT Press, 1990), 428; Michael Martin, "'Example' and 'Imitation' in the Thessalonian Correspondence," *Southwestern Journal of Theology* 42, no. 1 (1999): 40–41. For an observation on the concept of imitation in other New Testament writers, classical writers, and Early Church Fathers, see James G. Samra, *Being Conformed to Christ in Community: A Study of Maturity, Maturation, and the Local Church in the Undisputed Pauline Epistles* (London: T & T Clark, 2006), 126–128.

to follow the pattern of his own story. Abraham Malherbe writes, "Paul's method of shaping a community was to gather converts around himself and by his own behavior to demonstrate what he taught."[67] It is natural that imitation is an effective process to build up a new community like the Thessalonian community with the new converts. Apprentices of faith cannot be expected to have mastered the demands of their new faith in their lives. Such converts do not only need instruction in their new faith but also concrete examples of how to embody their new faith in the various contexts of their lives. Stephen Fowl therefore notes, "No amount of abstract verbal instruction can bring about mastery of a craft without the concrete example of a master to imitate."[68] Telling of his story is Paul's way of asking the listeners to follow him.

In addition, it should not be underestimated that imitation of Paul's story is fundamental to his construction of communal identity within the community. Paul's story functions as an "in-group prototype," which can be defined as the "shared cognitive representation of the ideal group member."[69] Within the community, Paul's story is the exemplar that prescribes to the converts who they are and how they should behave. Therefore, telling of Paul's story manifests the consensus of the community, and the listeners can ground their common identity by remembering and imitating his story.

Paul's presentation of his own story as the prototype of the community increases his influence and authority within the community. As Rikard Roitto writes, "prototypicality is therefore the basis of a leader's influence within the group."[70] However, Paul's intention in telling his story as the exemplar of the community is not an exercise of power designed to produce a "docile body" that submits to his instruction or to a privatized community.[71] Imitation of Paul's story is not imitation of his own person but is an

---

67 Abraham J. Malherbe, *Paul and the Thessalonians: The Philosophic Tradition of Pastoral Care* (Philadelphia: Fortress Press, 1987), 52.
68 Fowl, 430.
69 Rikard Roitto, "Behaving Like a Christ-Believer: A Cognitive Pespective on Identity and Behavor Norms in the Early Christ-Movement," in *Exploring Early Christian Identity*, ed. Bengt Holmberg (Tübingen: Mohr Siebeck, 2008), 107.
70 Ibid., 108.
71 Stephen Moore distrusts what he perceives in Paul's instruction of imitation as a technique designed to render the community "docile" with no initiative. See Stephen D. Moore, *Poststructural-Ism and the New Testament: Derrida and Foucault at the Foot of the Cross* (Minneapolis: Fortress Press, 1994), 109.

imitation of Christ as one who lives in Paul.[72] Paul presents his story as an example for the community because his own life follows the example of Christ. By imitating Paul's story, consequently, his converts imitate Christ, whom they cannot see.[73] Though Hellenistic teachers in Paul's days typically provided themselves as exemplars for their students,[74] this Christological dimension of Paul's concept of imitation is unique. 1 Thessalonians is no exception as the Thessalonian converts are commended for having become imitators "of us and of the Lord (1:6)."[75] Paul correlates the imitation of his story with the imitation of the story of Christ, the ultimate model. Wannamaker therefore writes, "Paul understood his own life as a form of mediation between Christ and his converts. His life provided the model of a Christ-like life for those who had no firsthand knowledge of Christ."[76] In telling his story, Paul is not concern with promoting "Paul-likeness" but Christ-likeness.[77] By remembering and imitating together Paul's story patterned by Christ's life, the listeners ultimately recognize their collective identity, which derives from the life of Christ.

While Paul's telling of his story about the founding ministry strengthens cohesion among those who know and imitate his story, the story provides the listeners with a strong sense of distinction from those who are not

---

[72] Charles A. Gieschen, "Christian Identity in a Pagan Thessalonica: The Imitation of Paul's Cruciform Life," *Concordia Theological Quarterly* 72, no. 1 (2008): 12.

[73] Frank J. Matera, *New Testament Theology: Exploring Diversity and Unity* (Louisville: Westminster John Knox Press, 2007), 108. Matera writes, "Paul speaks of imitation rather than following Christ in the way of discipleship. For whereas Jesus' disciples could see and follow him, Paul's converts could not. Consequently, they had to imitate someone who could present him with a model of what it means to be a believer. By imitating Paul, they imitate Christ since Paul has perfectly conformed himself to Christ's death and resurrection."

[74] Malherbe, *Paul and the Thessalonians: The Philosophic Tradition of Pastoral Care*, 52–53. This pattern of setting forward examples to be imitated is also found in Second Temple Jewish literature. See Gieschen: 9.

[75] The order "of us and of the Lord" does not suggest that Paul was more concerned with his own status than with that of the Lord. Paul seems to put the more powerful party second as seen in other cases such as 2:5 and 2:10. See Beverly R. Gaventa, *First and Second Thessalonians* (Louisville: Westminster John Knox Press, 1998), 16. Paul's emphasis on Christ in the concept of imitation can be found here and there in Paul's other letters (1 Cor. 4:16; 11:1; Phil. 3:17).

[76] Wanamaker, *The Epistles to the Thessalonians: A Commentary on the Greek Text*, 80.

[77] Marion Carson, "For Now We Live: A Study of Paul's Pastoral Leadership in 1 Thessalonians," *Themelios* 30, no. 3 (2005): 32.

in the community. Those who are not in the community do not know Paul's story and do not imitate it. Paul's story functions as the distinction between the in-group and the out-group. Undoubtedly, remembering and imitating Paul's story highlights the symbolic distinction between the two groups.

When it comes to Paul's story after his departure from Thessalonica, his telling also strengthens the solidity of the in-group community and stresses its distinction from the outside community. It is critical that Paul does not accentuate conveying information to the listeners by telling the story after his departure. Although Paul does not use the recall motif in telling his story, as explored in the above section, the converts appear to know much of the information about what happened to Paul after his departure. By telling the story, Paul wants to communicate affection rather than information. The story is mainly related to "the theme of friendship."[78] In the story, Paul maintains that physical separation does not mean emotional separation, demonstrating his unchanged deep feelings and concern for the converts. Beverly Gaventa comments on this portion: "In common with the crafters of love letters, Paul does not write to convey data but to express his affection and communicate his concerns."[79] By telling the story, Paul intends to sustain and intensify his intimate friendship with the converts.

Paul's intention to reassure his listeners about his close relationship becomes more explicit in his use of highly emotional language. In his story, Paul tells about his distress at being separated from the converts and describes himself and his coworkers as having "been made orphans" without them. He adds, "all the more, with great desire, we were eager to see your face" (2:17, NASB). Paul also mentions that Timothy's visit, which shows his deep affection for the converts, is reciprocated in Timothy's favorable report, which shows the converts' affection for Paul. This story is filled with warm, heartfelt, and emotional language. This moving language of the story increases the warmth between Paul and his listeners. Therefore, Paul's telling of his story filled with emotion-laden language strengthens the close relationship between Paul and the converts, and creates a common sense of intimate ties with Paul within the community. While Paul's story creates the group cohesion, the story also functions to exclude those who are not in the community. Those who have a close

---

78 Wanamaker, *The Epistles to the Thessalonians: A Commentary on the Greek Text*, 119.
79 Gaventa, 40.

relationship with Paul are the members of the community; those who do not have a close relationship with Paul are not members.

The communal identity is also strengthened by Paul's telling of the conversion story accompanied with the kerygmatic narrative, since the converts reacted to the kerygmatic narrative *in the same way* – that is, their collective story. Hearing and remembering their collective story together constructs a collective identity among the listeners. Their collective identity is reinforced by remembering their collective story. In particular, their suffering story is fundamental to Paul's construction of collective identity for those in the community. "For Paul" as Burton Mack notes, "Christian existence was understood as an imitation of the sufferings and sacrificial death of Christ."[80] Their suffering story not only functions to establish a connection between Christ, Paul, and the community but also maintains their cooperated identity – all shared in persecution. Persecution marks those who are in the community. It is obvious that their suffering story also identifies those who are not in the community. The outsiders do not follow Christ and thus do not suffer; they even oppress the Christ-following community. Paul's telling of their suffering strengthens the boundary between "us" and "them."

4.4. Preaching of Ethical Norms to Create Boundaries

4.4.1. Ethical Norms Incorporated

When Paul preaches his ethical instructions to the Thessalonians, he mainly focuses on sexual matters (4:3–8) and brotherly love (4:9–12). Paul's exhortations about sexual conduct are closely connected to with holiness. While the theme of holiness is prominent throughout 1 Thessalonians,[81] the concern for holiness is most obvious in 4:3–8, where Paul addresses sexual immorality. Starting to issue his sexual norms,

---

80 Burton L. Mack, *Who Wrote the New Testament?: The Making of the Christian Myth* (San Francisco: Harper, 1995), 184.
81 Jeffrey A. D. Weima, "'How You Must Walk to Please God': Holiness and Discipleship in 1 Thessalonians," in *Patterns of Discipleship in the New Testament* (Grand Rapids: W. B. Eerdmans Pub., 1996), 98–101.

Paul clearly refers to God's will to the converts' "sanctification" (4:3). The term ἁγιασμὸς functions as the backbone of the entire following discussion on sexual conduct, leading Paul's three-fold use of the holy word in 4:3–8. Based on the reference to God's will for holy living, Paul states that the believers are to acquire a wife or control their own body in "holiness (ἁγιασμῷ)" (4:4). The purpose of holiness is negatively stated again: God did not call the converts to uncleanness but to "holiness (ἁγιασμῷ)" (4:7). Paul also states that it is for the purpose of holy living that God gives them his Spirit, which is "holy (ἅγιον)" (4:8). According to Jeffrey Weima, therefore, Paul's reference that God's will for lives of the believers are connected with holiness is "a thesis-like statement" encompassing all of the subsequent treatments of sexual matters.[82]

Though it is true that holiness is extensive enough to cover all aspects of believers' behavior, Paul in 1 Thessalonians deals with the specific subject of sexual morality. It has been debated whether or not Paul's focus on sexual morality in his exhortations reflects the situation of the community. Some scholars suggest that Paul's exhortations are ascribed to his use of traditional parenetic materials common in those times, consequently arguing that Paul's focus on sexual morality is unrelated to the situation of the community.[83] Others maintain that some converts fell into the immoral behavior as seen in the part where the community was not well so that he might "supply what is lacking in your faith" (3:10).[84] Still other scholars claim that Paul was concerned that the converts might revert to the immorality of their previous lifestyle though the problem had not yet emerged in the community.[85] Given the situation of the community, although it cannot be known whether some converts actually went back to their former immoral life style, Paul's ethical instructions on sexual morality likely reflect the situation of the community. As explored in the previous chapter, the Thessalonian community was facing massive pressure to conform to the

---

82   Ibid., 107.
83   Helmut Koester, "1 Thessalonians – Experiment in Christian Writing," in *Continuity and Discontinuity in Church History: Essays Presented to George Huntston Williams*, eds. F. Forrester Church and Timothy George (Leiden: E. J. Brill, 1979), 38–39.
84   Fee, 143; Wanamaker, *The Epistles to the Thessalonians: A Commentary on the Greek Text*, 158–159.
85   William Neil, *The Epistle of Paul to the Thessalonians* (New York: Harper & Brothers, 1950), 77; Still, *Conflict at Thessalonica: A Pauline Church and Its Neighbours*, 237. Still states: "Paul's purpose in this pericope (i.e. 4:1–8) appears to be preventative, not corrective."

pattern of the pagan society. As a result of such pressure, it may be possible that some of the immature converts returned to their former pagan practices, many of which were related to sexual corruption. Therefore, Paul's focus on sexual morality reflects the very real danger of the Thessalonian converts reverting to previous pagan cultic practices.

Paul issues three ethical norms of sexual conduct. The first is general: "You should avoid sexual immorality" (4:3). The term πορνεία, which in the Greek world had to do with prostitution, in biblical usage can mean sexual immorality of any kind.[86] This ethical norm fundamentally originated from moral instructions, both of Diaspora Judaism and early Christianity. Frequently, in Judeo-Christian literature, sexual immorality metaphorically referred to the practice of idolatry. However, the social norms in Greco-Roman society of Paul's time normally permitted sexual behavior that the Jews or Christian ethic prohibited. Though a few groups such as the Stoics were concerned with moral behavior,[87] the society in general had a very tolerant attitude toward sexual conduct, particularly for men. It was typical that married men would have sexual intercourse with prostitutes, female slaves, and mistresses. The very tolerant view toward sexual conduct was reflected in the phases of life of the day. Concubinage was common. Prostitution was regarded as a normal business. Owners of inns and cook shops frequently kept female slaves for sexual entertainment for their customers.[88] In the context of the sexual customs of the era, Paul issues the moral norm that the converts should avoid sexual immorality.

The second of Paul's three ethical norms in 4:4–5 has engendered numerous scholarly debates. The debate centers on the meaning of the noun σκεῦος, which literally means "vessel" and its verb κτάομαι, which normally means "to acquire." The RSV and the NAB take σκεῦος as a metaphorical reference to "wife," so that here Paul's ethical norm is: Each of you should

---

86 Fee, 145. Bruce Malina, however, argues that this term does not include pre-marital sexual relationships. See Bruce J. Malina, "Does Porneia Mean Fornication?," *Novum testamentum* 14, no. 1 (1972): 10–17.

87 O. Larry Yarbrough provides many examples of Greco-Roman philosophical and rhetorical treatments of marriage. Many individuals cited advised loyalty in marriage. See O. Larry Yarbrough, *Not Like the Gentiles: Marriages Rules in the Letters of Paul* (Atlanta: Scholars press, 1985), 31–63.

88 Weima, 104–105. Wayne Meeks writes, "The specific moral expectations that Paul expresses, of the sort that one could state as moral rules, are hardly different from those widely accepted as 'decent' in Greco-Roman society." Wayne A. Meeks, *The Moral World of the First Christians* (Philadelphia: Westminster Press, 1986), 128.

learn how to acquire a wife for yourself in holiness and honor. Scholars advocating this translation[89] generally appeal to the alleged similarity between 4:4 and 1 Corinthians 7:2, where Paul says, "Since there is so much immorality, each man should have his own wife, and each woman her own husband." They also consider the use of σκεῦος in 1 Peter 3:7, where the wife is the "weaker vessel." Additionally, it is suggested that in a number of references in rabbinic literature wife or woman is referred to as a vessel.[90] However, it is necessary to consider that Paul in 1 Corinthians 7:2 clearly says "wife (γυνή)" to refer to wife, not the use of this metaphor. The evidence of 1 Peter 3:7 also seems ambiguous because in the passage both husbands and wives are "vessels." Moreover, the rabbinic usage could be peripheral but not essential to establish Pauline usage. Furthermore, this ethical norm is not directed to a particular group in the community – married men, because Paul provides the norm for "each of you" in the Thessalonians community (4:4).

The NIV, the NRSV, the NEB, the ESV, and the NET also take a metaphorical meaning of σκεῦος as referring to one's own "body" so Paul's norms are to learn how to control one's own body in holiness and honor. Scholars holding to this interpretation[91] find Paul's same usage of σκεῦος referring to the human body in 2 Corinthians 4:7, where Paul says that "we have this treasure in earthen vessels" (NASB). They also suggest that self-control is the common theme in Christian teaching of sexual morality by Paul and other writers of the New Testament (Acts 15:20, 29; 21:25; 1 Cor. 6:12–20; Eph. 5:3; Col. 3:5; 2 Tim. 2:21–22). Some of scholars

---

89 See Best, 163–164; Trevor J. Burke, *Family Matters: A Socio-Historical Study of Kinship Metaphors in 1 Thessalonians* (New York: T & T Clark International, 2003), 187–196; James E. Frame, *A Critical and Exegetical Commentary on the Epistles of St. Paul to the Thessalonians* (New York: C. Scribner's Sons, 1912), 149; Victor Paul Furnish, *1 Thessalonians, 2 Thessalonians* (Nashville: Abingdon Press, 2007), 89–90; Joseph B. Lightfoot, *Notes on Epistles of St Paul from Unpublished Commentaries* (London: Macmillan, 1904), 54–55; Malherbe, *The Letters to the Thessalonians: A New Translation with Introduction and Commentary*, 226–228; D. Michael Martin, *1, 2 Thessalonians* (Nashville: Broadman & Holman, 1995), 124–125; Witherington, 114; Yarbrough, 65–87.
90 See Yarbrough, 72–73.
91 See Beale; Green, 193–194; Michael W. Holmes, *1 and 2 Thessalonians: The Niv Application Commentary* (Grand Rapids: Zondervan, 1998), 126; Leon Morris, *The First and Second Epistles to the Thessalonians* (Grand Rapids: W. B. Eerdmans Pub., 1991), 121; Earl Richard, *First and Second Thessalonians* (Collegeville: Liturgical Press, 1995), 198.

holding to the second interpretation have regarded σκεῦος as a euphemistic reference particularly to the male sex organ based on the LXX of 1 Samuel 21:5–6.[92] Given the phallic character of the Cabirus and Dionysian cults popular in Thessalonica, this opinion may be reasonable. However, there are no parallels for this usage in the New Testament. The major problem of the translation is not related to σκεῦος but the verb κτάομαι. The meaning of "to control" taken for this translation is not supported by solid lexical evidence. Therefore, it can be said that neither translations escaped unscathed. The choice between the two options still remains difficult "not because both are equally appropriate, but because neither is free from serious difficulty," as Joseph Lightfoot noted.[93]

It is important to note, however, that the Thessalonian converts knew what the ethical norm accurately means, even though the contemporary readers do not. Presumably, this is because Paul has already instructed the converts during his founding mission (4:2). Whatever Paul actually means in the passage, it is certain that the converts should live in a way that is holy and honorable, instead of falling into sexual immorality as was the custom of their pagan Thessalonians.

The last of the three ethical norms is provided in 4:6: "In this matter no one should wrong his brother or take advantage of him." Some suggest that Paul moves on to a new topic, a business matter,[94] since the normal usage of the verb πλεονεκτεῖν is not for sexual immorality but for improperly acquiring material gain. Paul's use of the verb, however, is not limited to only business matters, as seen in 2 Corinthians 2:11:[95] "In order that Satan might not *outwit* us." Moreover, the verses 3–6 in the Greek text constitute one long sentence that appears to structurally have a thematic unity, which is in favor of addressing one subject.[96] Furthermore, one's sexual immorality in the Christ-following community is not just regarded as a private activity; on the contrary, it is completely related to one's relationship with others.

---

92 In this passage, the Hebrew word כְּלִי translated to σκεῦος in the LXX, has been understood to refer to the male sex organ. This idea was initially suggested by J. Whitton. See J. Whitton, "A Neglected Meaning for *SKEUOS* in 1 Thessalonians 4:4," *New Testament Studies* 28, no. 1 (1982). Also see Bruce; Fee, 149; Wanamaker, *The Epistles to the Thessalonians: A Commentary on the Greek Text*, 152.
93 Lightfoot, 54.
94 See Jürgen Becker, *Christian Beginnings: Word and Community from Jesus to Post-Apostolic Times* (Louisville: Westminster John Knox Press, 1993), 160; Richard, 200.
95 Martin, *1, 2 Thessalonians*, 129.
96 Burke, 182–183.

Dishonorable sexual activity with someone else's spouse is to "wrong" and "take advantage of" someone in the community. Thus, Paul's business expression in this context can be understood as a euphemistic reference to sexual immorality.

In addition to the sexual matters, Paul in 4:9–12 issues ethical norms of brotherly love (φιλαδελφία). Though one might think that in the pericope Paul deals with two separated topics, brotherly love and work matters, the theme of brotherly love is closely related to how the converts should conduct themselves while working. The overarching topic of brotherly love is introduced in 4:9–10a, then 4:10b functions as a bridge, linking the topic of brotherly love with what Paul discuss in 4:11–12, as seen in the way that the only directive "we urge" (παρακαλοῦμεν) of 4:10b is completed by four following infinitives in 4:10b–12: "to bound" (περισσεύειν), "to aspire (φιλοτιμεῖσθαι) to live quietly," "to mind (πράσσειν) your own affairs," and "to work (ἐργάζεσθαι) with your own hands."[97] This grammatical structure shows that the second half of the pericope is a continuation of the main topic of brotherly love.

The topic of brotherly love is not new to the community as Paul in 4:9 informs the converts: "About brotherly love we do not need to write to you." Though such expressions were not uncommon in the parenetic literature of the day,[98] Paul still does not just follow the regular custom without any consideration of the real conditions of the community. Brotherly love not only belongs to the knowledge of the believers but also is acted out as "to love each other" within the community on the basis of what they have been taught. Moreover, such brotherly love was toward "all the brothers throughout Macedonia" (4:10).

Paul's first ethical norm about brotherly love is "to do so more and more" (4:10). What Paul urges the community "to do" is not explicitly stated, but it is assumed that the first norm is to abound in brotherly love. Followed by the first norm, Paul's three-fold norms are unpacked in 4:11–12: "to make it your ambition to lead a quiet life, to mind your own business, and to work with your hands."

These moral norms, which appear to be related to only work ethic in a cursory reading, have provoked much debate among scholars regarding

---

[97] See Jacob W. Elias, *1 and 2 Thessalonians* (Scottdale: Herald Press, 1995), 157; Martin, *1, 2 Thessalonians*, 132.

[98] See Stanley K. Stowers, *Letter Writing in Greco-Roman Antiquity* (Philadelphia: Westminster Press, 1986), 103.

the background of the community, which motivated Paul to give the instructions to the converts. Some scholars have advocated that these norms followed "undue eschatological excitement that had induced a restless tendency in some of the Thessalonian Christians and made them disinclined to attend to their ordinary business."[99] This is the thought behind the opinion that some converts affected by the eschatological excitement ceased working and then depended on others in the community. Though the eschatological expectation was vibrant in the community, however, it is necessary to consider that Paul does not connect he imminent return of Christ with the question of work in the pericope. Other scholars who are inclined to a social hypothesis have thought that the patron-client relationship in the Greco-Roman world produced the problem of idleness in the community.[100] Clients from lower classes attached themselves to patrons of higher status, receiving benefits from them while giving their patrons honor and expressions of gratitude. Thus, some convert who found new patrons in the community became excessively dependent on the generosity of their patrons. However, it cannot be assumed that a patron-client relationship was in operation in the community. If it were, the typical duties of clients in a patronage relationship were not so small that clients would be accused of idleness.[101] Some also have suggested that these ethical norms were ascribed to the negative attitude toward physical work, which was common in the Greco-Roman society.[102] However, this negative view on manual work was only held by the upper class. This perspective must have had little to do with laborers or artisans, who probably were not negligible numbers in the community.[103]

---

99 Bruce, 91. Also see Best, 175–176; Frame, 161; Marshall, 117; Morris, 131.
100 See Green, 208–209; R. Russell, "The Idle in 2 Thess 3.6–12: An Eschatological or a Social Problem?," *New Testament Studies* 34, no. 1 (1988): 105–119; David J. Williams, *1 and 2 Thessalonians* (Peabody: Hendrickson Publishers, 1992), 150.
101 Weima, 115.
102 Marshall, 116. For the negative perspective on physical work in the Greco-Roman world, see Moses I. Finley, *The Ancient Economy* (Berkeley: University of California Press, 1973), 35–61; Ronald F. Hock, *The Social Context of Paul's Ministry: Tentmaking and Apostleship* (Philadelphia: Fortress Press, 1980), 35–36.
103 Many scholars believe that the majority of the Thessalonian converts were manual workers. See Richard S. Ascough, *Paul's Macedonian Associations: The Social Context of Philippians and 1 Thessalonians* (Tübingen: Mohr Siebeck, 2003), 174; Best, 176; Robert Jewett, *The Thessalonian Correspondence: Pauline Rhetoric and Millenarian Piety* (Philadelphia: Fortress Press, 1986), 120–121; Wayne A. Meeks,

Alternatively, some scholars, those who consider the converts' conflict with the larger society, including family,[104] propose that their social unrest could be the context of Paul's ethical norms.[105] For the converts who experienced the dislocation of the traditional family unit, Paul attempted to shape the community into a surrogate family. Thus, these norms were designed for Paul's project of construction of a new family and are regarded not only as ethical teachings for the converts but also family rules that all members of the family should keep, contributing toward the construction of the alternative family. This opinion seems more pervasive. First of all, these norms are not independent but subordinate to the overarching topic of brotherly love, as argued earlier. In addition, these norms reflect the ideal ethos of family in the ancient Greco-Roman world where members of a family cooperated with each other to discharge their responsibilities toward the family. About the ethos of the ancient family, David DeSilva states, "Solidarity and cooperation, rather than competition, should be the hallmark of the interactions between siblings."[106] All members in a family were expected to work together in craft or trade for the good of the whole family, and collaboratively contribute to the family's wealth.[107] Thus, Paul's ethical norms about work are not disparate with brotherly love but fit the family ethos. Lastly, Paul's emphasis on the lifestyle that will "win the respect of outsiders" could be understood in the context of the first-century Greco-Roman culture where honor or respect functioned as the central value when making decisions.[108] In this honor culture, every member of the family ought to behave in accordance with the honor or respect for the family, even from the viewpoint of outsiders. Therefore, Paul uses the concept of family life at the time to issue ethical

---

The First Urban Christians: The Social World of the Apostle Paul (New Haven: Yale University Press, 1983), 64–65; Steve Walton, *Leadership and Lifestyle: The Portrait of Paul in the Miletus Speech and 1 Thessalonians* (Cambridge: Cambridge University Press, 2000), 169.

104 See § 3.3.
105 For example, see John M. G. Barclay, "Conflict in Thessalonica," *Catholic Biblical Quarterly* 55, no. 3 (1993): 523–524; Burke, 216.
106 David A. deSilva, *Honor, Patronage, Kinship & Purity: Unlocking New Testament Culture* (Downers Grove: InterVarsity Press, 2000), 166.
107 Carolyn Osiek and David L. Balch, *Families in the New Testament World Households and House Churches* (Louisville: Westminster John Knox Press, 1997), 54.
108 See David A. deSilva, *Despising Shame: Honor Discourse and Community Maintenance in the Epistle to the Hebrews* (Atlanta: Scholars Press, 1995), 1–144.

norms closely associated with brotherly love for the converts who need new sibling relationships.

While no one is exactly sure why some converts stopped working,[109] it is evident that Paul in these norms exhorts them "to work with your hands" (4:11b) so "that you will not be dependent on anybody" (4:12b). One might understand that here Paul simply teaches a common ethical topic of the day: self-sufficiency.[110] Given the overarching topic of brotherly love, however, Paul's norms are regarded as relating to the brothers not being a burden on other brothers in the community. To those who are able to work, work itself is an expression of brotherly love. Whereas Paul seeks to encourage brotherly love in the community as he exhorts them to abound in love more and more, Paul does not want to allow his ethical teaching of brotherly love to be exploited. John Stott explains it this way: "It is an expression of love to support others who are in need; but it is also an expression of love to support ourselves, so as not to need to be supported by others."[111] By providing ethical norms relating brotherly love to the matter of work, Paul makes it clear that refusing to work by taking advantage of other brothers' generosity is not driven by brotherly love, and therefore in appropriate for the community as a new family.

According to Paul, the problem with brotherly love is not just an intra-community matter. As Michael Holmes explains, Paul's concept of brotherly love is "bi-directional,"[112] the problem relating to brotherly love is also related to the outsiders of the community. The converts should be mindful that their behavior affects not only one another in the community but also the perspective of the outsiders. Therefore, another reason for the converts to work and to provide for their families' needs is "so that your daily life may win the respect of outsiders" (4:12). Paul thinks that brotherly love is not just a restricted issue within the community but also a matter of how the community is perceived by those not part of it. "Thus, the exhortation to brotherly love carries with it not only the necessity for providing for one's

---

109 Besides reasons described above, Barclay ascribes the problem of idleness in the community to the converts' engagement in evangelic activities. Barclay: 522.
110 See Best, 178; Craig de Vos, *Church and Community Conflicts: The Relationships of the Thessalonian, Corinthian, and Philippian Churches with Their Wider Civic Communities* (Atlanta: Scholars Press, 1999), 175 n. 198.
111 John R. W. Stott, *The Gospel and the End of Time: The Message of 1 and 2 Thessalonians* (Downers Grove: InterVarsity Press, 1991), 90.
112 Holmes, 142.

own needs, but failure to do so could endanger the reputation of the group on the part of those outside,"[113] Trevor Burke aptly writes. Paul's recognition that the ethical norms of brotherly love should properly work toward the external relation with the larger society squares with the situation that the converts were subject to enormous suffering and pressure from the larger society. Although Paul would not want the believers to abandon their faith to win the respect of their unbelieving compatriots, he might hope that their honorable conduct based on the ethical norms of brotherly love would dispel the suspicions about them and so alleviate the conflict with the surrounding world.

4.4.2. Ethical Norms Functioned as Symbolic Boundaries

While Paul's exhortations are undoubtedly related to the morality of the converts, his concerns about the norms are more than a matter of morality. His ethical norms have social functions. The moral discipline of the converts could operate as the symbolic boundary for the community and distinguish the converts from the outside world.

Paul's sexual norms have social functions. His prescription for sexual practice is not only for the advancement of virtue among the converts but also for the task of community formation, by maintaining the collective identity of the believing community and separating it from the pagan society. The corporate identity formed by the attitudes and behaviors in accordance with Paul's sexual norms is qualified as holiness. The concept of holiness is never found in known pagan literature, and no Greco-Roman moralist was concerned with holy living.[114] Paul's attention to holiness must be from his Jewish background such as the Holiness Code in Leviticus 17–26. Just as God called Israel to be holy as God is holy, Paul reminds the converts that God "called" them not to impurity but "in holiness" (4:7). In Jeffery Weima's argument, Paul suggests the gentile converts in Thessalonica to be "the renewed Israel" by applying the holiness that has been the exclusive privilege of Israel.[115] Though it could not be affirmed whether

---

113 Burke, 221–222.
114 Fee, 144–145.
115 Weima, 102–103. Likewise, Andy Johnson suggests that the believing community in Thessalonica functioned as "an eschatological instantiation of Israel" as a result of their becoming an embodiment of holiness. Andy Johnson, "The Sanctification of the

the gentile converts unfamiliar with the Jewish tradition fully understood Paul's intention connecting them with Israel's identity, the shared manners of lifestyle that conform to Paul's exhortations on sexual morality must have cultivated the communal identity of the community: holiness.[116]

It may be supposed that Paul's sexual norms would enhance the social stability and internal cohesion of the community. While some might advocate that sexual activity should be placed only in the private sphere, Paul believes that it ought to be practiced by social relations. Paul prescribes practicing sexual norms in a way that is not only holy but also "honorable" (4:4). Honor in the Greco-Roman society was a high value acquired from social relations. Paul's use of terms having connotations of business ethics also implies that his sexual norms have a social dimension. Lone Fatum thus concludes that Paul in the sexual instructions "addresses the socio-sexual activities."[117] Therefore, Paul believes that dishonorable sexual activities should be prohibited since they would increase tension among the converts and threaten the harmony of the community, which consequently could head to the collapse of the community. Jouette Bassler writes, "The emphasis here on holiness/sanctification is clear, yet when Paul defines more precisely what this means, it also becomes clear that actions that lead to holiness *also* lead to peace."[118] Paul's sexual norms involve attributes of inner harmony of the community.

The other function of Paul's moral exhortations on sexual conduct is emphasis on separation. Paul's sexual norms play a role in the distinction between those inside and outside of the community. From the Jewish perspective, holiness, the ideal of Paul's sexual morality, is associated with the concept of separation: "You are to be holy to me because I, the LORD, am holy, and I have set you apart from the nations to be my own" (Lev. 20:26).

Imagination in 1 Thessaloninas," in *Holiness and Ecclesiology in the New Testament*, eds. Kent E. Brower and Andy Johnson (Grand Rapids: W. B. Eerdmans Pub., 2007), 276–279.

116 Paul always uses the word holiness in a communal context, not to refer to an individual. See James Thompson, *Moral Formation According to Paul: The Context and Coherence of Pauline Ethics* (Grand Rapids: Baker Academic, 2011), 55.

117 Lone Fatum, "Brotherhood in Christ: A Gender Hermeneutical Reading of 1 Thessalonians," in *Constructing Early Christian Families: Family as Social Reality and Metaphor*, ed. Halvor Moxnes (New York: Routledge, 1997), 190.

118 Jouette M. Bassler, "Peace in All Ways: Theology in the Thessalonian Letters. A Response to R. Jewett, E. Krentz, and E. Richard" in *Pauline Theology Vol. 1*, ed. Jouette M. Bassler (Minneapolis: Fortress Press, 1994), 83. Italics original.

Holiness was the boundary maker that separates God's people from the people around them. Given the pagan culture where sexual immorality was pervasive, Paul undoubtedly expects this boundary maker in matters of sexual conduct to separate the converts from the pagan society to which they previously belonged. By insisting that the converts practice sexual behave in holiness, Paul draws a symbolic boundary around the community.

The distinction created by the moral boundary is also clearly found in Paul's use of terms of reference to represent two opposing groups, each with its own distinctive features and conduct. Regarding the group to which the converts belong, there is the intimate relationship among "brothers" (4:1, 6) who have been "called" by God (4:7). Their lifestyle is qualified as "holiness" (4:3, 7, 8). In contrast, the divergent group is defined by "sexual immorality" (4:3), "passionate lust" (4:5), being "impure" (4:7), and as "the heathens who do not know God" (4:5). Paul's contrasting way of telling serves to mark the difference between the two groups and draws a clear line of demarcation between them. Craig de Vos, therefore, writes, "This in itself creates, or at least encourages, a dichotomy between those inside and outside the Christian community."[119]

It is necessary to note that Paul's contrasting language – positive language for in-group and negative language for out-group – indicates Paul's attempt to install the superiority of the in-group within the community. It is no wonder that there are qualitative differences between the in-group lifestyle, defined as holiness, and the out-group, defined as sexual immorality. For this reason, Philip Esler claims,

> Paul's insistence on behavioural norms falls within the larger purpose of recommending to the Thessalonian Christ-followers a positive identity. In other words, Paul may want to tell them how they should behave, but only in the course of installing in their consciousness the larger and more important reality of who they are.[120]

Their holy lifestyle provides them with a sense of righteousness, especially in the eyes of God who "will punish men for all such sins" (4:6). God's favor would create the sense of the superiority over those "who do not know God" (4:5).

Paul's ethical norms of brotherly love also have a social function as the symbolic boundary to create the collective identity of the community and

---

119 de Vos, 173.
120 Esler, "'Keeping It in the Family': Culture, Kinship and Identity in 1 Thessalonians and Galatians," 171.

develop group solidarity. With the norms of brotherly love, Paul intends to shape the believing community into a surrogate family group. This intent can be inferred from his usage of φιλαδελφία. Prior to Paul's usage of it, the word was used almost exclusively for the love of biological siblings. The term is also rarely used in the New Testament.[121] In fact, Paul uses φιλαδελφία only twice, including this case.[122] Thus, one might think that there is no apparent explanation for Paul's usage of the term instead of ἀγάπη normally used in the New Testament.[123] In this context, nevertheless, Paul's metaphorical application of φιλαδελφία shows that he intended to construct the believing community as a surrogate kinship group by encouraging a genuine feeling of kinship among the listeners who had no basis for a reciprocal relationship before entering the community.

Paul, however, recognizes that the kinship community in Thessalonica cannot be constructed only by the metaphorical use of family language. For its formation, each member, as a brother, is evidently expected to have and perform habits and ways of living in accordance with the kinship community. Members are required to act to be brothers in the same family. In this regard, David Horrell thus labels Paul's ethics as "role-ethics," a set of expectations about how behavior should be shaped according to a role-designation as brothers.[124] Paul advises the Thessalonian converts about how they can behave as brothers in the new family group – the role of brothers in brotherly love. The awareness about the presence of the role of brothers and the attitudes and behaviors governed by the role provide the converts with an unambiguous brotherhood to which they belong in the same family. Clearly, the brotherhood constructs the kinship community.

For the construction of the community, the norms are also designed to solve problems that may disserve the community. The norms mean that brothers are supposed to work together, which reflects the family ethos of the ancient Mediterranean world. It was expected that cooperation among brothers not only uphold the family but also bolster the brotherhood. The

---

121 Heb. 13:1; 1 Peter 1:22; 2 Peter 1:7.
122 The other case is found in Rom. 12:10.
123 Similarly, see Hans Dieter Betz, "De Fraterno Amore," in *Plutarch's Ethical Writings and Early Christian Literature*, ed. Hans Dieter Betz (Leiden: Brill, 1978), 232.
124 David G. Horrell, *Solidarity and Difference: A Contemporary Reading of Paul's Ethics* (New York: T & T Clark International, 2005), 113.

norms also imply that brothers are not supposed to be a burden on one another. The norms would curtail the possibility of internal tensions and relational difficulties that could arise from over-dependence or exploitation of one another.

The apparent awareness of brotherhood and its lifestyle necessarily accompanies the awareness of those who are not truly brothers. By Paul's norms of brotherly love, the line of separation is drawn between the brothers and those who do not belong, the non-brothers. The social function of Paul's ethical norms of brotherly love is twofold: internal cohesion and external separation. Raymond Collins appropriately encapsulates this idea:

> For Paul to write of the church of the Thessalonians as a brotherhood is to say something about that community *ab intra* and *ad extra*. Brotherhood speaks of togetherness and apartness. The recognition of their existence as a specific religious brotherhood marks a distinctive stage in the ecclesial self-awareness of the Thessalonians. […] The recognition of brotherhood is a recognition of distinctness, yet the recognition is also a recognition of togetherness. *Ab intra* the description of a community as a brotherhood draws attention to the bonds that link the matters together.[125]

It is necessary to point out that the external dynamic of Paul's norms of brotherly love is not restricted to the separation from non-brothers. The ethical norms are involved in the concern to "win the respect of outsiders" (4:12). This concern shows Paul's hope that the converts' behavior "will be such as to no conflict with certain ideals which even the non-Christian would accept,"[126] but more importantly, he assumes that the family group is superior to any other group and thus the honor of the family is to be maintained in the eyes of those outside the community. By the exhortation to honorable conduct suitable for the family honor, Paul shares a sense of superiority with the listeners and reinforces the hierarchical status of the community. Paul's norms of brotherly love embody the honor of the family, and its superiority, in external relationships.

---

125 Raymond F. Collins, *Studies on the First Letter to the Thessalonians* (Leuven: University Press, 1984), 296. Italics original.
126 Best, 177.

4.5. Conclusion

Paul proficiently intertwines the kerygmatic narrative, the local narratives, and the ethical norms with his preaching in 1 Thessalonians. Paul's aim to incorporate these resources into his preaching is not primarily to convey information unfamiliar to the listeners, since he indicates that he already taught them, they already knew them, and they even already did them well in a variety of ways. Rather, his chief goal is to enhance and to maintain the community facing a serious challenge that could destroy it. Paul's primary goal is not informative; it's formative. In other words, the kerygmatic narrative, the local narratives, and the ethical norms take on a social function in Paul's preaching.

The sociological concept of symbolic boundaries is probably the best way to explain the social function of these resources in Paul's preaching. Serving as criteria through which members of a group include insiders and exclude outsiders, the symbolic boundaries provide the members with a collective identity and distinguish them from other groups with a sense of distinctiveness or superiority. Boundary building is absolutely indispensable to the formation of a community. To create and maintain boundaries, Paul inserts the kerygmatic narrative, the local narratives, and ethical norms. Functioning as symbolic boundaries, these resources in Paul's preaching take an important role to promote the converts to derive a cooperative identity from the community to which they belong and strengthen the distinction between them and the larger society. By providing the converts with internal consensus and external separation, Paul's preaching of the kerygmatic, the local narratives, and the ethical norms in 1 Thessalonians serves to construct and maintain the Christ-following community that is internally united and externally distinct.

Chapter Five
Homiletical Implications of Paul's Preaching for Community Formation with Regard to the Post-Christian Context

This chapter examines the homiletical implications of Paul's community formation preaching in the post-Christian culture. The chapter first will attempt to discover congruities between the pagan context that Paul was facing in his ministry for the Thessalonian community and the post-Christian context that contemporary preachers face in the ministry, and then connect the two. This connection will indicate that Paul's preaching for community formation provides a model for the contemporary preachers who have an essential task of building Christian communities in a post-Christian culture. Suggestions will then be offered for contemporary homiletics whose duty is to equip and train preachers who work in a post-Christian society. For community formation in a post-Christian culture, it will be suggested that preaching as Paul does in 1 Thessalonians is to provide shared narratives and communal ethical norms that are not in accordance with those in a non-Christian culture.

5.1. Connecting the Post-Christian Context to Paul's Pre-Christian Context

Fred Craddock, a pioneer of the New Homiletic, has written that "there is no lack of information in a Christian land; something else is lacking, and this is a something which the one cannot directly communicate to the other."[1] Listeners have "overheard" the gospel. Preachers face the task of preaching to those who are familiar with Christian messages and have heard it week after week. It is Craddock's fundamental assumption that the preacher and listeners are under the influence of Christian culture.

---
1   Fred B. Craddock, *Overhearing the Gospel* (Nashville: Abingdon Press, 1978), 9.

Craddock's assumption, however, should be reconsidered. Many Western countries with a rich Christian heritage are moving into a post-Christian outlook. When Lesslie Newbigin, a British missionary in India, returned to England in the 1970s, he observed that an enormous decline of the church and Christian influence had occurred during his absence. At the time he left England, main cultural institutions of society were generally in harmony with the Christian faith and the churches could gather without much difficulty those who were in favor of Christianity. However, things had changed. The Christian West had vanished. In Europe, including England, church attendance precipitously fell. Christianity lost much influence. Newbigin found that the West was becoming not only a secular society without God but also a pagan society filled with false gods. Therefore, he suggested that modern Western societies should be understood as a mission field. In a series of books, Newbigin calls for the "missionary encounter of the gospel with our Western culture."[2] It can no longer be assumed that the Western societies are not in need of evangelization, since they have been heavily influenced by a post-Christian culture. The West has entered a post-Christian age.

Although a reaction against Christianity came to the United States more slowly than it did in Britain and Europe,[3] the country once regarded as "Christian America"[4] is also becoming a post-Christian and unchurched nation.

---

2 See Lesslie Newbigin, *The Other Side of 1984: Questions for the Churches* (Geneva: WCC Publications, 1983); Lesslie Newbigin, *Foolishness to the Greeks: The Gospel and Western Culture* (Grand Rapids: W. B. Eerdmans Pub., 1986); Lesslie Newbigin, *The Gospel in a Pluralist Society* (Grand Rapids: W. B. Eerdmans Pub., 1989).

3 Some observers conclude that this phenomenon is related to evangelical Christianity popular among Americans in the 1970s and 1980s. The appeal of evangelical Christianity, which has never occurred as strongly elsewhere, has served to keep the United States more religious. Among others, see Robert D. Putnam and David E. Campbell, *American Grace: How Religion Divides and Unites Us* (New York: Simon & Schuster, 2012), 100–120. However, evangelical churches also have been in decline. Robert Putnam and David Campbell report, "Since this fact is not widely understood, it is worth reemphasizing – *the evangelical boom that began in the 1970s was over by the early 1990s, nearly two decades ago. In twenty-first century America expansive evangelicalism is a feature of the past, not present.*" Italics original. Ibid., 105.

4 See Robert T. Handy, *A Christian America: Protestant Hopes and Historical Realities* (New York: Oxford University Press, 1971). Handy writes, "From the beginning American Protestants entertained a lively hope that someday the civilization of the country would be fully Christian. The ways in which the hope was expressed and the

Since the 1960's,[5] church membership in the United States has plummeted. The decline is most obviously observed in main Protestant churches. By the 1950s, mainline Protestant denominations represented the dominant religious tradition in the United States. However, mainline churches have experienced dramatic losses in membership. They lost 5 million members between 1960 and 2000, while the population grew by over 100 million people, which means that the mainline churches lost 20 percent of their membership in 40 years.[6]

In addition to the decrease of church membership, the number of people who say they do not have a religion has increased. The General Social Survey has been tracking trends in American religious preference since 1972. According to the Survey, just 5 percent of Americans in 1972 stated that they have "no religion." However, the percentage has continually increased. In the 2012 data, 20 percent answered "no religion." Robert Putnam and David Campbell states, "[T]he fraction of Americans who said they were 'none' suddenly began to rise, and at virtually the same time the fraction of people said that they 'never' attend church also began to rise."[7] They aptly describe this nationwide phenomenon as "emptying pews and increasing nones."[8] Americans who attend churches have greatly decreased; those who do not have religion have abruptly increased. Tom Clegg and Warren Bird observe:

> The unchurched population in the United States is so extensive that, if it were a nation, it would be the fifth most populated nation on the planet after China, the former Soviet Union, India and Brazil. Thus our unchurched population is the largest mission field in the English-speaking world and the fifth largest globally.[9]

The entry into a post-Christian American society also becomes apparent as the influence of Christian practice has lessened in culture. For example,

---

activities it engendered varied somewhat from generation to generation, but for more than three centuries Protestants drew direction and inspiration from the vision of a Christian America." Handy, viii.

5   For the massive cultural shift of the 1960s in the Unites States, see § 2.1.1.
6   Martha Grace Reese, *Unbinding the Gospel: Real Life Evangelism* (St. Louis: Chalice Press, 2006), 25–27.
7   Putnam and Campbell, 122. They give this opinion based on the General Social Survey data between 1973 and 2010.
8   Ibid., 122.
9   Tom Clegg and Warren Bird, *Lost in America: How You and Your Church Can Impact the World Next Door* (Loveland: Group, 2001), 25.

a series of decisions by the Supreme Court were an acknowledgement that Christian practices would no longer receive state sanction. State-sponsored prayer in schools was banned in 1962, mandatory Bible reading in schools was forbidden in 1963, posting of the Ten Commandments in schools was found unconstitutional in 1980, and prayer by any clergy at an elementary or secondary school graduation was restricted in 1992. The main public and cultural institutions of the country no longer support Christianity. Contemporary American culture is much less receptive to Christian beliefs and ethics, and even has in many ways become hostile to Christianity.[10] Alan Hirsch, therefore, comments, "Even America, for so long a bastion of a distinct and vigorous form of cultural Christendom, is now experiencing a society that is increasingly moving away from that church's sphere of influence and becoming genuinely neo-pagan."[11] Christian faith is becoming marginalized.

Many scholars describe the current marginalization of faith as being in "exile."[12] Walter Brueggemann, for example, uses a biblical metaphor for understanding the current place of the church in American culture. Though the current situation does not involve physical exile, he believes that the similarity between Israel in the Babylonian exile and the current situation originates from the "loss of a structured, reliable world where treasured symbols of meaning are mocked and dismissed."[13] Like ancient Israel, the church finds itself in the situation where it does not fit in with its current surroundings. Similarly, Stanley Hauerwas and William Willimon state that "colony" is the apt designation for the church and "resident aliens" is the apt description for the identity of contemporary Christians.[14]

---

10   Compared to other generations, younger adults became more resistant and hostile to traditional Christianity. See Putnam and Campbell, 124–125.
11   Alan Hirsch, *The Forgotten Ways: Reactivating the Missional Church* (Grand Rapids: Brazos Press, 2006), 118.
12   See Walter Brueggemann, *Cadences of Home: Preaching among Exiles* (Louisville: Westminster John Knox Press, 1997); Erskine Clarke, *Exilic Preaching: Testimony for Christian Exiles in an Increasingly Hostile Culture* (Harrisburg: Trinity Press International, 1998); Michael Frost, *Exiles: Living Missionally in a Post-Christian Culture* (Peabody: Hendrickson Publishers, 2006); James Thompson, *The Church in Exile: God's Counterculture in a Non-Christian World* (Abilene: Leafwood Publishers, 2010).
13   Brueggemann, 2.
14   Stanley Hauerwas and William H. Willimon, *Resident Aliens: Life in the Christian Colony* (Nashville: Abingdon Press, 1989), 12.

In the midst of a post-Christian culture, the church is a countercultural community, and being a Christian means having an alternative way of identifying oneself relating to the dominant culture.

While it is clear that the current era is not identical with the first century, it is also true that the contemporary situation of the church cannot be considered completely different from the situation of the Thessalonian community. As discussed in chapter 3, the Thessalonian community also experienced marginalization and even hostile oppression from the surrounding pagan society. Despite the two millennia that separate them, both contexts assume the marginalization of faith and the dominant pagan culture. Timothy Keller describes the parallelism between Paul's era and our era thusly: "When Paul preached the gospel to the imperial elites, he called his message 'truthful and rational,' yet to the listeners he seemed out of his mind. Today again, what Christians think is true and reasonable now appears to be sheer madness to increasing numbers of the population."[15] N. T. Wright also makes a connection between Paul's pre-Christian context and the contemporary post-Christian context:

> There are all sorts of possibilities here for addressing the specific questions of the 1990s, and indeed the 2000s, and in doing so, discovering the relevance of parts of Paul formerly relegated to comparative obscurity. When, for instance, we confront the serious neo-paganism of the Western world, with its rampant materialism on the one hand and its 'new age' philosophies on the other, it is no bad time to remind ourselves that Paul's basic mission was to the pagans of his world, not to the Jews, and that he might just have something to say to contemporary paganism as well.[16]

We may find there is much to learn from Paul's preaching to the Thessalonian community in its pre-Christian, pagan context. Paul's preaching provides a model for contemporary preachers who work in a post-Christian, new pagan context.

---

15 Timothy Keller, *Preaching: Communicating Faith in an Age of Skepticism* (New York: Viking, 2015), 94.
16 N. T. Wright, *What Saint Paul Really Said* (Oxford: Lion, 1997), 22.

5.2. Essential Task of Preaching in a Post-Christian Culture: Community Formation

As previously explained in chapter 3, the main focus of Paul's preaching in 1 Thessalonians is to maintaining and reinforcing the newly born community in the dominant pagan society. Paul implements the process of community formation.

Community formation, Paul's fundamental task in preaching, contributes to a reconsideration of the listener-centered approach to preaching, especially since the development of the New Homiletic. As discussed in chapter 2, it is not an exaggeration to say that the "turn to the listener" is regarded as a catchphrase of the New Homiletic. O. Wesley Allen summarizes the listener-driven approach of the New Homiletic:

> The New Homiletic represented a turn to the hearer. Earlier homiletical works usually focused on how the preacher builds an argument. The New Homiletic focused instead on how people in the pew listen, how they experience spoken language. Instead of constructing language simply to serve the content, you play with language to invite hearers to *experience* something specific.[17]

Listener-oriented approach of the New Homiletic resulted in a paradigm shift in contemporary homiletics, which paved the way for many homileticians to offer abundant methods to appeal to the listener. It also led to a remarkable development in the field of homiletics. However, it is undeniable that the attention to the listener is restricted since the new homileticians have primarily focused on appeal to the individual listener and tended to view the listeners simply as individuals rather than as a part of a community of faith.[18] Homileticians have been little concerned with the communal identity of the listeners and the larger context of preaching. Consequently, their emphasis on the performative dimension of text and eventfulness of preaching – the New Homiletic's important contribution to contemporary homiletics – is finally limited to the individual level.[19] Charles Campbell

---

17 O. Wesley Allen, "Introduction: The Pillars of the New Homiletic," in *The Renewed Homiletic*, ed. O. Wesley Allen (Minneapolis: Fortress Press, 2010), 8. Italics original.
18 See § 2.3.4.
19 Robert Reid, Jeffery Bullock, and David Fleer explain the essential change triggered by the New Homiletic: "The New Homiletic appears more interested in what the sermon may do and even undo in the experience of the receiving audience, than pointedly

thus criticizes, "The problem is that up until now narrative homiletics has provided no resources for thinking carefully about the ways preaching contributes to the upbuilding of the church – the formation of the people of God – *beyond* the individual hearer."[20] The text wants something to happen as the new homileticians assert, but the something that the text wants is not just to provide an experiential event to appeal to individual listeners. The text also works to shape a community of faith. David Kelsey writes that the text is "taken as *doing* something that decisively shapes the community's identity."[21] Therefore, biblical preaching must be involved in the task that deals with more than personal experience but rather incorporates the formation of the Christian community. Contrary to the narrow listener-oriented approach of the New Homiletic, Paul's preaching moves the view of the listener and the task of preaching toward a communal direction. Directed by Paul's preaching, the task of preachers is regarded not only as delivery of an experience to individual listeners, but also that of the formation of community.

Paul's call for attention to preaching for community formation is appropriate to the situation of the church in a post-Christian culture. In Christendom, churches were communities into which people were born. The church was a part of the inherited order of things and the only legitimate source of forming religious identity. In a post-Christian culture, however, one's religion is regarded as a matter of preference instead of as a fixed characteristic. People no longer adopt the given religious identity; instead, they make their own religious choices.[22] Eddie Gibbs and Ryan Bolger thus write, "Religion

---

    conveying content." David Reid, Stephen Bullock, and Jeffrey Fleer, "Preaching as the Creation of an Experience: The Not-So-Rational Revolution of the New Homileitc," *The Journal of Communication and Religion* 18, no. 1 (1995): 1. For more specific details, see § 2.2.2. On critique against individualistic orientation of the New Homiletic, see § 2.3.4.

20 Charles L. Campbell, *Preaching Jesus: New Directions for Homiletics in Hans Frei's Postliberal Theology* (Grand Rapids: W. B. Eerdmans Pub., 1997), 144. Italics original. Campbell sees so-called narrative homiletics as tied directly to the New Homiletic. For similar positions, see John C. Holbert, "Toward a Story Homiletic: History and Prospects," *Journal for Preachers* 33, no. 3 (2000): 16; James Thompson, *Preaching Like Paul: Homiletical Wisdom for Today* (Louisville: Westminster John Knox Press, 2001), 2–14.

21 David H. Kelsey, *The Uses of Scripture in Recent Theology* (Philadelphia: Fortress Press, 1975), 208. Italics original.

22 Charles Taylor argues that a society is secular insofar as belief in God is understood to be one option among others. He notes that the shift to secularity, which he refers to

is now the burden of the solitary individual. He or she must work out his or her own solutions to the spiritual quest."[23] Individuals are allowed and even encouraged to pursue their religious identity, and are able to acquire religious or spiritual resources even outside of churches. In this state of religious diversity and flux, therefore, churches must provide a concrete and resilient religious identity for their congregations and must be created and maintained like other voluntary organizations. According to David Lose, the fact that most mainline churches in North America lose their congregations indicates that they have failed to compete against other institutions and associations that could provide potential resources for religious identity.[24] For this reason, it is significant and timely to stress that a church is much more than an inherited reception that can only be created via active construction. Christian churches are placed to accentuate the task of community formation for their survival and prosperity in a post-Christian culture.

The task of community formation is also a key factor in reaching emerging generations. Robert Putnam describes the weakening community bonds of the twenty-first century in the United States as "Bowling Alone." In his book of the same title, Putnam writes, "Given population growth, more Americans are bowling than ever before, but *league bowling* has plummeted in the last ten to fifteen years."[25] Based on extensive data that reveal Americans' behavior, he shows that civil society is breaking down as Americans become more alienated and disconnected from their families, neighbors, and communities. Especially, he concludes that the younger generations tend to feel more disconnection to communities.[26] However, this does not mean that the new generations, which are less embedded in communities, do not need community bonds. Jimmy Long gives an account of the new generations: Generation X and Millennials

---

as "secular$_3$," indicates a "move from a society where belief in God in unchallenged and indeed, unproblematic, to one in which it is understood to be one option among others, and frequently not the easiest to embrace." Charles Taylor, *A Secular Age* (Cambridge: Harvard University Press, 2007), 3.

23 Eddie Gibbs and Ryan K. Bolger, *Emerging Churches: Creating Christian Community in Postmodern Cultures* (Grand Rapids: Baker Academic, 2005), 23.

24 David J. Lose, *Preaching at the Crossroads: How the World – and Our Preaching – Is Changing* (Minneapolis: Fortress Press, 2013), 99–100.

25 Robert D. Putnam, *Bowling Alone: The Collapse and Revival of American Community* (New York: Simon & Schuster, 2010), 112. Italics original.

26 Ibid., 265–266.

> While my generation [Baby Boomers] was obsessed by the search for freedom, these generations are searching for roots, stability, order and identity. [...] These generations' legacy to our culture just may be a turning of the tide away from individualism toward community, something no generation has been able to do in the last four hundred years.[27]

The shift in the forms of radical individualism, broken families, and disconnection to civic communities has led them to long for a higher degree of human relationship and to desire participation in a community.[28] In this regard, Graham Johnston writes, "As society breaks down people become more alienated from one another, the church is uniquely poised to address the need for community. In fact, today's churches should supply not only a theological context for belief but also a sociological one."[29] It is no coincidence that a new stream of church ministry emerged in the context of the emerging generations, which emphasizes forming and belonging to a community. The general expectation of how people enter into a Christian community has been to believe first, then choose to belong followed by participation in the behaviors of the faith. Today's churches, however, have moved mainly from "believing before belonging" to "belonging before believing."[30] Alister McGrath summarizes the new emphasis among practitioners: "Where the rationality of European churches often seemed to rest on Descartes's celebrated (if enigmatic) axiom 'I think, therefore I am', such churches rest their appeal on a totally different axiom – 'I belong, and therefore I am'."[31] Therefore, we should ask how our preaching will actually cultivate community. Community formation that Paul's

---

27 Jimmy Long, *Emerging Hope: A Strategy for Reaching the Postmodern Generations* (Downers Grove: InterVarsity Press, 2004), 52. According to Long, the boomers were born between 1946 and 1964, the Gen Xers between 1964 and 1984, and the Millennials between 1984 and 2000. See Ibid., 20.

28 Electronic ties are more important to Gen Xers than the previous generations. However, cyber-friends are not enough for the young generation as a source of community. See Putnam, 275.

29 Graham Johnston, *Preaching to a Postmodern World: A Guide to Reaching Twenty-First-Century Listeners* (Grand Rapids: Baker Books, 2001), 124.

30 Stuart Murray, *Church after Christendom* (Milton Keynes: Paternoster, 2004), 36–38. Instead of the centuries old approach of believing, behaving, and belonging, Diana Butler Bass proposes the reversed order: belonging, behaving, and believing. See Diana Butler Bass, *Christianity after Religion: The End of Church and the Birth of a New Spiritual Awakening* (New York: Harper One, 2013), 103–214.

31 Alister E. McGrath, *The Future of Christianity* (Oxford: Blackwell, 2002), 59.

preaching reminds us must a significant portion of church ministry in the contemporary culture.

To accomplish the task of community formation, as argued in chapter 4, Paul in his preaching concentrates on creating a collective identity of the Thessalonian community different from the surrounding culture by using symbolic resources as boundaries. Building and maintaining symbolic boundaries between who is in and who is out of the community is the indispensable process of Paul's preaching to strengthen the collective identity that sustains the community.

With fresh understanding of the church in relation to the contemporary context of a post-Christian culture, some scholars and practitioners have pioneered an innovative approach to ministry, "missional church."[32] They understand the church as a countercultural community and seek to cultivate it in their own contexts as mission fields. Some of them argue that we move from bounded-set thinking to centered-set thinking in our understanding of structure and formation of the church. According to them, involvement in the bounded-set churches is predicated on adherence to their standards and the mechanism determines who is in and who is out. Centered-set thinking, however, is more fluid and members in the centered-set churches are regarded as moving toward the center of the community. Michael Frost and Alan Hirsch claim the legitimacy of centered-set thinking:

> Rather than seeing people as Christian or non-Christian, as in or out, we would see people by their degree of distance from the center, Christ. In this way, the missional-incarnational church sees people as Christian and not-yet-Christian. It acknowledges the contribution of not-yet-Christian to Christian community and values the contribution of all people. Jesus' faith community was clearly a centered set, with him at the center.[33]

Accepting others is imperative to a Christian community, as Frost and Hirsch suggest. Their idea that everyone is potentially a part of the community in a broad sense also deserves much attention. Yet, it is essential to note that community formation requires a certain form of boundary formation, just Paul did in his preaching for the Thessalonian community. If

---

32   For a brief discussion about the paradigm shift of the missional church, see Ed Stetzer and David Putman, *Breaking the Missional Code: Your Church Can Become a Missionary in Your Community* (Nashville: Broadman & Holman, 2006), 59–71.

33   Michael Frost and Alan Hirsch, *The Shaping of Things to Come: Innovation and Mission for the 21st-Century Church* (Grand Rapids: Baker Books, 2013), 68.

the nature of community is countercultural, what is more necessary is the creation and maintenance of boundaries. Alan Roxburgh, one of the proponents for the missional church, emphasizes that it is not enough to build only a centered-set community while presenting a bigger picture of the community structure. The community includes not only a congregation as a centered set but also a covenant community consisting of core members as a bounded set. He writes,

> A centered set [...] is not a sufficient understanding of the church: it is hardly the church as the sign, foretaste, agent, and instrument of the reign of God. But congregation as centered set begins to lay out a framework for forming congregations into missional communities. Missional communities are more than centered-set congregations. A pilgrim, covenant people require an alternative way of life. This calls for bounded-set identity.[34]

In a post-Christian culture, a Christian community must have some degree of countercultural identity. Stanley Hauerwas and William Willimon thus declare, "The call to be part of the gospel is a joyful call to be adopted by an alien people, to join a countercultural phenomenon, a new *polis* called church."[35] Timothy Keller writes in more detail:

> For centuries in the West, churches could limit themselves to specifically "religious" concerns and function as loose fellowship within a wider semi-Christian culture. Now, however, becoming a Christian involves a much more radical break with the surrounding non-Christian culture. The church can no longer be an association or a club but is a "thick" alternate human society in which relationships are strong and deep – and in which sex and family, wealth and possessions, racial identity and power, are all used and practiced in godly and distinct ways.[36]

Christian communities will be able to exist only if they are different from the surrounding culture. Without boundaries, the Christian communities cannot survive in the middle of a non-Christian context. The issue is not whether there are boundaries or not; it is what kind of boundaries and how

---

34 Alan J. Roxburgh, "Missional Leadership: Equipping God's People for Mission," in *Missional Church: A Vision for the Sending of the Church in North America*, ed. Darrell L. Guder (Grand Rapids: W. B. Eerdmans Pub., 1998), 207.
35 Hauerwas and Willimon, 30. Italics original.
36 Timothy Keller, *Center Church: Doing Balanced, Gospel-Centered Ministry in Your City* (Grand Rapids: Zondervan, 2012) 273.

they should be created and maintained.[37] Therefore, Paul's preaching to create boundaries provides a required model for contemporary preachers who face the task of forming Christian communities in a post-Christian culture.

5.3. Preaching Methods for Community Formation

5.3.1. To Preach Shared Narratives

This study has demonstrated that Paul in his preaching uses the elements of narratives to form a community. Paul intends the narratives to function as symbolic boundaries to shape communal identity from the Thessalonian converts and thus to shape and sustain the community of faith. Though contemporary homileticians have understood the prime function of narratives as facilitating the individual listener to experience a sermonic event,[38] Paul's preaching shows that narratives play a crucial role in community formation.

An essential narrative element that Paul uses for forming a community is the kerygmatic narrative. This teaches contemporary preachers that they should preach the kerygmatic narrative repeatedly. Preaching the kerygmatic narrative cannot be restricted to a method to evangelism for unbelievers. C. H. Dodd in *The Apostolic Preaching and Its Development* has claimed that the early church distinguished sharply between preaching

---

37   According to Miroslav Volf, Christian "boundaries must be permeable." He writes, "Without boundaries, groups lose identity and abdicate any possibility of social impact. But the boundaries of Christian communities cannot be the impenetrable walls of tall fortresses." Miroslav Volf, *A Public Faith, How Followers of Christ Should Serve the Common Good* (Grand Rapids: Brazos Press, 2011) 96. Similarly, Michael Gorman describes Paul's believing communities as "exclusivist-inclusivist" communities. He explains, "These communities exclude allegiance to every other so-called lord or god, but include people of all stations in life who confess and live Jesus as Lord, thus challenging the values of the day by their very existence." Michael J. Gorman, *Cruciformity: Paul's Narrative Spirituality of the Cross* (Grand Rapids: W. B. Eerdmans Pub., 2001), 366.
38   For a thorough analysis on contemporary narrative homiletics, see Campbell, 117–165. Also see § 2.2.3.

in a missionary setting and teaching in an established church. He writes, "The New Testament writers draw a clear distinction between preaching and teaching. [...] Teaching (*didaskein*) is in a large majority of cases ethical instruction. [...] Preaching, on other hand, is public proclamation of Christianity to the non-Christian world."[39]

Though Dodd's distinction between preaching and teaching, between *kerygma* and *didache*, has widely influenced contemporary homiletics,[40] it is also true that a considerable number of scholars have raised the question of whether the early church sharply separated preaching from teaching.[41] Moreover, it should be pointed out that the rigid distinction between preaching and teaching is not appropriate to the current situation of the church. In a culture that is in transition to post-Christianity, preachers can no longer assume that the listeners, just because they are in the pew, are familiar with the gospel story. Even though they might know it, it is uncertain that they hold established Christian beliefs and values with their understanding and reception of the gospel. In a post-Christian culture, Craig Loscalzo writes, "The great narratives of Judeo-Christian belief, the pivotal stories of the Bible's characters, the events of the life and ministry of Jesus Christ either are not known or do not carry the meaning-making significance they did for previous generations."[42] Preachers may expect challenge of preaching to congregations with conflicting worldviews and identities shaped by different stories.[43] In a matrix of rival stories, preaching must do more than reflect the stories of the listeners; preaching must emanate the gospel story. Preaching, then, concentrates on the formation

---

39 C. H. Dodd, *The Apostolic Preaching and Its Developments* (New York: Harper, 1964), 7.
40 David Buttrick writes, "From the 1940s until the 1990s, scarcely a book on homiletics appeared that did not refer to Dodd's *The Apostolic Preaching* and the idea of a primitive *kerygma*." David Buttrick, "Proclamation," in *Concise Encyclopedia of Preaching*, eds. William H. Willimon and Richard Lischer (Louisville: Westminster John Knox Press, 1995), 385.
41 Among others, see Victor Paul Furnish, *Theology and Ethics in Paul* (Nashville: Abingdon Press, 1968), 106–107.
42 Craig A. Loscalzo, *Apologetic Preaching: Proclaiming Christ to a Postmodern World* (Downers Grove: InterVarsity Press, 2000), 24.
43 Timothy Keller lists five main narratives which greatly influence Christian believers in late-modern times. See Keller, *Preaching: Communicating Faith in an Age of Skepticism*, 129–133. According to Keller, these narratives "are so pervasive, and felt to be so self-evident, that they are not visible as beliefs to those who hold them." Ibid., 127.

of the Christian community, as people find the identity in the gospel story instead of in the myriad of competing stories.

Walter Brueggemann in *Biblical Perspectives on Evangelism* widens the scope of evangelism. Outsiders are naturally the most obvious constituency for evangelism. However, he notes that there are many insiders who suffer from "amnesia" in the contemporary church. Those insiders who do not remember the gospel story are the other constituency for evangelism.[44] Therefore, there is no denying that one of the essential duties of contemporary preachers is to summon the insiders from amnesia to memory, which is only available through continuous preaching of the kerygmatic narrative following Paul's example of preaching.

It is worth noting that the kerygmatic narrative Paul incorporates into his preaching reflects the grand narrative of God's redemptive deeds.[45] Paul's understanding of the kerygmatic narrative leads preachers to see the necessity of understanding and preaching the big picture of the coherent narrative through the whole Bible, which has been sometimes ignored in the discussions about the narrative of the homiletical circle. Contemporary narrative homiletics is primarily concerned with narrative as a form that tends to shape a sermon,[46] taking little interest in the larger narrative of the Bible. In this regard, Charles Campbell proposes a new direction for narrative preaching: "Narrative preaching in this sense involves, in Richard Hays's terms, sermons shaped not simplistically by narrative forms, but by a deep narrative logic."[47] The grand narrative of the Bible, whatever it is called, should be seriously considered to overcome the limitations of contemporary narrative preaching.

The knowledge of the structure of God's grand story throughout the whole Bible is also essential for all preachers who want to preach the Bible faithfully. Interpretation of the Bible requires us not only to determine what a text means in its own context but also to see how the text functions in its broader contexts, even in the entire scope of Scripture. Sydney Greidanus claims, "A holistic interpretation of biblical texts demands further that

---

44 Walter Brueggemann, *Biblical Perspectives on Evangelism: Living in a Three-Storied Universe* (Nashville: Abingdon Press, 1993), 90.
45 See § 4.2.1.
46 See § 2.2.3.
47 Charles L. Campbell, "Apocalypse Now," in *Narrative Reading, Narrative Preaching: Reuniting New Testament Interpretation and Proclamation*, eds. Joel B. Green and Michael Pasquarello (Grand Rapids: Baker Academic, 2003), 165–166.

the interpreter see the message of the text not only in its immediate historical-cultural context but also in its broadest possible context, that is, Scripture's teaching regarding history as a whole."[48] Similarly, Walter Kaiser also declares that good exegesis considers the whole context, whether the context is immediate, sectional, within in a book, or canonical.[49] The holistic context of the Bible, the grand narrative, is frequently overlooked. There is no doubt, however, preachers need to interpret and preach a text with considerable understanding of the grand narrative that encompasses each individual text of the Bible.[50]

In addition to the kerygmatic narrative, Paul in his preaching weaves local narratives mostly related to the context of his initial ministry for the community formation. Paul's emphasis on preaching local narratives shows contemporary preachers the need for preaching the stories born of pastoral ministry for forming a community of faith. The local stories, which are only known within the community, establish the communal identity contributing to the community formation. The success of telling our story is a success of creating our community. Therefore, preachers who desire to form a community need to preach local narratives created in the pastoral context.

Paul's preaching of the local narratives reminds preachers of the close connection between preaching and pastoral ministry often forgotten in the enthusiasm about the latest "how to" ideas for satisfying the desire to be effective and relevant.[51] It is undeniable that contemporary homiletics, especially the New Homiletic, has endeavored to devise new techniques or strategies for effective communication and thus turned the attention of

---

48 Sidney Greidanus, *The Modern Preacher and the Ancient Text: Interpreting and Preaching Biblical Literature* (Grand Rapids: W. B. Eerdmans Pub., 1988), 94–95.

49 Walter C. Kaiser, *Toward an Exegetical Theology: Biblical Exegesis for Preaching and Teaching* (Grand Rapids: Baker Book House, 1981), 69–85.

50 In the circle of expository preaching, homiletical methods that reflect the understanding of the redemptive narrative throughout the Bible have been produced. See Bryan Chapell, *Christ-Centered Preaching: Redeeming the Expository Sermon* (Grand Rapids: Baker Academic, 2005); Graeme Goldsworthy, *Preaching the Whole Bible as Christian Scripture: The Application of Biblical Theology to Expository Preaching* (Grand Rapids: W. B. Eerdmans Pub., 2000); Sidney Greidanus, *Preaching Christ from the Old Testament: A Contemporary Hermeneutical Method* (Grand Rapids: W. B. Eerdmans Pub., 1999).

51 Michael Pasquarello, *Sacred Rhetoric: Preaching as a Theological and Pastoral Practice of the Church* (Grand Rapids: W. B. Eerdmans Pub., 2005), 6–9.

preachers to technical wisdom for preaching.[52] So long as preaching is primarily regarded as a skill for effective communication, it is not easy to conceive of the profound relationship between preaching and pastoral ministry, which distinguishes preaching radically from other kinds of communication. However, it should not be forgotten that preaching in most cases is enacted in the context of pastoral ministry and is in many significant ways influenced by the context.

For such a reason, Haddon Robinson categorizes three different worlds in which preachers must be involved in. He adds "the particular world in which we are called to preach"[53] on the two-world categorization found in much homiletical literature: the world of the Bible and the modern world. He comments on the particular world:

> A church has a postal code and stands near Fifth and Main in some town or city. The profound issues of the Bible and the ethical, philosophical questions of our times assume different shapes in rural villages, in middle-class communities, or in the ghettos of crowded cities. Ultimately we do not address everyone; we speak to a particular people and call them by name.[54]

The pastoral context gives the preacher rigorous understanding of the congregation. It is natural that the understanding of the listeners permits the preacher to preach with a power and effectiveness unavailable to the itinerant speaker, regardless of his or her skill or reputation.

Though a devaluation of the pastoral context in preaching is at work in television and internet preaching, it cannot be underestimated that the preaching ministry of local pastors who know their congregations through a pastoral relationship has huge advantages. It is not an exaggeration to say that great preaching and great preachers are local; that is, they arise out of pastoral contexts. Phillips Brooks writes,

> It is remarkable how many of the great preachers of the world are inseparably associated with the places where their work was done, where perhaps all their life was lived. In many cases their place has passed into their name as if it were a true part of themselves. Chrysostom of Constantinople, Augustine of Hippo, Savonarola of Florence, Baxter of Kidderminster, Arnold of Rugby, Robertson of Brighton, Chalmers of Glasgow [...][55]

---

52   See § 2.3.3.
53   Haddon W. Robinson, *Biblical Preaching: The Development and Delivery of Expository Messages* (Grand Rapids: Baker Academic, 2001), 73.
54   Ibid., 74.
55   Phillips Brooks, *Lectures on Preaching* (New York: E.P. Dutton, 1877), 189.

The preaching ministry thrives when it is deeply embedded in local soil from the pastoral context. Needless to say, it is also true that preaching intimately, by connecting to the local context, contributes to the formation of local communities of faith, which is why Paul incorporates the local narratives into his preaching.

Paul's local narratives include his own stories indicating his character and behavior. This requires preachers to pay attention to the integrity of the preacher, which has been virtually ignored in contemporary homiletics where the desire for effective communication diverts attention from the preacher to the use of proper technique.[56] The character of the preacher, however, was preeminent in previous epochs of church history and cannot be ignored for effective preaching. Phillips Brooks has given a widely quoted definition of preaching as "truth through personality." He writes, "Preaching is the communication of truth by men to men. It has in it two essential elements, truth and personality."[57] If preaching cannot be separated from the personality of the preacher, then the integrity and trustworthiness of the preacher must be the condition for effective preaching. Haddon Robison aptly describes this point: "Our listeners know us, trust us, and see in us lives that largely back up what we preach. That example accomplishes more than more homiletical skills ever can."[58] Only if the truth is embodied in the personal narrative of the preacher will the listeners trust the message of the preacher.

It is necessary to emphasize that most of the narratives in Paul's preaching, both the kerygmatic and the local, were not new to the listeners and had already been shared in the Thessalonian community. A considerable portion of Paul's preaching to the Thessalonians is a repetition of what they already knew, which means that an important purpose of Paul's preaching was to remind (*anamnesis*). The ability to remind someone about the past

---

56 Richard Lischer, "Before Technique: Preaching and Personal Formation," *Dialog* 29, no. 3 (1990): 178.
57 Brooks, 5. Susan Hedahl comments on Brooks's definition: "Brooks's statement echoed through homiletical literature and instruction for decades following. His statement signaled the growing preoccupation with issues of ethos that continues today – often at the expense of the listeners and the text." Susan K. Hedahl, "Character," in *Concise Encyclopedia of Preaching*, eds. William H. Willimon and Richard Lischer (Louisville: Westminster John Knox Press, 1995), 67.
58 Haddon W. Robinson, "Competing with the Communication Kings," in *Making a Difference in Preaching: Haddon Robinson on Biblical Preaching*, ed. Scott M. Gibson (Grand Rapids: Baker Books, 1999), 112.

does not seem to be a skill that is nurtured well among modern people, including preachers. In this age of overflowing information, massive quantity of fragmented information is poured on us via various forms of media, which causes us to not reflect on the information nor remember it. Moreover, preachers are under the subtle pressure that their sermons must fulfill the listeners' expectations, usually formed by the entertainment culture; hence, the preachers attempt to avoid boring the listeners by avoiding predictability and repetition. James Thompson describes the current situation:

> Just as predictability ultimately dooms the best television serial, we also sense that it reduces our capacity to maintain the vitality of the congregation. Consequently, those of us who preach attempt at all costs to avoid repetition. We hesitate to preach on time-honored texts or to repeat ourselves or what others have said before, and we measure the quality of preaching by its creativity and originality.[59]

The assumption is evidently that the effectiveness and interest of preaching rely on its newness, on the preacher delivering to the listeners something they have never heard. Nevertheless, preaching is often an exercise in reminding and remembering. The Scripture itself requires one to remember. Many biblical authors wanted their hearers to be gripped and formed by the past. Much of the Pentateuchal discourses and the book of Psalms is composed in the "rhetoric of recall," to represent God's saving story in such a way that the listeners affirm it as a present reality in their own lives.[60] The early sermons in the book of Acts (2:14–36; 3:12–26; 4:8–12; 5:29–32; 7:2–53) are based on the author's attempt to remind his audience about the memory of how God has acted in history and has acted in Christ to save the world.[61] From the outset, the church also has placed preaching in the context of worship in which God's people celebrate and remember His actions in history on their behalf.[62] Commenting on *First Apology of Justin Martyr*, one of the earliest accounts of the church at worship on Sunday, William Willimon describes an important pattern of the early church's Sunday gatherings: "*The church remembers* by encountering the 'writing' – the

---

59 Thompson, *Preaching Like Paul: Homiletical Wisdom for Today*, 128.
60 David L. Bartlett, "Sermon," in *Concise Encyclopedia of Preaching*, eds. William H. Willimon and Richard Lischer (Louisville: Westminster John Knox Press, 1995), 434.
61 Robert Webber, *Ancient-Future Worship: Proclaiming and Enacting God's Narrative* (Grand Rapids: Baker Books, 2008), 47.
62 On the issues with preaching in the context of worship, see David M. Greenhaw and Ronald J. Allen, *Preaching in the Context of Worship* (St. Louis: Chalice Press, 2000).

Scriptures that evoke, form, and critique the church."[63] By preaching the Scripture, the church remembers what she should remember. Preaching calls for the listeners to remember the saving acts of God to that they can build awareness of identity. Though reputation may not be considered a virtue in contemporary homiletics, Paul's preaching shows that a great need exists today to rediscover the reminding function of preaching, especially for community formation.

5.3.2. To Preach Ethical Norms

This study has shown that Paul does not hesitate to preach ethical norms to the Thessalonian community. Contemporary homiletics, influenced especially by the New Homiletic, has encouraged preachers to avoid ethical demands for change in the lives of their listeners, warning that such a deed may appear authoritarian.[64] Preachers are often advised not to be concerned about direct guidance or application. This tendency has been reinforced among homileticians and practitioners in the postmodern context where authority is suspect and people do not trust those in power. However, the Bible cannot be preached without authority because it requires our obedience for a new way of life. Eugene Peterson writes, "The most important question we ask of this text is not, 'What does this mean?' but 'What can I obey?'"[65] Preaching the Bible is not just for the sake of learning information but for obeying and following Jesus Christ. Brian Chapell states, "Biblical preaching moves from exegetical commentary and doctrinal exposition to life instruction. Such preaching exhorts as well as expounds because it recognizes that Scripture's own goal is not merely to share information about God but to conform his people to the likeness of Jesus Christ."[66] Preaching must press on with the call to the Christian way of life. Of course, preachers certainly need to avoid the trap of legalism. Salvation cannot be earned by following the Christian way of life. Instead, Christian behavior is an inevitable result of the gospel. However,

---

63 William H. Willimon, *Pastor: The Theology and Practice of Ordained Ministry* (Nashville: Abingdon Press, 2002), 77. Italics original.
64 See § 2.2.1.
65 Eugene H. Peterson, *Eat This Book: A Conversation in the Art of Spiritual Reading* (Grand Rapids: W. B. Eerdmans Pub., 2006), 71.
66 Chapell, 54.

this does not mean that those who receive the gospel automatically know how to live as a mature Christian. As Paul preached, they need to be taught the way they must live as Christ's disciples. John Stott thus writes, "To teach the standards of moral conduct which adorn the gospel is neither legalism nor pharisaism but plain apostolic Christianity."[67] Preaching should offer the occasion to look at ethical issues and offer ethical guidelines, which is obviously seen in Paul's preaching.

Preaching ethical norms to promote Christian life should be more emphasized in a post-Christian culture where there is no longer a common behavior fully based on Christian principles and values. Preachers must recognize that the current listeners do not arise from a world determined by a common understanding of Christian morality. In a culture that cannot be counted on to form the Christian way of life, preaching should move the listeners beyond a sense of feeling guilty to a point of decisive ethical actions that meet Christian standards.

It should be emphasized that Paul's purpose for preaching the ethical norms is related not only to the cultivation of individual morality for the converts but also to the social function for contributing to community formation. Victor Paul Furnish has aptly summarized Paul's ethics for community formation:

> The believer's life and action are always in, with, and for "the brethren" in Christ. For him, moral action is never a matter of an isolated actor choosing from among a variety of abstract ideals on the basis of how inherently "good" or "evil" each may be. Instead, it is always a matter of choosing and doing what is good for the brother and what will upbuild the whole community of brethren.[68]

For Paul, ethical norms were part of an active formation process wherein his believing communities were shaped.[69] Paul's emphasis on the social

---

67 John R. W. Stott, *Between Two Worlds* (Grand Rapids: W. B. Eerdmans Pub., 1994), 158.
68 Victor Paul Furnish, *Theology and Ethics in Paul* (Nashville: Abingdon Press, 1968), 233.
69 Wayne Meeks describes the role of Christian morality, including Paul's, as a device for a socialization process wherein believing communities were formed: "My thesis is that we cannot begin to understand that process of moral formation until we see that it is inextricable from the process by which distinctive communities were taking shape. Making morals means making community." Wayne A. Meeks, *The Origins of Christian Morality: The First Two Centuries* (New Heaven: Yale University Press, 1993), 5.

function of ethical norms reminds us that preachers who desire community formation should make their listeners ask not just "What should *I* do?" but "What should *we* do?"[70] Christians cannot exist in isolation from each other. Each is a part of another, all living together in a community. To be Christian corporately in a community is a crucial task for all Christians.[71] Therefore, preaching needs to include the establishment of concrete expectations for those who live in a community. If preaching establishes communal ethical norms, then a community is properly established. It is true that the establishment of communal norms is not an easy undertaking for the preacher in a culture focusing that values individual freedom. For the listeners who are shaped by the individualistic culture and the prime emphasis on individual rights, the imperative mood may sound legalistic and communal norms seem to inhibit their freedom. George Lindbeck writes,

> The suggestion that communities have the right to insist on standards of belief and practice as conditions of membership is experienced as an intolerable infringement of the liberty of the self. This reaction is intensified by the growing contradiction between the traditional standards and the prevailing values of the wider society as communicated by education, the mass media, and personal contacts.[72]

Though preaching to establish communal norms is likely to be unwelcome, preaching for community formation is to challenge the listeners to choose an ethical decision based on the communal norms. Preaching for community formation must be a place to teach and encourage shared rules and practices to the listeners, so that those who know and act on shared rules and practices can become a part of the community.[73] In this regard,

---

70 Richard Hays, *The Moral Vision of the New Testament: A Contemporary Introduction to New Testament Ethics* (San Francisco: Harper, 1996), 197. Italics original.
71 For Christian ethics, Stanley Grenz writes, "We live as individuals before a holy God, and we are individually responsible to this God. But the biblical ethic does not address the individual in isolation. Instead, knowing that we constantly live in social contexts, we can only speak to persons-in-relationship. The biblical writers call us to live as God's people in all our relationships, and as a result, the Christian ethic is never merely a 'personal' but always also a 'social' ethic." Stanley J. Grenz, *The Moral Quest: Foundations of Christian ethics* (Downers Grove: IVP Academic, 1997), 264.
72 George A. Lindbeck, *The Nature of Doctrine: Religion and Theology in a Postliberal Age* (Philadelphia: Westminster Press, 1984), 77.
73 David Gushee and Glen Stassen suggest that Christian communities could play a critical role as pioneering communities helping to correct the autonomous individualism that disintegrates our society. They argue, "So long as churches are merely associations of autonomous individuals and not pioneering communities, we will be

Walter Brueggemann writes, "The preacher is cast in a social role as voice of normativeness, in a society bereft of norms."[74] When the preacher does not neglect the social role in preaching in a community, the community is truly formed and enhanced.

5.4. Conclusion

Exact parallels between Paul's era and the present times have not been assumed; sufficient congruities between Paul's pre-Christian context and the current post-Christian context are enough to enable Paul's preaching to serve as a model for contemporary preaching. As seen in Paul's preaching, the essential task of contemporary preaching is also community formation. The community formation is completed by creating boundaries for the communal identity distinguished from the surrounding post-Christian culture. For the function of boundaries, the preacher should preach both the kerygmatic and the local narratives, and establish communal ethical norms. If the preaching enables post-Christian listeners, who do not know what they believe and how they behave, to find their identity in the shared narratives and communal norms, then a community that is internally cohesive and externally distinct can be formed. Therefore, the preacher who desires community formation in a post-Christian culture should preach the shared narratives and the communal norms.

---

weak puffs of air against the winds of fragmentation. [...] To become such communities, churches need *shared practices* that transform social experiences, that form and transform people morally, that provide a meaningful sense of membership, and that support critical teaching of the difference between obedience to the subtle powers and authorities of our society and obedience to the rule of God." David P. Gushee and Glen H. Stassen, *Kingdom Ethics: Following Jesus in Contemporary Context* (Grand Rapids: W. B. Eerdmans Pub., 2016), 205. Italics original.

74 Walter Brueggemann, *The Word Militant: Preaching a Decentering Word* (Minneapolis: Fortress Press, 2010), 90.

Chapter Six
Conclusion

6.1. Summary of the Findings

The main objective of this study has been to explore Paul's preaching for community formation in 1 Thessalonians as an alternative to contemporary homiletics, particularly the New Homiletic. Chapter 1, as the introduction of the study, explained the necessity for and the structure of the study. It also provided evidence of correlation between Paul's letters and his preaching, justifying this homiletical study on Paul's preaching in 1 Thessalonians. Paul's letters, written according to the first-century letter-writing protocol shaped by the orally oriented culture, much reflect Paul's oral communication and preaching style. Moreover, Paul's letters were written primarily for the communities of faith, which means that Paul intended the letters to function as a substitute for his presence and preaching. Paul's letters provide unbroken continuity in his preaching.

Chapter 2 described and evaluated the New Homiletic, which has had enduring consequences for the contemporary homiletical field, especially in North America. The chapter first described the essential background features that incubated the New Homiletic. The background context connects the cultural situation of the 1960s, dissatisfaction with traditional preaching, and the new hermeneutic. Furthermore, the chapter identified the common characteristics of the New Homiletic by analyzing the homiletical theories of main figures of the homiletical approach: the elevation of the listener's role, experience as the primary purpose of preaching, and attention to alternative sermon forms. By presenting a critique of the common features of the New Homiletic, the chapter argued that the New Homiletic has an inherently individualistic orientation, which neglects the cooperative identity of listener in the community. This criticism in turn resulted in a search for an alternative approach to preaching for community formation.

Chapter 3 explored one of the most important intentions of Paul's preaching in 1 Thessalonians: to maintain and solidify the young believing community in the face of challenges by the larger pagan society. Thessalonica was a pagan city where cults encompassed all spheres of life. In this context, the fledgling Christ-following community, primarily composed of former pagans, experienced conflicts with pagan compatriots and pressures from the larger pagan society, due to their sudden disapproval of certain cultic practices. The chapter showed that, in this critical situation in which the young community could have been damaged, Paul attempts to strengthen the process of community formation and its continuous well-being.

Chapter 4 explained in depth Paul's preaching for community formation in 1 Thessalonians, which is the core subject of this study. To provide the necessary background, the sociological concept of symbolic boundaries was introduced. By clearly drawing a line between insiders and outsiders, symbolic boundaries provide the members of a community with a collective identity and distinguish them from other groups. Doing so also gives a community a sense of distinctiveness or superiority. The creation of the boundary is absolutely indispensable to the formation of a community. The chapter also showed that Paul in his preaching of 1 Thessalonians used three symbolic resources to create boundaries for the Thessalonian community: the kerygmatic narrative, local narratives, and ethical norms. The three resources functioned as symbolic boundaries to aid the converts in deriving a communal identity and strengthening the distinction between them and the larger society. Paul's preaching of the kerygmatic narrative, the local narratives, and the ethical norms contributed to the formation of Thessalonica's believing community that was internally cohesive and externally distinct.

Chapter 5 examined the homiletical implications of Paul's community formation preaching in the context of the post-Christian culture. First, it demonstrated that there are sufficient congruities between Paul's pre-Christian context and contemporary post-Christian context and therefore Paul's preaching also provides a model for contemporary preachers who work in a post-Christian society. It also demonstrated that community formation must remain a fundamental task for contemporary preachers. Yet, contemporary homiletics has not paid much attention to the task. The community formation is completed by creating boundaries for the collective Christian identity distinguished from the surrounding non-Christian culture. Therefore, the chapter suggested that contemporary preachers, who face the task of forming Christian communities in a post-Christian society, should preach shared narratives and communal norms for the creation of boundaries.

6.2. Suggestions for Further Study

Though the primary motivation of this study was to increase awareness about preaching for community formation, one cannot neglect the need for further homiletical study on community formation. As explored in chapters 2 and 5, the topic of community formation has been often ignored in contemporary discussions about homiletics. As seen in chapter 5, it is normal for the identity of a Christian community to remain fragile and fluid in this current post-Christian culture. Thus, the issue of community formation is crucial for the survival and health of the Christian community in a non-Christian society. Therefore, preaching for community remains a promising area for further research.

While 1 Thessalonians was paramount in this study, further study could explore Paul's preaching for community formation in Paul's other letters. For instance, studies tracing Romans, 1 and 2 Corinthians, and Galatians as was done in this study would be beneficial. This further research could illuminate areas of similarity as well as difference in Paul's preaching for community formation, from which can be deduced Paul's various approaches to preaching for community formation.

While this study provided the framework of preaching for community formation, another area for further study could be case studies in actual communities. This kind of project could examine how preaching of the kerygmatic narrative, local narratives, and ethical norms as proposed in this study actually form and solidify a community, considering a given preacher's practice in it. Such a study could yield more insights for contemporary preachers.

Bibliography

Abney, Corey Len. "The Apostle Paul's Methodology of Preaching in Acts and 1 Corinthians and Its Implications for Expository Preaching." Ph.D. diss., Southern Baptist Theological Seminary 2009.

Achtemeier, Paul J. *An Introduction to the New Hermeneutic*. Philadelphia: Westminster Press, 1969.

—. "Omne Verbum Sonat: The New Testament and the Oral Environment of Late Western Antiquity." *Journal of Biblical Literature* 109, no. 1 (1990): 3–27.

Ahlstrom, Sydney E. *A Religious History of the American People*. New Heaven: Yale University Press, 1972.

Allen, David L. "A Tale of Two Roads: Homiletics and Biblical Authority." *Journal of the Evangelical Theological Society* 43, no. 3 (2000): 489–516.

Allen, O. Wesley. "Introduction: The Pillars of the New Homiletic." In *The Renewed Homiletic*, edited by O. Wesley Allen. Minneapolis: Fortress Press, 2010.

Allen, Ronald J. "The Turn to the Listener: A Selective Review of a Recent Trend in Preaching." *Encounter* 64, no. 2 (2003): 167–196.

—. "Celebration Renewed: Responses." In *The Renewed Homiletic*, edited by O. Wesley Allen. Minneapolis: Fortress Press, 2010.

Allen, Ronald J., Barbara Shires Blaisdell, and Scott Black Johnston. *Theology for Preaching: Authority, Truth, and Knowledge of God in a Postmodern Ethos*. Nashville: Abingdon Press, 1997.

Altizer, Thomas J. J. *The Gospel of Christian Atheism*. Philadelphia: Westminster Press, 1966.

Ascough, Richard S. *Paul's Macedonian Associations: The Social Context of Philippians and 1 Thessalonians*. Tübingen: Mohr Siebeck, 2003.

Ashcraft, Morris. *Rudolf Bultmann* Makers of the Modern Theological Mind. Waco: Word Books, 1972.

Barclay, John M. G. "Thessalonica and Corinth: Social Contrasts in Pauline Christianity." *Journal for the Study of the New Testament* 15, no. 47 (1992): 49–74.

———. "Conflict in Thessalonica." *Catholic Biblical Quarterly* 55 no. 3 (1993): 512–530.

Barclay, William. "A Comparision of Paul's Missionary Preaching and Preaching to the Church." In *Apostolic History and the Gospel: Biblical and Historical Essays Presented to F. F. Bruce on His 60th Birthday*, edited by W. Ward Gasque and Ralph P. Martin. Grand Rapids: Eerdmans, 1970.

Barnett, Kristopher Kim. "A Historical/Critical Analysis of Dialogical Preaching." Ph.D. diss., Southwestern Baptist Theological Seminary, 2008.

Bartlett, David L. "Text Shaping Sermons." In *Listening to the Word: Studies in Honor of Fred B. Craddock*, edited by Gail R. O'Day and Thomas G. Long. Nashville: Abingdon Press, 1993.

———. "Sermon." In *Concise Encyclopedia of Preaching*, edited by William H. Willimon and Richard Lischer. Louisville: Westminster John Knox Press, 1995.

———. *Between the Bible and the Church: New Methods for Biblical Preaching*. Nashville: Abingdon Press, 1999.

Barton, Stephen C. "Review of Jewett 1986." *Expository Times* 99 no. 3 (1987): 90.

Bass, Diana Butler. *Christianity after Religion: The End of Church and the Birth of a New Spiritual Awakening*. New York: Harper One, 2013.

Bassler, Jouette M. "Peace in All Ways: Theology in the Thessalonian Letters. A Response to R. Jewett, E. Krentz, and E. Richard" In *Pauline Theology Vol. 1*, edited by Jouette M. Bassler. Minneapolis: Fortress Press, 1994.

Bauer, Walter. *A Greek-English Lexicon of the New Testament and Other Early Christian Literature*. Chicago: University of Chicago Press, 2000.

Beale, G. K. *1–2 Thessalonians*. Downers Grove: InterVarsity Press, 2003.

Becker, Jürgen. *Christian Beginnings: Word and Community from Jesus to Post-Apostolic Times*. Louisville: Westminster John Knox Press, 1993.

Beker, J. Christiaan. *Heirs of Paul: Paul's Legacy in the New Testament and in the Church Today*. Minneapolis: Fortress Press, 1991.

Berger, Peter L., and Thomas Luckmann. *The Social Construction of Reality: A Treatise in the Sociology of Knowledge*. New York: Anchor Books, 1967.

Best, Ernest. *A Commentary on the First and Second Epistles to the Thessalonians*. New York: Harper & Row, 1972.

Betz, Hans Dieter. "De Fraterno Amore." In *Plutarch's Ethical Writings and Early Christian Literature*, edited by Hans Dieter Betz. Leiden: Brill, 1978.

Bird, Michael F. *Introducing Paul: The Man, His Mission, and His Message*. Downers Grove: InterVarsity Press, 2008.

Botha, Pieter J. J. "The Verbal Art of the Pauline Letters: Rhetoric, Performance and Presence." In *Rhetoric and the New Testament*, edited by Thomas H. Olbricht and Stanley Porter, 409–428. Sheffield: JSOT Press, 1993.

Braxton, Brad R. *Preaching Paul*. Nashville: Abingdon Press, 2004.

Broadus, John Albert, and Jesse Burton Weatherspoon. *On the Preparation and Delivery of Sermons*. New York: Harper & brothers, 1944.

Brooks, Phillips. *Lectures on Preaching*. New York: E.P. Dutton, 1877.

Brown, Raymond E. *An Introduction to the New Testament*. New York: Doubleday, 1997.

Brown, Robert MacAfee. *The Spirit of Protestantism*. New York: Oxford University Press, 1965.

Brown, Rupert. "Tajfel's Contribution to the Reduction of Intergroup Conflict." In *Social Groups and Identities: Developing the Legacy of Henri Tajfel*, edited by William Robinson. Oxford: Butterworth-Heinemann, 1996.

Bruce, F. F. "Is the Paul of Acts the Real Paul?" *Bulletin of John Rylands Library* 58 no. 2 (1976): 282–305.

—. *1 and 2 Thessalonians*. Waco: Word Books, 1982.

Brueggemann, Walter. *Biblical Perspectives on Evangelism: Living in a Three-Storied Universe*. Nashville: Abingdon Press, 1993.

—. *Cadences of Home: Preaching among Exiles*. Louisville: Westminster John Knox Press, 1997.

—. *The Word Militant: Preaching a Decentering Word*. Minneapolis: Fortress Press, 2010.

Bullock, Jeffrey Francis. *Preaching with a Cupped Ear: Hans-Georg Gadamer's Philosophical Hermeneutics as Postmodern Wor(l)d*. New York: Peter Lang, 1999.

Bultmann, Rudolf Karl. "Is Exegesis without Presuppositions Possible?" In *Existence and Faith: Shorter Writings of Rudolf Bultmann*, edited by Schubert Miles Ogden. New York: Meridian Books, 1960.

———. "New Testament and Mythology." In *New Testament and Mythology and Other Basic Writings*, edited by Schubert Miles Ogden. Philadelphia: Fortress Press, 1984.

———. "The Problem of Hermeneutics." In *New Testament and Mythology and Other Basic Writings*, edited by Schubert Miles Ogden. Philadelphia: Fortress Press, 1984.

Burke, Trevor J. *Family Matters: A Socio-Historical Study of Kinship Metaphors in 1 Thessalonians*. New York: T & T Clark International, 2003.

Buttrick, David. "Interpretation and Preaching." *Interpretation* 35, no. 1 (1981): 46–58.

———. *Homiletic: Moves and Structures*. Philadelphia: Fortress Press, 1987.

———. *A Captive Voice: The Liberation of Preaching*. Louisville: Westminster John Knox Press, 1994.

———. "Proclamation." In *Concise Encyclopedia of Preaching*, edited by William H. Willimon and Richard Lischer. Louisville: Westminster John Knox Press, 1995.

Calvin, John. *Institutes of the Christian Religion*. Philadelphia: Westminster Press, 1960.

Campbell, Charles L. *Preaching Jesus: New Directions for Homiletics in Hans Frei's Postliberal Theology*. Grand Rapids: W. B. Eerdmans Pub., 1997.

———. "Apocalypse Now." In *Narrative Reading, Narrative Preaching: Reuniting New Testament Interpretation and Proclamation*, edited by Joel B. Green and Michael Pasquarello. Grand Rapids: Baker Academic, 2003.

Campbell, Douglas A. *The Quest for Paul's Gospel: A Suggested Strategy*. London: T & T Clark, 2005.

Carrell, Lori. *The Great American Sermon Survey*. Wheaton: Mainstay Church Resources, 2000.

Carson, Marion. "For Now We Live: A Study of Paul's Pastoral Leadership in 1 Thessalonians." *Themelios* 30, no. 3 (2005): 23–41.

Castelli, Elizabeth A. *Imitating Paul: A Discourse of Power*. Louisville: Westminster John Knox Press, 1991.

Chapell, Bryan. *Christ-Centered Preaching: Redeeming the Expository Sermon*. Grand Rapids: Baker Academic, 2005.

Clarke, Erskine. *Exilic Preaching: Testimony for Christian Exiles in an Increasingly Hostile Culture*. Harrisburg: Trinity Press International, 1998.

Clegg, Tom, and Warren Bird. *Lost in America: How You and Your Church Can Impact the World Next Door*. Loveland: Group, 2001.

Collins, Raymond F. *Studies on the First Letter to the Thessalonians*. Leuven: University Press, 1984.

—. *The Birth of the New Testament: The Origin and Development of the First Christian Generation*. New York: Crossroad, 1993.

Coser, Lewis A. *The Functions of Social Conflict*. Glencoe: Free Press, 1956.

Cousar, Charles B. *The Letters of Paul*. Nashville: Abingdon Press, 1996.

Cox, Claude E. "The Reading of the Personal Letters as the Background for the Reading of the Scripture in the Early Church." In *The Early Church in Its Context: Essays in Honor of Everett Ferguson*, edited by Abraham Malherbe, Frederick Norris and James Thompson. Leiden: Brill, 1998.

Craddock, Fred B. *As One without Authority: Essays on Inductive Preaching*. Enid: Phillips University Press, 1971.

—. *Overhearing the Gospel*. Nashville: Abingdon Press, 1978.

—. *As One without Authority*. Saint Louis: Chalice Press, 2001.

—. *Overhearing the Gospel*. St. Louis: Chalice Press, 2002.

—. "Inductive Preaching Renewed." In *The Renewed Homiletic*, edited by O. Wesley Allen. Minneapolis: Fortress Press, 2010.

Cranfield, C. E. B. "Change of Person and Number in Paul's Epistles." In *Paul and Paulinism: Essays in Honour of C.K. Barrett*, edited by Hooker M. D. and Wilson S. G. London: SPCK, 1982.

Dargan, Edwin Charles, and Ralph G. Turnbull. *A History of Preaching 3*. Grand Rapids: Baker, 1974.

Davis, Henry Grady. *Design for Preaching*. Philadelphia: Muhlenberg Press, 1958.

de Vos, Craig. *Church and Community Conflicts: The Relationships of the Thessalonian, Corinthian, and Philippian Churches with Their Wider Civic Communities*. Atlanta: Scholars Press, 1999.

Deissmann, Adolf. *Bible Studies: Contributions, Chiefly from Papyri and Inscriptions, to the History of the Language, the Literature, and the Religion of Hellenistic Judaism and Primitive Christianity*. Edinburgh: T. & T. Clark, 1901.

—. *Light from the Ancient East: The New Testament Illustrated by Recently Discovered Texts of the Graeco-Roman World*. London: Hodder & Stoughton, 1909.

deSilva, David A. *Despising Shame: Honor Discourse and Community Maintenance in the Epistle to the Hebrews*. Atlanta: Scholars Press, 1995.

—. "Worthy of His Kingdom: Honor Discourse and Social Engineering in 1 Thessalonians." *Journal for the Study of the New Testament* 19, no. 64 (1996): 49–79.

—. *The Hope of Glory Honor Discourse and New Testament Interpretation*. Collegeville: Liturgical Press, 1999.

—. *Honor, Patronage, Kinship & Purity: Unlocking New Testament Culture*. Downers Grove: InterVarsity Press, 2000.

Dewey, Joanna. "Textuality in an Oral Culture: A Survey of the Pauline Traditions." *Semeia* 65 (1994): 37–65.

Dibelius, Martin, and Werner Georg Kümmel. *Paul*. Philadelphia: Westminster Press, 1966.

Dodd, C. H. *The Apostolic Preaching and Its Developments*. New York: Harper, 1964.

Donfried, Karl P. "The Theology of 1 Thessalonians." In *The Theology of the Shorter Pauline Letters*, edited by Karl P. Donfried and I. Howard Marshall. Cambridge: Cambridge University Press, 1993.

—. "The Imperial Cults and Political Conflict in 1 Thessalonians." In *Paul and Empire: Religion and Power in Roman Imperial Society*, edited by Richard A. Horsley. Harrisburg: Trinity Press International, 1997.

—. *Paul, Thessalonica, and Early Christianity*. Grand Rapids: W. B. Eerdmans Pub., 2002.

Doty, William G. *Letters in Primitive Christianity*. Philadelphia: Fortress Press, 1973.

Dunn, James D. G. *The Theology of Paul the Apostle*. Grand Rapids: W. B. Eerdmans Pub., 1998.

Durkheim, Émile. *The Elementary Forms of the Religious Life*. New York: Free Press, 1965.

Ebeling, Gerhard. *Word and Faith*. Philadelphia: Fortress Press, 1963.

Ebeling, Gerhard, and David James Randolph. *On Prayer: Nine Sermons*. Philadelphia: Fortress Press, 1966.

Edgell, Penny, Joseph Gerteis, and Douglas Hartmann. "Atheists as 'Other': Moral Boundaries and Cultural Membership in American Society." *American Sociological Review* 71, no. 2 (2006): 211–234.

Gibbs, Eddie, and Ryan K. Bolger. *Emerging Churches: Creating Christian Community in Postmodern Cultures*. Grand Rapids: Baker Academic, 2005.

Edson, Charles. "Cults of Thessalonica." *Harvard Theological Review* 41, no. 3 (1948): 153–204.

Edwards, O. C. "History of Preaching." In *Concise Encyclopedia of Preaching*, edited by William H. Willimon and Richard Lischer. Louisville: Westminster John Knox Press, 1995.

—. *A History of Preaching*. Nashville: Abingdon Press, 2004.

Eichorn, Christian David. "Ecclesial Preaching: The Homiletical Theology of Vatican II and Its Influence Upon Protestant Homiletics of the Twentieth Century." Ph.D. diss., Drew University, 2001.

Elias, Jacob W. *1 and 2 Thessalonians*. Scottdale: Herald Press, 1995.

Elliott, W. A. *Us and Them: A Study of Group Consciousness*. Aberdeen: Aberdeen University Press, 1986.

Elson, John T. "Theology: Toward a Hidden God." *Time*, April 8, 1966, 82–87.

Esler, Philip F. "Group Boundaries and Intergroup Conflict in Galatians: A New Reading of Galatians 5:13–6:10." In *Ethnicity and the Bible*, edited by Mark G. Brett. Leiden: E. J. Brill, 1996.

—. *Galatians*. London: Routledge, 1998.

—. "Jesus and the Reduction of Intergroup Conflict: The Parable of the Good Samaritan Jesus and the Reduction of Intergroup in the Light of Social Identity Theory." *Biblical Interpretation* 8, no. 4 (2000): 325–357.

—. "'Keeping It in the Family': Culture, Kinship and Identity in 1 Thessalonians and Galatians." In *Families and Family Relations as Represented in Early Judaisms and Early Christianities: Texts and Fictions*, edited by Jan Willem van Henten and Athalya Brenner. Leiden: Deo, 2000.

Eslinger, Richard L. *A New Hearing: Living Options in Homiletic Methods*. Nashville: Abingdon Press, 1987.

—. *The Web of Preaching: New Options in Homiletical Method*. Nashville: Abingdon Press, 2002.

Fant, Clyde E. *Preaching for Today*. New York: Harper & Row, 1975.

Fatum, Lone. "Brotherhood in Christ: A Gender Hermeneutical Reading of 1 Thessalonians." In *Constructing Early Christian Families: Family as Social Reality and Metaphor*, edited by Halvor Moxnes. New York: Routledge, 1997.

Fee, Gordon D. *The First and Second Letters to the Thessalonians*. Grand Rapids: W. B. Eerdmans Pub., 2009.

Fee, Gordon D., and Douglas K. Stuart. *How to Read the Bible Book by Book: A Guided Tour*. Grand Rapids: Zondervan, 2002.

Ferguson, Everett. *Backgrounds of Early Christianity*. Grand Rapids: W. B. Eerdmans Pub., 1993.

Finley, Moses I. *The Ancient Economy*. Berkeley: University of California Press, 1973.

Fowl, Stephen E. *The Story of Christ in the Ethics of Paul: An Analysis of the Function of the Hymnic Material in the Pauline Corpus*. Sheffield: JSOT Press, 1990.

Frame, James E. *A Critical and Exegetical Commentary on the Epistles of St. Paul to the Thessalonians*. New York: C. Scribner's Sons, 1912.

Fredricksmeyer, E. A. "On the Background of the Ruler Cult." In *Ancient Macedonian Studies in Honor of Charles F. Edson*, edited by Harry J. Dell. Thessaloniki: Institute for Balkan Studies, 1981.

Frost, Michael. *Exiles: Living Missionally in a Post-Christian Culture*. Peabody: Hendrickson Publishers, 2006.

Frost, Michael, and Alan Hirsch. *The Shaping of Things to Come: Innovation and Mission for the 21st-Century Church*. Grand Rapids: Baker Books, 2013.

Fuchs, Ernst. "The New Testament and the Hermeneutical Problem." In *The New Hermeneutic*, edited by James M. Robinson and John B. Cobb. New York: Harper & Row, 1964.

Funk, Robert. "The Apostolic Parousia: Form and Significance." In *Christian History and Interpretation: Studies Presented to John Knox*, edited by William R. Farmer, Charles Francis D. Moule and Richard R. Niebuhr. Cambridge: University Press, 1967.

Furnish, Victor Paul. *Theology and Ethics in Paul*. Nashville: Abingdon Press, 1968.

—. *1 Thessalonians, 2 Thessalonians*. Nashville: Abingdon Press, 2007.

Gamble, Harry Y. *Books and Readers in the Early Church: A History of Early Christian Texts*. New Haven: Yale University Press, 1995.

Garnsey, Peter, and Richard Saller. "Patronal Power Relations." In *Paul and Empire: Religion and Power in Roman Imperial Society*, edited by Richard A. Horsley. Harrisburg: Trinity Press International, 1997.

Gatzke, Nicholas G. "Preaching in the Emerging Church and Its Relationship to the New Homiletic." Ph.D. diss., Brunel University, 2008.

Gaventa, Beverly R. *First and Second Thessalonians*. Louisville: Westminster John Knox Press, 1998.

Gibson, Scott M. "Defining the New Homiletic." *The Journal of the Evangelical Homiletics Society* 5, no. 2 (2005): 19–28.

Gieryn, Thomas F. "Boundary-Work and the Demarcation of Science from Non-Science: Strains and Interests in Professional Ideologies of Scientists." *American Sociological Review* 48, no. 6 (1983): 781–795.

Gieschen, Charles A. "Christian Identity in a Pagan Thessalonica: The Imitation of Paul's Cruciform Life." *Concordia Theological Quarterly* 72, no. 1 (2008): 3–18.

Goldsworthy, Graeme. *Preaching the Whole Bible as Christian Scripture: The Application of Biblical Theology to Expository Preaching*. Grand Rapids: W. B. Eerdmans Pub., 2000.

Gorman, Michael J. *Cruciformity: Paul's Narrative Spirituality of the Cross*. Grand Rapids: W. B. Eerdmans Pub., 2001.

—. *Apostle of the Crucified Lord: A Theological Introduction to Paul and His Letters*. Grand Rapids: W. B. Eerdmans Pub., 2004.

Green, Gene L. *The Letters to the Thessalonians*. Grand Rapids: W. B. Eerdmans Pub., 2002.

Greenhaw, David M. "As One with Authority." In *Intersections: Post-Critical Studies in Preaching*, edited by Richard L. Eslinger. Grand Rapids: W. B. Eerdmans Pub., 1994.

Greenhaw, David M., and Ronald J. Allen. *Preaching in the Context of Worship*. St. Louis: Chalice Press, 2000.

Greidanus, Sidney. *The Modern Preacher and the Ancient Text: Interpreting and Preaching Biblical Literature*. Grand Rapids: W. B. Eerdmans Pub., 1988.

—. *Preaching Christ from the Old Testament: A Contemporary Hermeneutical Method*. Grand Rapids: W. B. Eerdmans Pub., 1999.

Grenz, Stanley J. *The Moral Quest: Foundations of Christian ethics*. Downers Grove: IVP Academic, 1997.

Grieb, A. Katherine. *The Story of Romans: A Narrative Defense of God's Righteousness*. Louisville: Westminster John Knox Press, 2002.

Gross, Nancy Lammers. *If You Cannot Preach Like Paul*. Grand Rapids: W. B. Eerdmans Pub., 2002.

Gushee, David P., and Glen H. Stassen. *Kingdom Ethics: Following Jesus in Contemporary Context*. Grand Rapids: W. B. Eerdmans Pub., 2016.

Halbwachs, Maurice. *On Collective Memory*. Chicago: University of Chicago Press, 1992.

Handy, Robert T. *A Christian America: Protestant Hopes and Historical Realities*. New York: Oxford University Press, 1971.

Harris, William V. *Ancient Literacy*. Cambridge: Harvard University Press, 1989.

Harvey, John D. *Listening to the Text: Oral Patterning in Paul's Letters*. Grand Rapids: Baker Books, 1998.

—. "Orality and Its Implications for Biblical Studies: Recapturing an Ancient Paradigm." *Journal of the Evangelical Theological Society* 45, no. 1 (2002): 99–109.

Hauerwas, Stanley, and William H. Willimon. *Resident Aliens: Life in the Christian Colony*. Nashville: Abingdon Press, 1989.

Havener, Ivan. "The Pre-Pauline Christological Credal Formulae of 1 Thessalonians." *Society of Biblical Literature Seminar Papers*, no. 20 (1981): 105–128.

Hays, Richard. *Echoes of Scripture in the Letters of Paul*. New Haven: Yale University Press, 1989.

—. *The Moral Vision of the New Testament: A Contemporary Introduction to New Testament Ethics*. San Francisco: Harper, 1996.

—. *The Faith of Jesus Christ: The Narrative Substructure of Galatians 3:1–4:11*. Grand Rapids: W. B. Eerdmans Pub., 2002.

Hedahl, Susan K. "Character." In *Concise Encyclopedia of Preaching*, edited by William H. Willimon and Richard Lischer. Louisville: Westminster John Knox Press, 1995.

Heidegger, Martin. *Existence and Being*. London: Vision Press, 1949.

Heil, John Paul. *The Letters of Paul as Rituals of Worship*. Eugene: Cascade Books, 2011.

Hendrix, Holland L. "Thessalonicans Honor Romans." 1984.

—. "Thessalonica." In *Anchor Bible Dictionary Vol. 6*, edited by David Noel Freedman. New York: Doubleday, 1992.

Hester, James D. "The Use and Influence of Rhetoric in Galatians 2:1–14." *Theologische Zeitschrift* 42, no. 5 (1986): 386–408.

Hill, Judith L. "Establishing the Church in Thessalonica." Ph.D. diss., Duke University, 1990.
Hirsch, Alan. *The Forgotten Ways: Reactivating the Missional Church.* Grand Rapids: Brazos Press, 2006.
Hock, Ronald F. *The Social Context of Paul's Ministry: Tentmaking and Apostleship.* Philadelphia: Fortress Press, 1980.
Hogg, Michael A. "Social Identity Theory." In *Contemporary Social Psychological Theories*, edited by Peter J. Burke. Stanford: Stanford Social Sciences, 2006.
Hogg, Michael A., and Deborah J. Terry. *Social Identity Processes in Organizational Contexts.* Philadelphia: Psychology Press, 2001.
Holbert, John C. "Toward a Story Homiletic: History and Prospects." *Journal for Preachers* 33, no. 3 (2000): 16–29.
Holmberg, Bengt. *Paul and Power: The Structure of Authority in the Primitive Church as Reflected in the Pauline Epistles.* Philadelphia: Fortress Press, 1980.
Holmes, Michael W. *1 and 2 Thessalonians: The Niv Application Commentary.* Grand Rapids: Zondervan, 1998.
Horrell, David G. "Models and Methods in Social-Scientific Interpretation: A Response to Philip Esler." *Journal for the Study of the New Testament* 22, no. 78 (2000): 83–105.
—. "'Becoming Christian': Solidifying Christian Identity and Content." In *Handbook of Early Christianity: Social Science Approaches*, edited by Anthony J. Blasi, Jean Duhaime and Paul-André Turcotte. Walnut Creek: AltaMira Press, 2002.
—. *Solidarity and Difference: A Contemporary Reading of Paul's Ethics.* New York: T & T Clark International, 2005.
—. *An Introduction to the Study of Paul.* New York: T & T Clark, 2006.
Howe, Reuel L. *Partners in Preaching: Clergy and Laity in Dialogue.* New York: Seabury Press, 1967.
Howell, Mark A. "Hermeneutical Bridges and Homiletical Methods: A Comparative Analysis of the New Homiletic and Expository Preaching Theory 1970–1995." Ph.D. diss., Sourthen Baptist Seminary, 1999.
Jeanrond, Werner G. *Theological Hermeneutics: Development and Significance.* New York: Crossroad, 1991.
Jenkins, Richard. *Social Identity.* London: Routledge, 2008.
Jensen, Richard A. *Telling the Story: Variety and Imagination in Preaching.* Minneapolis: Augsburg Pub., 1980.

Jewett, Robert. "The Form and Function of the Homiletical Benediction." *Anglican Theological Review* 51 (1969): 18–34.

—. *The Thessalonian Correspondence: Pauline Rhetoric and Millenarian Piety*. Philadelphia: Fortress Press, 1986.

—. "Tenement Churches and Communal Meals in the Early Church: The Implications of a Form-Critical Analysis of 2 Thessalonians 3:10." *Biblical Research* 38 (1993): 23–43.

—. *Paul the Apostle to America: Cultural Trends and Pauline Scholarship*. Louisville: Westminster John Knox Press, 1994.

Johnson, Andy. "The Sanctification of the Imagination in 1 Thessalonians." In *Holiness and Ecclesiology in the New Testament*, edited by Kent E. Brower and Andy Johnson. Grand Rapids: W. B. Eerdmans Pub., 2007.

Johnston, Graham. *Preaching to a Postmodern World: A Guide to Reaching Twenty-First-Century Listeners*. Grand Rapids: Baker Books, 2001.

Johnston, Scott Black. "Who Listens to Stories?: Cautions and Challenges for Narrative Preaching." *Insights* 111, no. 2 (1996): 4–13.

Kaiser, Walter C. *Toward an Exegetical Theology: Biblical Exegesis for Preaching and Teaching*. Grand Rapids: Baker Book House, 1981.

Kaiser, Walter C. and Moisés Silva. *An Introduction to Biblical Hermeneutics: The Search for Meaning*. Grand Rapids: Zondervan, 2007.

Kay, James F. *Preaching and Theology*. Saint Louis: Chalice Press, 2008.

Keightley, Georgia M. "The Church's Memory of Jesus: A Social Science Analysis of 1 Thessalonians." *Biblical Theology Bulletin* 17, no. 4 (1987): 149–156.

Keller, Timothy. *Center Church: Doing Balanced, Gospel-Centered Ministry in Your City*. Grand Rapids: Zondervan, 2012.

—. *Preaching: Communicating Faith in an Age of Skepticism*. New York: Viking, 2015.

Kelley, Dean M. *Why Conservative Churches Are Growing: A Study in Sociology of Religion*. New York: Harper & Row, 1972.

Kelsey, David H. *The Uses of Scripture in Recent Theology*. Philadelphia: Fortress Press, 1975.

Knowles, Michael P. *We Preach Not Ourselves: Paul on Proclamation*. Grand Rapids: Brazos Press, 2008.

Koester, Helmut. "1 Thessalonians – Experiment in Christian Writing." In *Continuity and Discontinuity in Church History: Essays Presented to George Huntston Williams*, edited by F. Forrester Church and Timothy George. Leiden: E. J. Brill, 1979.

Krabbendam, Hendrik. "The New Hermeneutic." In *Hermeneutics, Inerrancy, and the Bible: [Papers from ICBI Summit II]*, edited by Earl D. Radmacher and Robert D. Preus. Grand Rapids: Academie Books, 1984.

Kreitzer, L. Joseph. "Eschatology." In *Dictionary of Paul and His Letters*, edited by Gerald F. Hawthorne, Ralph P. Martin and Daniel G. Reid. Downers Grove: InterVarsity Press, 1993.

Lüdemann, Gerd. *Paul, Apostle to the Gentiles: Studies in Chronology.* Philadelphia: Fortress Press, 1984.

Lamont, Michèle. *Money, Morals, and Manners: The Culture of the French and American Upper-Middle Class.* Chicago: University of Chicago Press, 1992.

Lamont, Michèle, and Marcel Fournier. *Cultivating Differences: Symbolic Boundaries and the Making of Inequality.* Chicago: University of Chicago Press, 1992.

Lamont, Michèle, and Virág Molnár. "The Study of Boundaries in the Social Sciences." *Annual Review of Sociology* 28 (2002): 167–195.

Levy, Peter B., ed. *America in the Sixties – Right, Left, and Center: A Documentary History.* Westport: Greenwood Press, 1998.

Lightfoot, Joseph B. *Notes on Epistles of St Paul from Unpublished Commentaries.* London: Macmillan, 1904.

Lindbeck, George A. *The Nature of Doctrine: Religion and Theology in a Postliberal Age.* Philadelphia: Westminster Press, 1984.

Lischer, Richard. "The Limits of Story." *Interpretation* 38, no. 1 (1984): 26–38.

—. "Before Technique: Preaching and Personal Formation." *Dialog* 29, no. 3 (1990): 178–182.

—. "The Interrupted Sermon." *Interpretation* 50, no. 2 (1996): 169–181.

Lischer, Richard, and William H. Willimon. "Interview with Richard Lischer & William Willimon." *Homiletic* 20, no. 2 (1995): 15–21.

Long, Jimmy. *Emerging Hope: A Strategy for Reaching the Postmodern Generations.* Downers Grove: InterVarsity Press, 2004.

Long, Thomas G. *Preaching and the Literary Forms of the Bible.* Philadelphia: Fortress Press, 1989.

—. "And How Shall They Hear?" In *Listening to the Word: Studies in Honor of Fred B. Craddock*, edited by Gail R. O'Day and Thomas G. Long. Nashville: Abingdon Press, 1993.
—. "When the Preacher Is a Teacher." *Journal for Preachers* 16, no. 2 (1993): 21–27.
—. "Form." In *Concise Encyclopedia of Preaching*, edited by William H. Willimon and Richard Lischer. Louisville: Westminster John Knox Press, 1995.
—. *The Witness of Preaching*. Louisville: Westminster John Knox Press, 2005.
—. *Preaching from Memory to Hope*. Louisville: Westminster John Knox Press, 2009.
Longenecker, Bruce W., ed. *Narrative Dynamics in Paul*. Louisville: Westminster John Konx Press, 2002.
Longenecker, Richard N. "On the Form, Function, and Authority of the New Testament Letters." In *Scripture and Truth*, edited by D. A. Carson and John D. Woodbridge. Grand Rapids: Zondervan, 1983.
—. "The Nature of Paul's Early Eschatology." *New Testament Studies* 31, no. 1 (1985): 85–95.
Loscalzo, Craig A. *Preaching Sermons That Connect: Effective Communication through Identification*. Downers Grove: InterVarsity Press, 1992.
—. *Apologetic Preaching: Proclaiming Christ to a Postmodern World*. Downers Grove: InterVarsity Press, 2000.
Lose, David J. *Preaching at the Crossroads: How the World – and Our Preaching – Is Changing*. Minneapolis: Fortress Press, 2013.
Lose, David L. "Whither Hence, New Homiletic?" In *the Academy of Homiletics*, 255–266. Perkins School of Theology: Academy of Homiletics, 2000.
Lovejoy, Grant Irven. "A Critical Evaluation of the Nature and Role of Authority in the Homiletical Thought of Fred B. Craddock, Edmund A. Steimle, and David G. Buttrick." Ph.D. diss., Southwestern Baptist Theological Seminary, 1990.
Lowry, Eugene L. *Doing Time in the Pulpit: The Relationship between Narrative and Preaching*. Nashville: Abingdon Press, 1985.
—. *How to Preach a Parable: Designs for Narrative Sermons*. Nashville: Abingdon Press, 1989.

—. "The Revolution of Sermonic Shape." In *Listening to the Word: Studies in Honor of Fred B. Craddock*, edited by Gail R. O'Day and Thomas G. Long. Nashville: Abingdon Press, 1993.

—. "Narrative Preaching." In *Concise Encyclopedia of Preaching*, edited by William H. Willimon and Richard Lischer. Louisville: Westminster John Knox Press, 1995.

—. *The Sermon: Dancing the Edge of Mystery*. Nashville: Abingdon Press, 1997.

—. *The Homiletical Plot: The Sermon as Narrative Art Form*. Louisville: Westminster John Knox Press, 2001.

—. *The Homiletical Beat: Why All Sermons Are Narrative*. Nashville: Abingdon Press, 2012.

Lyons, George. "Modeling the Holiness Ethos: A Study Based on First Thessalonians." *Wesleyan Theological Journal* 30, no. 1 (1995): 187–211.

MacDonald, Margaret Y. *The Pauline Churches: A Socio-Historical Study of Institutionalization in the Pauline and Deutero-Pauline Writings*. Cambridge: Cambridge University Press, 1988.

Mack, Burton L. *Who Wrote the New Testament?: The Making of the Christian Myth*. San Francisco: Harper, 1995.

MacMullen, Ramsey. *Paganism in the Roman Empire*. New Haven: Yale University Press, 1981.

Malherbe, Abraham J. "'Gentle as a Nurse': The Cynic Background to I Thess II." *Novum testamentum* 12, no. 2 (1970): 203–217.

—. *Paul and the Thessalonians: The Philosophic Tradition of Pastoral Care*. Philadelphia: Fortress Press, 1987.

—. "God's New Family in Thessalonica." In *The Social World of the First Christians: Essays in Honor of Wayne A. Meeks*, edited by L. Michael White and O. Larry Yarbrough. Minneapolis: Fortress Press, 1995.

—. *The Letters to the Thessalonians: A New Translation with Introduction and Commentary*. New York: Doubleday, 2000.

Malina, Bruce J. "Does Porneia Mean Fornication?" *Novum testamentum* 14, no. 1 (1972): 10–17.

—. *The New Testament World: Insights from Cultural Anthropology*. Louisville: Westminster John Knox Press, 1993.

Manson, Thomas Walter. *Studies in the Gospels and Epistles*. Philadelphia: Westminster Press, 1962.

Marshall, I. Howard. *1 and 2 Thessalonians: Based on the Revised Standard Version*. Grand Rapids: W. B. Eerdmans Pub., 1983.

Martin, D. Michael. *1, 2 Thessalonians*. Nashville: Broadman & Holman, 1995.

Martin, Michael. "'Example' and 'Imitation' in the Thessalonian Correspondence." *Southwestern Journal of Theology* 42, no. 1 (1999): 39–49.

Marx, Karl. *The Eighteenth Brumaire of Louis Napoleon*. New York: International Publishers, 1963.

Matera, Frank J. *New Testament Theology: Exploring Diversity and Unity*. Louisville: Westminster John Knox Press, 2007.

McClure, John S. *The Roundtable Pulpit: Where Leadership and Preaching Meet*. Nashville: Abingdon Press, 1995.

—. *Preaching Words: 144 Key Terms in Homiletics*. Louisville: Westminster John Knox Press, 2007.

McGrath, Alister E. *The Future of Christianity*. Oxford: Blackwell, 2002.

McGuire, Martin R. P. "Letters and Letter Carriers in Christian Antiquity." *The Classical World* 53, no. 5 (1960): 148–153, 184–185.

Meeks, Wayne A. "Since Then You Would Need to Go out of the World: Group Boundaries in Pauline Christianity." In *Critical History and Biblical Faith: New Testament Perspectives*, edited by Thomas J. Ryan. Villanova: Horizons, 1979.

—. *The First Urban Christians: The Social World of the Apostle Paul*. New Haven: Yale University Press, 1983.

—. "Social Functions of Apocalyptic Language in Pauline Christianity." In *Apocalypticism in the Mediterranean World and the near East*, edited by David Hellholm. Tübingen: J. C. B. Mohr, 1983.

—. *The Moral World of the First Christians*. Philadelphia: Westminster Press, 1986.

—. *The Origins of Christian Morality: The First Two Centuries*. New Heaven: Yale University Press, 1993.

Miller, Calvin. "Narrative Preaching." In *Handbook of Contemporary Preaching*, edited by Michael Duduit. Nashville: Broadman Press, 1992.

Mitchell, Henry H. *The Recovery of Preaching*. San Francisco: Harper & Row, 1977.

—. *Celebration and Experience in Preaching*. Nashville: Abingdon Press, 1990.

Mitchell, Margaret M. "New Testament Envoys in the Context of Greco-Roman Diplomatic and Epistolary Conventions: The Example of Timothy and Titus." *Journal of Biblical Literature* 111, no. 4 (1992): 641–662.

—. "1 and 2 Thessalonians." In *The Cambridge Companion to St. Paul*, edited by James D. G. Dunn. Cambridge: Cambridge University Press, 2003.

Moore, Stephen D. *Poststructural-Ism and the New Testament: Derrida and Foucault at the Foot of the Cross*. Minneapolis: Fortress Press, 1994.

Morris, Leon. *The First and Second Epistles to the Thessalonians*. Grand Rapids: W. B. Eerdmans Pub., 1991.

Mounce, R. H. "Preaching, Kerygma." In *Dictionary of Paul and His Letters*, edited by Gerald F. Hawthorne, Ralph P. Martin and Daniel G. Reid. Downers Grove: InterVarsity Press, 1993.

Mulligan, Mary Alice, Diane Turner-Sharazz, Dawn Ottoni Wilhelm, and Ronald J. Allen. *Believing in Preaching: What Listeners Hear in Sermons*. St. Louis: Chalice Press, 2005.

Murray, Stuart. *Church after Christendom*. Milton Keynes: Paternoster, 2004.

Neil, William. *The Epistle of Paul to the Thessalonians*. New York: Harper & Brothers, 1950.

Newbigin, Lesslie. *The Other Side of 1984: Questions for the Churches*. Geneva: WCC Publications, 1983.

—. *Foolishness to the Greeks: The Gospel and Western Culture*. Grand Rapids: W. B. Eerdmans Pub., 1986.

—. *The Gospel in a Pluralist Society*. Grand Rapids: W. B. Eerdmans Pub., 1989.

Neyrey, Jerome H. "Eschatology in 1 Thessalonians: The Theological Factor in 1:9–10; 2:4–5; 3:11–13; 4:6 and 4:13–18." *Society of Biblical Literature Seminar Papers*, no. 19 (1980): 219–231.

Nilsson, Martin P. *The Dionysiac Mysteries of the Hellenistic and Roman Age*. New York: Arno Press, 1975.

Nock, Arthur D. *St. Paul*. New York: Harper and Brothers, 1937.

O'Day, Gail R., and Thomas G. Long. "Introduction." In *Listening to the Word: Studies in Honor of Fred B. Craddock*, edited by Gail R. O'Day and Thomas G. Long. Nashville: Abingdon Press, 1993.

Osiek, Carolyn, and David L. Balch. *Families in the New Testament World Households and House Churches*. Louisville: Westminster John Knox Press, 1997.

Osmer, Richard R. *Practical theology: An Introduction*. Grand Rapids: W. B. Eerdmans Pub., 2008.

Pasquarello, Michael. *Sacred Rhetoric: Preaching as a Theological and Pastoral Practice of the Church*. Grand Rapids: W. B. Eerdmans Pub., 2005.

Penn, Michael P. "Performing Family: Ritual Kissing and the Construction of Early Christian Kinship." *Journal of Early Christian Studies* 10, no. 2 (2002): 151–174.

Perkins, Pheme. "1 Thessalonians and Hellenistic Religious Practices." In *To Touch the Text: Biblical and Related Studies in Honor of Joseph A. Fitzmyer*, edited by Maurya P. Horgan and Paul J. Kobelski. New York: Crossroad, 1989.

Petersen, Norman R. *Rediscovering Paul: Philemon and the Sociology of Paul's Narrative World*. Philadelphia: Fortress Press, 1985.

Peterson, Eugene H. *Eat This Book: A Conversation in the Art of Spiritual Reading*. Grand Rapids: W. B. Eerdmans Pub., 2006.

Plummer, Alfred. *A Commentary on St. Paul's Second Epistle to the Thessalonians*. London: Robert Scott, 1918.

Pobee, John S. *Persecution and Martyrdom in the Theology of Paul*. Sheffield: JSOT Press, 1985.

Polhill, John B. *Paul and His Letters*. Nashville: Broadman & Holman, 1999.

Porter, Stanley E. "A Functional Letter Perspective: Towards a Grammar of Epistolary Theory." in *Paul and the Ancient Letter Form*, edited by Stanley E. Porter and Sean A. Adams. Leiden: Brill, 2010.

Putnam, Robert D. *Bowling Alone: The Collapse and Revival of American Community*. New York: Simon & Schuster, 2000.

Putnam Robert D. and David E. Campbell. *American Grace: How Religion Divides and Unites Us*. New York: Simon & Schuster, 2012.

Randolph, David James. *The Renewal of Preaching*. Philadelphia: Fortress Press, 1969.

Randolph, David James, and Robert Stephen Reid. *The Renewal of Preaching in the Twenty-First Century: The Next Homiletics Commentary*. Eugene: Cascade Books, 2009.

Reese, Martha Grace. *Unbinding the Gospel: Real Life Evangelism.* St. Louis: Chalice Press, 2006.
Reid, Clyde H. *The Empty Pulpit: A Study in Preaching as Communication.* New York: Harper & Row, 1967.
Reid, David, Stephen Bullock, and Jeffrey Fleer. "Preaching as the Creation of an Experience: The Not-So-Rational Revolution of the New Homileitc." *the Journal of Communication and Religion* 18, no. 1 (1995): 1–9.
Reid, Robert Stephen. "Postmodernism and the Function of the New Homiletic in Post-Christendom Congregations." *Homiletic* 20, no. 2 (1995): 1–13.
Rice, Charles L. *Interpretation and Imagination: The Preacher and Contemporary Literature.* Philadelphia: Fortress Press, 1970.
Richard, Earl. *First and Second Thessalonians.* Collegeville: Liturgical Press, 1995.
Richards, E. Randolph. *Paul and First-Century Letter Writing: Secretaries, Composition, and Collection.* Downers Grove: InterVarsity Press, 2004.
Robinson, Haddon W. *Biblical Preaching: The Development and Delivery of Expository Messages.* Grand Rapids: Baker Book House, 1980.
—. "Competing with the Communication Kings." In *Making a Difference in Preaching: Haddon Robinson on Biblical Preaching*, edited by Scott M. Gibson. Grand Rapids: Baker Books, 1999.
—. *Biblical Preaching: The Development and Delivery of Expository Messages.* Grand Rapids: Baker Academic, 2001.
—. "Preaching Trends: A Riview." *Journal of the Evangelical Theological Society* 6, no. 2 (2006): 23–31.
Robinson, James M. "Hermeneutic since Barth." In *The New Hermeneutic*, edited by James M. Robinson and John B. Cobb. New York: Harper & Row, 1964.
Roetzel, Calvin J. *The Letters of Paul: Conversations in Context.* Louisville: Westminster John Knox Press, 2015.
Roitto, Rikard. "Behaving Like a Christ-Believer: A Cognitive Pespective on Identity and Behavor Norms in the Early Christ-Movement." In *Exploring Early Christian Identity*, edited by Bengt Holmberg. Tübingen: Mohr Siebeck, 2008.
Rose, Lucy Atkinson. *Sharing the Word: Preaching in the Roundtable Church.* Louisville: Westminster John Knox Press, 1997.

Roxburgh, Alan J. "Missional Leadership: Equipping God's People for Mission." In *Missional Church: A Vision for the Sending of the Church in North America*, edited by Darrell L. Guder. Grand Rapids: W. B. Eerdmans Pub., 1998.

Russell, R. "The Idle in 2 Thess 3.6–12: An Eschatological or a Social Problem?" *New Testament Studies* 34, no. 1 (1988): 105–119.

Ryoo, David Eung-Yul. "Paul's Preaching in the Epistle to the Ephesians and Its Homiletical Implications." Ph.D. diss., Southern Baptist Theological Seminary, 2003.

Samra, James G. *Being Conformed to Christ in Community: A Study of Maturity, Maturation, and the Local Church in the Undisputed Pauline Epistles*. London: T & T Clark, 2006.

Schlueter, Carol J. *Filling up the Measure: Polemical Hyperbole in 1 Thessalonians 2:14–16*. Sheffield: JSOT Press, 1994.

Schmithals, Walter. *Paul and the Gnostics*. Nashville: Abingdon Press, 1972.

Schnabel, Eckhard J. *Early Christian Mission*. Downers Grove,: InterVarsity Press, 2004.

Scroggs, Robin. "The Earliest Christian Communities as Sectarian Movement: Studies for Morton Smith at Sixty." In *Christianity, Judaism and Other Greco-Roman Cults*, edited by Jacob Neusner, 1–23. Leiden: Brill, 1975.

Selby, Gary S. "'Blameless at His Coming': The Discursive Construction of Eschatological Reality in 1 Thessalonians." *Rhetorica* 17, no. 4 (1999): 385–410.

Sider, Ronald J., and Michael A. King. *Preaching About Life in a Threatening World*. Philadelphia: Westminster Press, 1987.

Simmel, Georg. *Conflict and the Web of Group-Affiliations*. New York: Free Press, 1955.

Simpson, John W. "Shaped by the Stories: Narrative in 1 Thessalonians." *Asbury Theological Journal* 53, no. 2 (1998): 15–25.

Smith, Sarah Jane. "Hearing Sermons: Reader-Response Theory as a Basis for a Listener-Response Homiletic." Th.D. diss., Univesrity of Toronto, 2003.

Smith, Steven W. *Dying to Preach: Embracing the Cross in the Pulpit*. Grand Rapids: Kregel Publications, 2009.

Somers, Margaret R. "Reclaiming the Epistemological 'Other': Narrative and the Social Constitution of Identity." In *Social Theory and the*

Politics of Identity, edited by Craig J. Calhoun. Cambridge: Blackwell, 1994.

Soulen, Richard N. "Ernst Fuchs: New Testament Theologian." *Journal of the American Academy of Religion* 39, no. 4 (1971): 467–487.

Steimle, Edmund A., Morris J. Niedenthal, and Charles L. Rice. *Preaching the Story*. Philadelphia: Fortress Press, 1980.

Stetzer, Ed, and David Putman. *Breaking the Missional Code: Your Church Can Become a Missionary in Your Community*. Nashville: Broadman & Holman, 2006.

Still, Todd D. *Conflict at Thessalonica: A Pauline Church and Its Neighbours*. Sheffield: Sheffield Academic Press, 1999.

—. "Eschatology in the Thessalonian Letters." *Review and Expositor* 96, no. 2 (1999): 195–210.

Stott, John R. W. *The Preacher's Portrait: Some New Testament Word Studies*. Grand Rapids: W. B. Eerdmans Pub., 1979.

—. *The Gospel and the End of Time: The Message of 1 and 2 Thessalonians*. Downers Grove: InterVarsity Press, 1991.

—. *Between Two Worlds*. Grand Rapids: W. B. Eerdmans Pub., 1994.

Stowers, Stanley K. "Social Status, Public Speaking and Private Teaching: The Circumstances of Paul's Preaching Activity." *Novum testamentum* 26, no. 1 (1984): 59–82.

—. *Letter Writing in Greco-Roman Antiquity*. Philadelphia: Westminster Press, 1986.

Surburg, Raymond F. "New Hermeneutic Versus the Old Hermeneutics in New Testament Interpretation." *Springfielder* 38, no. 1 (1974): 13–21.

Swidler, Ann. *Talk of Love: How Culture Matters*. Chicago: University of Chicago Press, 2001.

Tajfel, Henri. "Social Categorization, Social Identity and Social Comparison." In *Differentiation between Social Groups: Studies in the Social Psychology of Intergroup Relations*, edited by Henri Tajfel. London: Academic Press, 1978.

Taylor, Charles. *A Secular Age*. Cambridge: Harvard University Press, 2007.

Tellbe, Mikael. *Paul between Synagogue and State: Christians, Jews, and Civic Authorities in 1 Thessalonians, Romans, and Philippians*. Stockholm: Almqvist & Wiksell, 2001.

Thompson, James. *Preaching Like Paul: Homiletical Wisdom for Today*. Louisville: Westminster John Knox Press, 2001.

—. "Reading the Letters as Narrative." In *Narrative Reading, Narrative Preaching: Reuniting New Testament Interpretation and Proclamation*, edited by Joel B. Green and Michael Pasquarello. Grand Rapids: Baker Academic, 2003.

—. *The Church in Exile: God's Counterculture in a Non-Christian World*. Abilene: Leafwood Publishers, 2010.

—. *Moral Formation According to Paul: The Context and Coherence of Pauline Ethics*. Grand Rapids: Baker Academic, 2011.

Tidball, Derek. "Social Setting of Maission Churches." In *Dictionary of Paul and His Letters*, edited by Gerald F. Hawthorne, Ralph P. Martin and Daniel G. Reid. Downers Grove: InterVarsity Press, 1993.

—. *Ministry by the Book: New Testament Patterns for Pastoral Leadership*. Downers Grove: IVP Academic, 2008.

Tite, Philip L. "How to Begin, and Why? Diverse Function of the Pauline Prescript within a Greco-Roman Context," In Paul and the Ancient Letter Form, edited by Stanley E. Porter and Sean A. Adams. Leiden: Brill, 2010.

Towner, Philip H. "Household and Household Codes." In *Dictionary of Paul and His Letters*, edited by Gerald F. Hawthorne, Ralph P. Martin and Daniel G. Reid. Downers Grove: InterVarsity Press, 1993.

Vahanian, Gabriel. *The Death of God: The Culture of Our Post-Christian Era*. New York: G. Braziller, 1961.

Vakalopoulos, Apostolos E. *A History of Thessaloniki*. Thessalonike: Institute for Balkan Studies, 1963.

van Buren, Paul. *The Secular Meaning of the Gospel: Based on an Analysis of Its Language*. New York: Macmillan, 1963.

van Eck, Ernest. "Social Memory and Identity: Luke 19:12b–24 and 27." *Biblical Theology Bulletin* 41, no. 4 (2011): 201–212.

Volf, Miroslav. *A Public Faith, How Followers of Christ Should Serve the Common Good*. Grand Rapids: Brazos Press, 2011.

Wallace-Hadrill, Andrew. "Patronage in Roman Society: From Republic to Empire." In *Patronage in Ancient Society*. London: Routledge, 1989.

Walton, Steve. "What Has Aristotle to Do with Paul? Rhetorical Criticism and 1 Thessalonians." *Tyndale Bulletin* 46, no. 2 (1995): 229–250.

—. *Leadership and Lifestyle: The Portrait of Paul in the Miletus Speech and 1 Thessalonians*. Cambridge: Cambridge University Press, 2000.

Wanamaker, Charles A. *The Epistles to the Thessalonians: A Commentary on the Greek Text.* Grand Rapids: W. B. Eerdmans Pub., 1990.

—. "Apocalyptic Discourse, Paraenesis and Identity Maintenance in 1 Thessalonians." *Neotestamentica* 36, no. 1 (2002): 131–145.

Ward, Richard F. "Pauline Voice and Presence as Strategic Communication." *Semeia*, no. 65 (1994): 95–107.

Wardlaw, Don M. "The Need for New Shapes." In *Preaching Biblically*, edited by Don M. Wardlaw. Philadelphia: Westminster Press, 1983.

Warner, R. Stephen. "Work in Progress toward a New Paradigm for the Sociological Study of Religion in the United States." *American Journal of Sociology* 98, no. 5 (1993): 1044–1093.

Waston, Duane. "Paul's Appropriation of Apocalyptic Discourse: The Rhetorical Strategy of 1 Thessalonians." In *Vision and Persuasion: Rhetorical Dimensions of Apocalyptic Discourse*, edited by Greg Carey and L. Gregory Bloomquist. St. Louis: Chalice Press, 1999.

Webber, Robert. *Ancient-Future Worship: Proclaiming and Enacting God's Narrative.* Grand Rapids: Baker Books, 2008.

Weber, Max. *Economy and Society Vol. 1.* Berkeley: University of California, 1978.

Weima, Jeffrey A. D. "'How You Must Walk to Please God': Holiness and Discipleship in 1 Thessalonians." In *Patterns of Discipleship in the New Testament*, 98–119. Grand Rapids: W. B. Eerdmans Pub., 1996.

—. "'But We Became Infants among You': The Case of NHITIOI in 1 Thess 2.7." *New Testament Studies* 46 no. 4 (2000): 547–564.

Weis, Lois, Amira Proweller, and Craig Centrie. "Re-Examining 'a Moment in History': Loss of Privilege inside White Working-Class Masculinity in the 1990s." In *Off White: Readings on Race, Power, and Society*, edited by Michelle Fine, Lois Weis, Linda C. Powell and L. Mun Wong. New York: Routledge, 1997.

Wells, C. Richard, and A. Boyd Luter. *Inspired Preaching: A Survey of Preaching Found in the New Testament.* Nashville: Broadman & Holman, 2002.

Wenham, David. *Paul and Jesus: The True Story.* Grand Rapids: W. B. Eerdmans Pub., 2002.

Whitfield, Stephen J. *The Culture of the Cold War.* Baltimore: Johns Hopkins University Press, 1991.

Whitton, J. "A Neglected Meaning for *SKEUOS* in 1 Thessalonians 4:4." *New Testament Studies* 28, no. 1 (1982): 142–143.

Wilkins, Amy C. *Wannabes, Goths, and Christians: The Boundaries of Sex, Style, and Status*. Chicago: University of Chicago Press, 2008.

Williams, David J. *1 and 2 Thessalonians*. Peabody: Hendrickson Publishers, 1992.

Williams, Randal Alan. "The Impact of Contemporary Narrative Homiletics on Interpreting and Preaching the Bible." Ph.D. diss., Southern Baptist Theological Seminary, 2006.

Willimon, William H. *Peculiar Speech: Preaching to the Baptized*. Grand Rapids: W. B. Eerdmans Pub., 1992.

—. *Pastor: The Theology and Practice of Ordained Ministry*. Nashville: Abingdon Press, 2002.

Wilson, Paul Scott. *The Practice of Preaching*. Nashville: Abingdon Press, 1995.

—. *Preaching and Homiletical Theory*. Saint Louis: Chalice Press, 2004.

Winkler, Allan M. "Modern America: The 1960s, 1970s, and 1980s." In *Encyclopedia of American Social History Vol. 1*, edited by Mary Kupiec Cayton, Elliott J. Gorn, and Peter W. Williams. New York: Charles Scribner's Sons, 1993.

Witherington, Ben. *Paul's Narrative Thought World: The Tapestry of Tragedy and Triumph*. Louisville: Westminster John Knox Press, 1994.

—. *The Acts of the Apostles: A Socio-Rhetorical Commentary*. Grand Rapids: W. B. Eerdmans Pub., 1998.

—. *1 and 2 Thessalonians: A Socio-Rhetorical Commentary*. Grand Rapids: W. B. Eerdmans Pub., 2006.

—. *New Testament Rhetoric: An Introductory Guide to the Art of Persuasion in and of the New Testament*. Eugene: Cascade Books, 2009.

Witt, Rex E. "The Kabeiroi in Ancient Macedonia." In *Ancient Macedonia Vol. 2*. Thessaloniki: Institute for Balkan Studies, 1977.

Wright, John W. *Telling God's Story: Narrative Preaching for Christian Formation*. Downers Grove: IVP Academic, 2007.

Wright, N. T. *The New Testament and the People of God*. Minneapolis: Fortress Press, 1992.

—. *What Saint Paul Really Said*. Oxford: Lion, 1997.

—. *Paul in Fresh Perspective*. Minneapolis: Fortress Press, 2009.

Yarbrough, O. Larry. *Not Like the Gentiles: Marriages Rules in the Letters of Paul*. Atlanta: Scholars press, 1985.

Zanker, Paul. "The Power of Image." In *Paul and Empire: Religion and Power in Roman Imperial Society*, edited by Richard A. Horsley. Harrisburg: Trinity Press International, 1997.

Zink-Sawyer, Beverly. "The Word Purely Preached and Heard." *Interpretation* 51, no. 4 (1997): 342–357.